Citizenship in Contemporary Europe

Michael Lister and Emily Pia

D1313619

Edinburgh U

Acknowledgements: We would like to thank Thomas Diez, Roberta Guerrina, Colin Hay, David Marsh, Magnus Ryner, Matthew Watson and Daniel Wincott for their help and guidance.

Edinburgh University Press Ltd
22 George Square, Edinburgh

Typeset in Goudy Old Style
by Norman Tilley Graphics Ltd, Northampton
and printed and bound in Great Britain
by Antony Rowe Ltd, Chippenham, Wilts

A CIP record for this book is available from the British Library

ISBN 978 0 7486 3341 8 (hardback)
ISBN 978 0 7486 3342 5 (paperback)

Contents

Tables and figures

For our families

Introduction

Citizenship is a concept which speaks to the relationships between individuals and political communities. Yet, increasingly in Europe the precise terms of this relationship are subject to question. What citizenship means is contested amongst academics, as established liberal theories of citizenship are confronted with communitarian, multicultural and postnational critiques which challenge the conception of what the relationships between individuals and political communities should look like. Parallel to this, citizenship also faces challenges in terms of contemporary social and political developments. In an era of globalisation, European integration, mass migration, and changing patterns of political participation and welfare state provision, the precise shape and structure of citizenship in Europe seems to be altering. This book seeks to analyse and, crucially, connect these developments. A key theme of the book is that the theoretical debates over the meaning of citizenship shape how we view contemporary social, political and economic developments which impact upon citizenship.

As Taylor-Gooby (1991: 94) notes, citizenship is both a normative and an empirical concept. It refers to a status which we might recognise as citizenship of a particular state or community and the rights and obligations which this status confers. In addition, such a description frequently also contains arguments about how citizenship should be developed, expanded or changed and, hence, normative arguments about what citizenship should be like. Another way of thinking about this is to say that citizenship is both theoretical and empirical. Citizenship refers to the relationship between the political community and the individual and between individuals themselves. This relationship has two aspects: a theoretical one, which considers what the relationship should be like, and an empirical one, which examines what the actual relationship is between political communities and individuals and between individuals in such communities. It is, one might argue, difficult to disentangle these two elements. If we wish to consider what we might ideally think citizenship should look like, some context of how citizenship *is*, empirically, might be thought useful. Equally, if we wish to know and understand citizenship empirically, it seems reasonable that some theoretical ideas about what citizenship is are important. Yet, things are not quite that simple. We shall return to this point below.

If influence is measured in terms of the amount of attention relative to the length of the work, then almost certainly the most influential work written on citizenship is T. H. Marshall's 'Citizenship and Social Class' (1963). Despite its relatively short length (around fifty pages), it has become a touchstone piece for a number of debates around citizenship. He is frequently credited with introducing the distinction of civil, political and social rights of citizenship. Yet, an overlooked argument within this essay is the argument that citizenship should be seen as a unified concept, with civil, political and social aspects which impact upon one another. There is a practical element of unification, as the exercise of one aspect of citizenship depends upon the existence and nature of other citizenship rights. There is also a theoretical connection, as the different elements of citizenship are all underpinned by the principle of equality of status. This is entrenched differently in the different spheres, such that equality of status can be taken to mean different things in the civil, political and social spheres, meaning that the relationship between them is one of complex interdependence (Lister 2005). This framework offers an interesting hypothesis, namely that the nature of one aspect of citizenship is related to the nature of other aspects of citizenship.

Despite this, generally, citizenship rights are viewed in isolation from one another. Social citizenship is a key theme in comparative welfare state literature, but is too infrequently related to the political and civil elements of citizenship. Equally, research on political citizenship is isolated from social and civil elements. There are notable exceptions to this, such as the power resource literature which analyses how the development of political rights were crucial in welfare state development (Esping-Andersen 1990; Korpi 1989). Equally, a number of feminist authors examine how social citizenship has influenced political and civil resources and opportunities for women (Hernes 1988; Orloff 1993). Ideas about cultural rights of specific groups have loomed large in recent years. There is a specific debate about how and whether these rights are compatible with other rights of citizenship and Marshall's conception of citizenship more generally. Yet, this remains a relatively small section of research on citizenship, which is dominated by considerations of one element of citizenship in isolation from others. Numerous books and articles consider and evaluate in great detail and depth the politics of migration and its relationship to citizenship, for example. These are important and valuable works, which shed light on important issues and developments. Yet, there are relatively few texts which seek to take seriously Marshall's arguments about citizenship. Marshall's conception of citizenship points to the unified nature of citizenship and the need to consider civil, political and social rights in relation to, not isolation from, each other.

A holistic analysis of citizenship is, therefore, one which brings together theories of citizenship with an empirical analysis of citizenship. Yet, this empirical focus should be broadly understood, such that it is not only theories of citizenship and one particular empirical aspect of citizenship that is examined, but a range of empirical aspects of citizenship, and crucially, *an examination of the ways in which they impact upon one another*. This book seeks to contribute to such a holistic analysis of citizenship in contemporary Europe. We will consider a range of ideas about what citizenship should be like, before going on to use these theoretical lenses to assess developments and trends in four key areas of citizenship in Europe: political participation, the welfare state, migration and citizenship of the European Union. In so doing, the ways in which the different spheres, or elements, impact upon one another will be clearer. It is not the intention of this book to specify all the ways in which such elements interact; indeed, these are theoretical and empirical questions which are deserving of much attention. However, by viewing these developments side by side, some of these links will be seen, and it may also serve to prompt interest and debate in such connections. As such, the book makes two key arguments. Firstly, that if we are to interpret and understand developments and trends in citizenship in Europe, theory is vital. As we shall see, there are a range of different theories as to what citizenship should be like. Each of these theories thus understands contemporary debates and developments in different terms. Any assessment of citizenship in contemporary Europe is thus heavily dependent upon which theory of citizenship one adopts. The second key argument is that in order to understand the developments in one area of citizenship politics, such as the welfare state, we must appreciate the relation that this has to other areas of citizenship, such as migration and political participation.

OUTLINE OF THE BOOK

The book is divided into two sections. In the first section we examine a range of different theories of citizenship. In Chapter One we will consider about three different classical conceptions of citizenship. The first is the liberal conception, which, unsurprisingly, takes the individual as the main focus. A liberal theory of citizenship emphasises the equality of rights which each citizen holds, and how these rights enable the individual to pursue their aims and goals. The second theory, communitarianism, is critical of this position. For communitarians, the individual does not exist prior to the community. As such, they argue that the liberal theory fails to consider duty or loyalty to the community, ignores the social nature of individuals and, in emphasising rights, ignores responsibilities and duties owed to the community. The essential argument is that liberal theories of citizenship allow the pursuit of individual ends at the expense of the wider social formation or community. A third theory of citizenship is the republican tradition. It emphasises participation in government as the foundation for the promotion of the civic good. It is critical of both the liberal perspective, which it sees as too fragmentary, and also, the communitarian view, as it is wary of local identities being placed above wider civic goals.

In addition to the classical theories of citizenship there are some critical theories of citizenship, which are orientated around the issues of identity, difference and inclusion/exclusion, which we will look at in Chapter Two. Despite having the same rights as other members of the community, there are many groups, such as ethnic minorities and women, who feel that citizenship does not take account of their differences and as such, feel excluded from the community. The multicultural critique, therefore, criticises the 'universal' theories of citizenship, seeing them as a reflection of the dominant groups' identity. It instead argues for a differentiated citizenship which takes account of and respects difference, and in doing so, includes them into the community. This position has, in turn, been criticised by those who see a retreat from universalism as highly damaging to the concept of citizenship. In a similar way, a number of feminist theorists have pointed out how citizenship is a gendered concept and have sought to develop a feminist theory of citizenship.

The traditional model of citizenship is one based at the state level. Yet, developments (processes of globalisation along with growing pluralisation of western societies) have led some to call this state-centric model into question. As rights become increasingly based not upon nationality but residency (as human rights discourses become more prominent), and political activism on global causes is directed beyond the nation-state, citizenship seems to be changing its locus. In Chapter Three we will examine these theories of postnational and cosmopolitan citizenship, and probe similarities and differences. Thinking about citizenship conceived of as rights, political participation and identity, we will examine and analyse developments which might be said to lead towards, or prompt, post-national or global citizenship.

The second section of the book focuses on four key social, economic and political developments which pose challenges for citizenship in Europe. They are: political participation, the welfare state, migration and European citizenship. These issues have been chosen as the authors feel they represent the most significant challenges to and for citizenship in contemporary Europe. They raise questions of identity, belonging, participation, welfare; all key themes for citizenship. They also reflect T. H. Marshall's civil, political and social spheres of citizenship. In each of these areas, changes and/or developments raise crucial questions for citizenship. Two main themes of the book will be clear in this section. The first is to emphasise that the way in which we view these trends and developments is crucially related to how we view citizenship theoretically. The second is to emphasise that developments in these areas are interrelated.

In Chapter Four we consider political participation in Europe. A range of contemporary European societies have witnessed a decline in formal political participation. In many countries turnout at elections, and membership of political parties and trade unions, is in decline. Yet, there seem to be counter trends, with an increase in activist political participation (marches and demonstrations). In this chapter we will examine these developments to assess how citizens in contemporary Europe express themselves politically. We will go on to consider the explanations for these patterns and trends observed, arguing that the reasons for these may lie in the impact of changing (state) institutions (such as the welfare state, or social citizenship rights) along with broader changes in social trends. We will investigate whether declining engagement with formal politics should be seen as a problem for citizenship. To a large extent, the answer to this question depends upon how one views citizenship theoretically.

The welfare state in Europe is commonly held to be under pressure. There is disagreement as to whether the welfare state has been cut back or not. In Chapter Five we will begin by analysing empirical data to assess whether welfare state retrenchment has occurred. What we will find is that there is some evidence of retrenchment, although, for most countries, it does not constitute significant cutbacks. We will then go on to consider how we might explain this. Some argue that globalisation, an ageing population and other factors, make the expansive welfare state of the post-war era unaffordable in contemporary Europe. However, whether the welfare state has to be cut back due to inexorable economic and demographic pressures, is debated. We will examine these debates to ascertain whether social citizenship provision provided by the welfare state is in decline. We will also assess whether globalisation does necessitate retrenchment of the welfare state, or whether other factors, such as Economic and Monetary Union (EMU) and the process of European integration, play a role. Having done this we will be in a position to assess what any decline in social provision may mean for citizenship. Since T. H. Marshall, social rights have been seen as a vital element of citizenship. If social citizenship rights must be cut, what does this mean for citizenship? Again, different theories of citizenship have different answers to this question.

Contemporary European societies are marked by migration – the movement of people across national boundaries. This poses challenges to conventional definitions of citizenship which draw a connection between citizenship and national identity. In Chapter Six we will begin by assessing patterns and trends in migratory levels in Europe, observing large rises for some countries, but greater stability in migration patterns for other countries. We will examine the different responses to immigration by three European countries (the Netherlands, Germany and Italy) and relate this to their different conceptions and practices of citizenship. We will also examine how the European Union (EU) has impacted upon these questions of migration, identity and citizenship. The EU (and indeed, national) agenda has become dominated by a securitised conception of migration, which we will examine, before thinking about how citizenship and migration impact upon one another theoretically.

The process of European integration is the final contemporary challenge to citizenship considered in this book, in Chapter Seven. In this chapter we will return to the issues and debates surrounding questions of belonging and identity and reflect on how the ongoing process of European integration affects citizenship. Some have identified Europe as an example, par excellence, of postnational citizenship (Soysal 1994). We begin by examining the history of EU citizenship. At present two issues dominate thinking and debates about European integration and European citizenship: constitutionalism and European identity. We will examine each in turn to consider the arguments (and counter arguments) that the EU can and should have both a constitution and an identity, although it should look to the nation-state for the precise form and model for these.

In these empirical chapters we will focus, for the most part, on nine European countries: Belgium, Denmark, France, Germany, Italy, the Netherlands, Spain, Sweden and the Netherlands. The aim of the empirical chapters is also to trace processes over time; to analyse and compare, for example, levels of migration in each of the countries. The choice of time scale is rather dictated by availability of cross-national time series data; for some chapters and processes, the time scale will be longer (voter turnout from the late 1960s onwards), for others, it will be shorter (migration levels from 1995).

The choice of these countries is a mixture of theoretical and practical considerations. Theoretically, the countries represent a mixture of different social, economic, political and cultural formations. Esping-Andersen's *Three Worlds of Welfare Capitalism* (1990) pointed to three different types of welfare capitalism: the liberal, the conservative and the social democratic. It is problematic (and removed from Esping-Andersen's intentions for his model) to put countries into boxes. However, the range of countries here do reflect these different models, along with a putative 'fourth' world of welfare capitalism, the Southern European (Ferrera 1996). Geography is also an important consideration, particularly so for migration, and again the countries selected represent the different areas of Europe – with a major exception. We have not included an Eastern European country, not for theoretical reasons, but for practical ones. A major aim of the book is to examine not just the present nature of citizenship, but also, crucially, trends in citizenship. To do this requires comparable empirical information over time, which, in a number of key ways, is lacking (or at least is not available for the same time span as the other countries considered) in this region. This is regrettable, but perhaps, unavoidable. No book or volume can include everything. Indeed, it is an interesting question as to what extent the patterns and trends that are observed in this volume, for more established European countries, are to be found in the newer European countries.

CHAPTER I

Theories of citizenship

INTRODUCTION

Citizenship in its many different theoretical and actual existing (state) forms might be seen as an attempt to grapple with the question of belonging and membership. How do states, or other political entities, coalesce individuals into some form of unit capable of living with one another? Each of the different theories we will examine in this and the coming chapters has a different answer to this. Frequently they contradict one another and are often incommensurable. To an extent this reflects the context and situations to which the different theories of citizenship are opposed. To simplify somewhat, liberal citizenship developed in opposition to absolutism in the sixteenth and seventeenth centuries; communitarianism might be seen as a reaction to problems of social cohesion which began in the 1960s and 1970s; (modern) republicanism is in many ways a response to the perceived decline of civic participation. Clearly, some, if not all, of these theories have antecedents and do not spring up simply in response to a particular development, but they do gain significant elements of their analytical thrust through their rejection or opposition towards particular processes.

Citizenship is, as Delanty points out, about membership of a political community. He argues that it involves a relationship between rights, duties, participation and identity; these are the core features of citizenship (Delanty 2000: 9). What we shall see in this chapter is that different theories of citizenship prioritise different elements of Delanty's core features of citizenship. This is not to say that they ignore the others, but rather that they may be said to emphasise certain ones over others. For liberal conceptions of citizenship, it is rights that are pre-eminent; for communitarian theories of citizenship, duties and identity are asserted; and for republican theories of citizenship, participation is stressed.

LIBERAL CITIZENSHIP

To the question of how political entities stimulate, encourage or produce membership and belonging, liberal theories of citizenship place rights at the centre of any answer. Liberal citizenship seeks to foster such membership through the granting of equal rights to all (Marshall 1963). As such, liberal citizenship has an egalitarian impulse at its heart. In some ways, liberal citizenship has become a victim of its own successes. It is because its central ideal, that individuals are entitled to equal treatment *by right*, has become so engrained in western political culture (and beyond) that many are critical of it; critical that the priority it places on the private sphere inhibits delivery on the egalitarian promise inherent within. Yet, as Stephen Macedo (1990: 39) succinctly argues: 'the benefits of private citizenship are not to be sneezed at: they place certain basic human goods (security, prosperity and freedom) within the grasp of nearly all, and that is nothing less than a fantastic human achievement'. We might wish to question whether security, prosperity and freedom are within the grasp of nearly all, yet, it is undoubtedly the case that these basic human goods are within the grasp of rather more people now than in the sixteenth and seventeenth centuries, when such liberal ideals were born. The egalitarianism at the heart of liberalism is one which states that each person's fate should be determined by their own efforts rather than their birth. The individual should be given the same rights, and thereby, the conditions to pursue their own way in life, insofar as it does not harm others. To this civil egalitarianism, it is necessary to add political equality, as, in order to pursue one's own conception of a good life, it is necessary that political power be prevented from being concentrated and absolute. Therefore, each citizen is of equal political worth, such that the concentration of power (and hence, absolutism) might be prevented. The extent to which liberal citizenship pursues an egalitarian social agenda is rather more complex, and, as we shall see below, dependent upon which particular variety of liberalism one espouses.

Individualism and freedom

Liberal citizenship, as with all strands of liberalism, seeks to prioritise the individual. For liberals, the individual exists prior to society; the commitment to the individual is, thus, a core ontological belief. The individual is not a product of his or her society, but rather produces that society. As such, the idea of the social contract is a key one in liberal thought. One of the most influential early liberal thinkers, John Locke, held that all individuals have an equal capacity for reason. For Locke, prior to society, in the state of nature, individuals are free to do whatever they want, as long as they respect others' right to do the same; this is the law of nature. This law of nature also concerns property; the freedom to do whatever one wants includes protection of property. '[R]eason [...] teaches all mankind, who will but consult it, that being all equal and independent, no one ought to harm another in his life, health, liberty or possessions' (Locke [1683] 1993: 117). As Plamenatz argues, property is equated with freedom and in this sense, is prior to society and government.

> Property in the larger sense, which makes it equivalent to freedom, is prior to government; it is man's right, under God, to dispose of himself and of what he sets aside for his own use in whatever ways seem best to him. (Plamenatz 1963: 216)

The purpose of government is the protection of this freedom. For Locke, men consent to government because the enjoyment of life, liberty and property is uncertain in the state of nature, as there is no common law, no judge or arbiter in disputes and no power to enforce decisions. The individual consents to government, and thus gives up some of his or her freedom in exchange for the certainty of enjoying his or her freedoms. Yet, it is clear that government is limited to the securing of the common good and rectifying the above three deficiencies in the state of nature (Locke [1683] 1993: 178–80). Government is thus to be limited, based on consent, and have the aim of protecting the liberty and freedoms of the individual, that is, the choices of the individual in the private sphere. This chiefly involves the protection of private property. Locke states that the 'great end' of men entering society is 'the enjoyment of their properties in peace and safety' (Locke [1683] 1993: 182).

In this characterisation of the law of nature we see the key elements of liberal thought: individualism, universalism, rights, reason, equality and property. Thus, for liberal citizenship, the individual becomes a member of the political community through the granting of universal rights which secure for the individual the freedom to life, liberty and property. There is a clear antagonism and opposition to community; for Locke, the only obligation which the individual is under is to respect in others the rights he or she enjoys. All other obligations are based upon consent; an individual may choose to take on certain other obligations, but they remain his or her choice. 'The fear is that the community will seek to impose obligations upon the individual that constrain or contradict his or her self-interest' (Faulks 2002: 57).

It is important to bear in mind that liberalism originally developed, primarily, in opposition to absolutism. Its main concern, therefore, was to stand against arbitrary government.

> Both logically and historically the first point of attack is arbitrary government, and the first liberty to be secured is the right to be dealt with in accordance with law. A man who has no legal rights against another, but stands entirely at his disposal, to be treated according to his caprice, is a slave to that other. He is 'rightless,' devoid of rights. (Hobhouse [1911] 1999: 11)

It is this attack on and opposition to absolutism which informs the priority given to the individual, which entails a suspicion and hostility towards society and particularly societal obligations. These represent a restriction on liberty, which unless consented to, are of dubious legitimacy.

It is also this opposition to absolutism and concern with liberty that informs liberalism's universalism. The law and, by implication, rights, must be universal, the same for all, for if they are not, then the freedom provided is not freedom for all. For liberals, a system of differential rights and freedoms does not represent freedom for all (Hobhouse [1911] 1999: 12). As such, for liberal citizenship, each individual is to be granted the same rights; in this way, each individual is brought into the political community on the same footing. Universalism is both a way of securing membership as well as a principle of justice.

Similarly, the emphasis on citizenship as rights reflects a concern to protect the individual from the overweening power of the state. Freedom and liberty are seen as the highest aims in life and it is freedom which liberal citizenship pursues; the freedom for the individual to pursue his or her life in whichever way he or she sees fit, as long as this does not harm others. In this way, liberal citizenship has little concern with public participation; in contrast to republicans, both ancient and modern, it is not through participation in the public sphere that the individual attains the highest good, but rather the enjoyment of the private sphere. In fact, liberalism extols the virtues of a retreat into the private sphere; privatism is not something to be lamented, but rather something to be celebrated. 'Liberal politics do not merely permit their citizens to retreat into their private pursuits if they wish; liberal ideology [...] affirmatively valorises the privatisation of personality, commitment and activity' (Schuck 2002: 137). Liberal citizenship provides rights which enable the individual to pursue his or her conception of the good life. This may involve participation in the public sphere, or it may not; it is for the individual to choose. Rights are the means of securing and valorising the individual. They protect the individual, their property and their choices. 'Most importantly, the possession of rights denotes individual autonomy. Rights give space to the individual to develop their interests and fulfil their potential free from interference from other individuals or from the community as a whole' (Faulks 2002: 56). Even in the more social variants of liberal citizenship, as we will see below, rights are justified as a means to enhance liberty and enable individuals to pursue their goals.

The protection of property is seen as a core value of liberal citizenship. It is what enables the individual to be free; even social liberals such as T. H. Marshall (see below) see property as central to liberty. It is, as Schuck (2002: 133) notes, a precondition for freedom as well as the goal of freedom's exercise. In this instance, Marshall justifies redistribution of property on the basis that all should be free to participate in society, that this requires a certain level of material well-being for all and that, hence, some redistribution is justified in order to enhance the liberty of all. Other, libertarian, strands of liberalism, are firmer in their affirmation and protection of civil rights. Nozick argues for a minimal state; his argument is that if individuals justly own their possessions, then a just distribution of goods is the outcome of a free (market) exchange. In this instance, the distribution of property and goods is just and the state has no justification for interfering. The state's only justifiable role is the provision of basic systems which allow free exchange and the protection of property rights (the judicial system) (Nozick 1974).

T. H. Marshall

This minimal state is based on a negative conception of liberty; that freedom consists of the absence of barriers. Other liberals favour a more positive conception of liberty, where freedom is the ability to pursue one's chosen ends (on positive and negative liberty see Berlin 1969). This requires that all individuals have a basic level of material well-being. The most developed version of this form of liberal citizenship comes from T. H. Marshall. It also perhaps represents the classic conception of (positive) liberal citizenship, emphasising membership through equal, universal rights.

Marshall sees citizenship as 'a status bestowed on those who are members of the community. All who possess the status are equal with respect to the rights and duties with which the status is endowed' (Marshall 1963: 87). These citizenship rights are divided into three categories or elements: civil, political and social. Marshall describes the evolution of these citizenship rights in England, with civil rights being established in the eighteenth century, political rights in the nineteenth century, and social rights coming into being in the twentieth century. Civil rights include personal liberties, the right to own property and other rights associated with individual freedom. Political rights refer to those rights which enable individuals to participate in the exercise of political power and social rights refer to the right to a certain level of economic well-being and a share in society (Marshall 1963). In many ways, the development of citizenship rights may be seen as the development, or unfolding, of the principle of equality of status (Lister 2005). Civil rights consist of basic individual free-doms – freedom of conscience, speech and the right to enter contracts and hold property and recognise, in contrast to societies of feudal estates, a fundamental legal equality between individuals. This principle of equality of status is also enshrined in political rights which ensure that individuals who are recognised as equals in the civil, legal sphere, are equal in the political sphere.

Marshall points out that initially, social provision, as provided by the Poor Law, was based on the rescinding of citizenship rights; the poor forfeited their citizenship rights in order to gain social assistance. As Delanty notes, this is because the policy was aimed as much at controlling the destitute as it was with providing assistance (Delanty 2002: 16). Social rights become a part of citizenship partly through practical reasons; the full enjoyment of basic civil and political rights is to some extent, reliant upon a basic level of material well-being. As Marshall succinctly phrases it, 'The right to freedom of speech has little real substance if, from lack of edu-cation, you have nothing to say that is worth saying' (Marshall 1963: 91). They also represent the extension of the principle of equality of status to the social sphere. The accumulation and enjoyment of property which civil rights ensures, threatens to create massive inequalities, which in turn, threaten the equality of status which citizenship represents.

Civil rights of citizenship aimed at destroying systems of class based on a hierarchy of status, through different legal rights and customs. Yet, these rights encourage a second system of social class which is 'not established and defined by the laws and customs of the society [...] but emerge[s] from the interplay of a variety of factors related to the institutions of property and education and the structure of the national economy' (Marshall 1963: 88–9). Citizenship is compatible with this system of social class, designed not to destroy or eliminate such inequalities emanating from activity in the private sphere, but rather aimed at 'class abatement', that is, reducing the worst excesses of inequality. In this way, Marshall argues, citizenship (the granting of equal rights) replaces status differentiations with market differentiations. The aim is not substantive equality but an equal freedom to pursue different aims and goals, with inevitable inegalitarian con-sequences. 'Differential status, associated with class, function and family, was replaced by the single uniform status of citizenship, which provided the foundation of equality on which the structure of inequality could be built' (Marshall 1963: 91).

Classically liberal in its orientation, citizenship is seen as 'the architect of legitimate social inequality' (Marshall 1963: 73), that is, a status which bestows a fundamental equality, which fosters freedom and allows, even encourages, market-based inequalities. Yet, should these inequalities become too pronounced, the equal freedom to pursue one's own conception of the good life, denied by feudalist systems, is similarly threatened by a capitalist system of vast inequalities. Thus social rights, defined as 'a universal right to real income which is not proportionate to the market value of the claimant' (Marshall 1963: 100), might be seen as rights which enhance the (positive) liberty of individuals, for it is only through a basic level of material well-being that an individual can enjoy their rights and liberties.

Thus, citizenship, for Marshall, provides membership of the community through the establishment of equal rights which give each individual an equal chance to pursue their own, private, goals. It aims at equality, but it is a public equality permitting, encouraging, even, a private (market) inequality.

Marshall's theory is not unproblematic and has been subject to a great deal of criticism. The periodization of the development of citizenship has been questioned, as has his account of the uni-directional unfolding of citizenship rights (Himmelfarb 1984; Giddens 1982; Mann 1987). Delanty (2002) identifies a number of key criticisms, which we will examine in further detail below and in subsequent chapters. The first is that Marshall ignores other forms of exclusion. His account privileges class inequalities and ignores other forms of inequality, such as gender and race (Pateman 1988; Young 1989). Secondly, authors have argued that his account of the development of citizenship is almost apolitical; citizens are granted rights passively. In fact, authors such as Mann (1987) argue that citizenship is a product of political struggle over time, something which is entirely missing from Marshall's account. Thirdly, Marshall assumes a connection between the nation and state, which cannot now be taken for granted (if it ever could). Citizenship rights and provisions are no longer provided solely by the state; as state power has passed upwards to supranational institutions like the EU, downwards to local and devolved assemblies, citizenship rights are provided by sources other than the state.

COMMUNITARIANISM

Liberal citizenship's emphasis, or even reification, of the rights of the individual has given rise to an extended critique from a wide range of political thinkers, who seek to (re)emphasise the role and importance of community. Liberal citizenship, as we have seen, seeks to create membership through the provision of rights. Communitarianism, however, seeks to emphasise the obligations of citizenship and sees membership as a prerequisite for rights. This is because where liberalism seeks to emphasise rights, communitarianism stresses the obligations that the individual owes to the community. These obligations will only be felt by a pre-existing community. Where such a community or common identification is not present, individuals will feel under no obligations to uphold the responsibilities which citizenship incurs. Hence, developing membership and belonging is less a case of making the community through citizenship rights but rather making citizenship reflect the community.

Communitarianism is a wide-ranging critique of liberal political philosophy, and a certain degree of care needs to be taken as there is perhaps not one, single, communitarian position. Indeed, it is worth bearing in mind that many of the concerns of modern communitarian thinkers have historical and philosophical antecedents. Although the liberal–communitarian debate took place in the 1970s and 1980s, in some ways, these kinds of arguments might be traced as far back as Hegel's critique of Kant and Locke. (Indeed, some authors have referred to the more modern debate as reinventing the wheel (Smith 1986: 123)). Hegel criticised the attempts of liberals like Locke and Kant to invoke an ahistorical conception of the individual (the state of nature and so on) which was then used to specify universal norms of justice around which society is to be organised. 'Hegel's point is that despite the claim to speak universally and ahistorically, these moralities presuppose and are dependent upon a social context for their validity' (Smith 1986: 133). The concept of community is also an important one for Marxism, as communism offers the prospect of an ideal community. As Delanty (2002: 25) notes, these conceptions of community differ from those of modern communitarians in emphasising the material, as opposed to the latter's emphasis on culture and morality.

Rawls and the communitarian critique

In many ways, modern communitarianism develops as a philosophical position in response and opposition to John Rawls' A *Theory of Justice*, first published in 1971. In order to understand communitarianism, it is worth beginning by considering Rawls' work and some of the principle objections to it, as these are the foundations of much modern communitarian thought. Rawls' work is not an explicit discussion of citizenship, but in acting as the spark for communitarian thinking, it does provide the launch pad for communitarian thinking about citizenship. The key point to carry forward is that, for communitarians, the community lies prior to the individual. It is this position which defines communitarian conceptions of citizenship.

Rawls seeks to identify what kind of social organisation is desirable. He proposes a scenario, called the original position (Rawls 1972: 118). In this original position, individuals are rational utility maximisers; they seek to maximise their goods and minimise their costs and pain. Crucially, for Rawls' argument, in the original position, individuals are placed behind a 'veil of ignorance'. In this hypothetical situation, no-one knows their class status, their talents or abilities, their psychological makeup (e.g. whether they are risk averse), the economic and political situation, or information about the society to which they belong (Rawls 1972: 137). Faced with this situation, Rawls argues that individuals would choose two principles of justice. The first principle is that everyone is entitled to the most extensive system of basic liberties which is compatible with the same liberties for all. The second principle states that social and economic inequalities are arranged such that they are attached to positions open to all (fair equality of opportunity principle) and to the greatest benefit of the least advantaged (the difference principle) (Rawls 1972: 302). These principles are in order of priority; 'equal liberty takes precedence over equal opportunity, which takes precedence over equal resources' (Kymlicka 2002: 56). In this formulation, inequality is only permissible if it benefits the less well-off.

Rawls' aim is to deduce principles which all rational persons, despite different faiths and conceptions of the good life, might agree to. The communitarian argument is that such an enterprise is fundamentally misguided as moral principles can only be understood within existing moral communities.

> For the communitarians, morality is something which is rooted in practice – in the particular practices of actual communities. So the idea of looking to uncover abstract principles of morality by which to evaluate or redesign society is an implausible one. There are no universal principles of morality or justice discoverable by reason. The foundations of morals lie not in philosophy but in politics. (Kukathas and Pettit 1990: 95)

Sandel takes issue with the conception of the self that Rawls relies upon. The Rawlsian account, Sandel argues, presents a conception of the 'unencumbered self, a self understood as prior to and independent of purposes and aims' (Sandel 1984: 86). Sandel's object of attack is the liberal idea that community is the product of independent individuals' associations. Sandel argues that it makes no sense to speak of community like this, as individuals capable of forming such associations are dependent upon a notion of community. Individuals shorn of community do not have the capacity to deliberate, choose or reflect. Sandel accuses Rawlsian liberalism of being 'parasitic on a notion of community it officially rejects' (Sandel 1984: 90–1).

The self and the community

At the heart of the liberal–communitarian debate lies an ontological difference. For liberals, the self is prior to and constitutive of society; in Rawls' famous phrase, 'prior to the ends which are affirmed by it' (Rawls 1971: 560). For communitarians, this abstract, or in Sandel's phrase 'unencumbered conception of the self' (Sandel 1984: 85), is profoundly mistaken. Instead, they argue that the individual is embedded in and constituted by social formations and communities. We cannot meaningfully speak of the individual outside of a particular social context, as that social context is constitutive of the individual. As we shall go on to see, this position means that communitarians are hostile to the liberal emphasis on rights; if the community is constitutive of the individual, then it is misguided to affirm the individual above the community, rights above obligations. Rather, for communitarians, the interests of the community should not be seen as conflicting with the interests of the individual, but more exactly as that which constitutes and gives meaning to the self. As MacIntyre argues:

> [W]e all approach our own circumstances as bearers of a particular social identity. I am someone's son or daughter, someone else's cousin or uncle; I am a citizen of this or that city, a member of this or that guild or profession; I belong to this clan, that tribe, this nation. Hence what is good for me has to be the good for one who inhabits these roles. As such, I inherit from the past of my family, my city, my tribe, my nation, a variety of debts, inheritances, rightful expectations and obligations. These constitute the given of my life, my moral starting point. This is in part what gives my life its own moral particularity. (MacIntyre 1984: 220)

The liberal–communitarian debate is wide-ranging with many variations and subtle shades of opinion (for more on this see Mulhall and Swift 1992). In this section we will consider what communitarian thinking means for citizenship and, specifically, the implications of this different conception of the self for citizenship. There are three main ways in which the communitarian conception of citizenship differs from the liberal one: a reassertion of the obligations of citizenship over the rights of citizenship; an emphasis on the importance of membership and identity; and the need for a substantive notion of the good life. We shall consider each in turn.

Rights and responsibilities

As discussed above, communitarians assert that the self is constituted by the community and, as a moral and ethical subject, is embedded in a cultural context. It is the community which gives the individual their subjectivity, sense of moral purpose and identity. They are heavily critical of the liberal notion of the subject as an autonomous, asocial individual. It is this 'thin' notion of the individual that communitarians reject. They believe that the liberal emphasis on individual rights and personal freedom ignores the extent to which these things are only possible within preexisting communities (Kymlicka 2002: 212). Liberalism, it is argued, ignores the real ties that bind individuals together. It is not autonomous rights bearing individual citizens that create communities, but communities who create autonomous, rights-bearing (and duty-owing) citizens.

The logical corollary of this is that liberal citizenships' emphasis on rights is misguided. If it is the community which creates autonomous, moral citizens, then, as the above quotation from MacIntyre suggests, it is the needs and interests of the community which should be prioritised, not the rights of the individual. Kymlicka explains:

> Once we recognize the dependence of human beings on society, then our obligations to sustain the common good of society are as weighty as our rights to individual liberty. Hence, communitarians argue, the liberal 'politics of rights' should be abandoned for, or at least supplemented by, a 'politics of the common good'. (Kymlicka 2002: 212)

In terms of citizenship, this concern with the priority of the community has translated into a recognition or (re)emphasis of the obligations of citizenship. Simply stated, a number of communitarians feel that there is an imbalance between the rights individuals hold and the requirements or obligations that they have towards the community. Over-emphasis of individuals' pursuit of happiness under the aegis of individual rights means that the concerns of the community, or 'the common good', are ignored, with the result that communities suffer. If liberal citizenship emphasises individual rights as constitutive or supportive of membership, then for communitarians it is in the obligations and duties of citizenship that membership is engendered.

This aspect of communitarian is probably most associated with the work of Amitai Etzioni. In *The Spirit of Community* (1995) Etzioni argues that there is, and perhaps has long been, an imbalance between rights and responsibilities. He argues that correcting this imbalance requires a four-point plan of action. Firstly, there should be a moratorium on new rights, likening the creation of rights to the printing of money – a process the leads to (rights) inflation (Etzioni 1995: 5). The second element is a reconnection of rights to responsibilities.

> Claiming rights without assuming responsibilities is unethical and illogical [...] To take and not to give is an amoral, self-centred pre-disposition that ultimately no society can tolerate [...] Hence, *those most concerned about rights ought to be the first ones to argue for the resumption of responsibilities.* One presumes the other. (Etzioni 1995: 9–10 original emphasis)

It is interesting to note that Etzioni is not arguing that rights are not important, but rather that the exercise of rights is dependent upon a stable, functioning community. If we all indulge our rights without heed of the obligations we owe to the community, to each other, then, ultimately, the community spirals into decline and the very existence of our rights is jeopardised. In some ways, this does not seem to be saying much more than J. S. Mill's ([1869] 1989) harm principle; that each of us has a right to as much liberty as is compatible with the same for all others. But Etzioni goes further, and thus clearly distinguishes the communitarian position. The third element in his agenda on rights and responsibilities is the assertion that, while all rights entail obligations, there are obligations which do not accord rights. Etzioni cites the environment as an example of an issue where we have a responsibility without any expected benefit. This is perhaps something noncontentious, even if liberals might be unhappy with the terminology. Yet, Etzioni continues and suggests that '*the same observations hold true for our responsibility to our moral, social and political environment*' (Etzioni 1995: 11, original emphasis). This suggests that we have responsibilities to support and maintain the community in a more general sense. Etzioni seems to be claiming that there is a parallel between environmental harm and moral, social and political harm. Remembering that for communitarians, the community is constitutive of the individual as a moral subject, Etzioni seems to be suggesting that moral, social and political degradation poses as serious a threat to future generations' existence as does environmental degradation. This seems to suggest that the environmental, social, moral and political 'health' of the community overrides individual rights and entitlements; the community comes first.

The final element of Etzioni's agenda is a readjustment of the interpretation of rights, such that public safety might be upheld. This is something that Etzioni, and others, have pursued with renewed vigour following 11 September 2001 (Etzioni and Marsh 2003; Etzioni 2004). They argue that in an age of international terrorism, of mass civilian casualties, that rights must be curtailed in order to guarantee public safety (for a critical analysis of this position see Waldron 2003).

Membership and identity

In asserting the priority of the individual, the abstract, 'unencumbered self' (Sandel 1984), liberals assert universalism. Justice and, relatedly, citizenship, is not particular. Principles of justice and the rights which uphold them, are universal; the same for all peoples, times and places. Yet, communitarians argue that the individual as a moral subject only exists within pre-existing communities. As such, justice and citizenship can only meaningfully exist with such communities. Walzer argues that there is no perspective outside of our community, that we cannot assume the Archimedean position and step outside our culture and history. Justice, for Walzer, is acting in accordance with the shared understandings of its members (Walzer 1983). This means that citizenship, for communitarians, is always citizenship of a particular place; there can be no universal concept of citizenship. A logical consequence of this idea is that different communities will have different notions of justice, and in terms of the present discussion, different conceptions of citizenship. Citizenship is therefore citizenship of *a particular place*, a particular community.

The rejection of universalism inherent in communitarianism reifies the community. As the community is, in effect, the locus of moral order, there is a sense in which it requires protection. Taylor argues that there may be a need for state recognition of minority *and* majority cultures (Taylor 1994; for more on this see Chapter Three). Miller, meanwhile argues that 'the duties we owe to our compatriots may be more extensive than the duties we owe to strangers, simply because they are compatriots' (Miller 1988b: 647). Delanty points out that communitarians are concerned with protecting the majority culture, and contra multiculturalism, 'incoming groups must adapt to this community in order to participate in its political community' (Delanty 2000: 27). If liberal citizenship promotes belonging and membership through the provision of equal rights, communitarianism seems to suggest that a sense of belonging and membership to the community are a prerequisite for such rights. It is only community, not abstract principles, that can provide 'enduring normative ties' (Delanty 2002: 159) that allow a coherent and strong conception of citizenship to develop and flourish. Identification with and belonging to this community are therefore con-stitutive elements of citizenship, not, as perhaps liberal accounts would suggest, an outcome.

The state and conceptions of the good

The third element of communitarian citizenship is a critique of the liberal idea of state neutrality. As Kymlicka points out, liberal citizenship rests on the idea that the state is neutral in terms of what constitutes the common good.

> In a liberal state, the common good is the result of a process of combining preferences all of which are counted equally (if consistent with the prin-ciples of justice) [...] Hence the common good in a liberal society is adjusted to fit the pattern of preferences and conceptions of the good held by individuals. (Kymlicka 2000: 220)

Liberal citizens are free to choose their conception of the good life and pursue it, as long as it does not infringe upon others' rights. This protects the private sphere and allows, even encourages, a plurality of conceptions of the good. Liberal thought is based on procedural justice; the right and the good are separated; abstract universal principles of justice are estab-lished (the right) and, as long as these are not violated, individuals are free to pursue whichever conception of the good they see fit. But for com-munitarians, the self is constituted by the community. It is the values of the community which provide individuals with their moral identity. There are stronger and weaker versions of this argument within communitarian thought. MacIntyre (1972), for example, argues for an Aristotelian con-ception of the good, where the good lies in the performance and achieve-ment of certain social roles. As such, individuals do not choose their own good, but rather discover it through the guidance of the community. Walzer has a more moderate version of the argument. As described above, in rejecting a universal conception of justice, Walzer argues that a com-munity's shared values provide guidance on what constitutes justice (Walzer 1983). As the community is constitutive of the individual and also fundamental to morality and ethics, it follows that for communitarians, the state cannot be neutral; there are no abstract principles beyond the conception of morality which lies in the community. Thus, Kymlicka argues: 'A communitarian state can and should encourage people to adopt conceptions of the good that conform to the community's way of life, while discouraging conceptions of the good that conflict with it' (Kymlicka 2000: 220). In terms of citizenship, this means a less privatist conception. For liberal citizenship, rights were the means by which individuals pursued their (generally) private conceptions of the good. For communitarians, the good is irrevocably bound to the good of the community; a privatist retreat is not possible. The community is constitutive of the individual, the moral and ethical order and our conceptions of the good.

Criticisms of communitarian citizenship

There is a recognition amongst communitarians that (re)emphasising obligations and duties may place the individual in a somewhat precarious position. The apparent primacy given to obligations, and, in some versions of communitarianism, the virtual or actual denial of the liberal doctrine of natural rights (MacIntyre 1984; Walzer 1983), leaves communitarianism exposed to charges of collectivism, or in emphasising responsibilities over rights, tilting the stick too far the other way. In such a system, individuals who dissent from the community position could be coerced into conformity and compliance. Other critics have charged communitarian thinking on citizenship with having little to say about the role of the state (Delanty: 2002), and coming close to a version of voluntarism (O'Neill 1997).

REPUBLICANISM

Republicanism shares with communitarianism a suspicion towards the privatism of liberal citizenship. There is a concern that 'liberalism gives too much concern to privacy and individual rights and too little to fostering the public virtues that lead people to do their duties as citizens' (Dagger 2002: 146). But whereas communitarianism relies upon the bonds of a pre-existing cultural or ethnic community, republicanism relies on public participation in the community. In other words, for communitarians, citizenship should be orientated around pre-existing cultural communities whereas for republicans, citizenship is created through the process of participation in public affairs. For it is in these encounters that individuals go beyond the concerns of their private life, the private world of their family and friends, and consider the public good. Like liberalism, however, republicanism shares a concern with individual liberty. It is, however, a rather different notion of freedom. If liberal citizenship seeks to promote the negative liberty of citizens, to enshrine rights which protect them from interference, republican citizenship seeks to foster a positive freedom (Berlin 1969), to create conditions where individuals are self-governing. Thus, citizenship for republicans, provides freedom, in the sense of self-government, and membership, in that when we participate in public life we encounter and integrate with other members of the community. For republican theories of citizenship, participation is the means by which both freedom and membership are created and sustained. Before going on to consider how participation sustains freedom and membership in more detail, we shall briefly consider the history of republican thinking.

Republicanism is, in origin, a classical ideal. It comes from the ancient societies of Greece and Rome, where citizens were those who partook in the governance of their societies. This was seen as an expectation rather than a right. As Dagger points out, the Greeks drew a distinction between the *politēs*, who was the citizen expected to participate in public life and the *idiōtēs*, the private person who would not or could not fulfil these responsibilities and expectations (Dagger 2002: 149). That the modern word idiot derives from a term for one who does not participate indicates the high value and regard placed upon participation. The classical republican tradition is one that comes from Cicero, through Machiavelli. These authors, and others, celebrated the active, participatory citizen, and supported a system of government marked by self-government, the rule of law and separation of powers (for more on the classical origins of republicanism see Oldfield 1990). These classical ideas and ideals were rediscovered in more modern times, and are influential in the writings of de Tocqueville ([1835–40] 2000), Rousseau ([1762] 1987), Jefferson (1999) and others. In turn, in the twentieth century, republican ideas have re-emerged in the works of Arendt (1958; 1963), Pocock (1975) and Barber (1984). The burgeoning literature on social capital, which argues that states and communities where individuals trust each other and engage in collective endeavours, are more vibrant, wealthy and healthy societies, might also be seen as drawing upon republican ideas (see Putnam 2000).

Republican freedom

Republican citizenship is, like liberal citizenship, concerned with promoting freedom. For liberal citizenship, the overriding aim is to provide certain rights, which provide and sustain the freedom of the individual. This is conceived of as freedom from interference so that individuals can pursue their (private) goals in life. Republican citizenship is also animated by a concern to protect and ensure freedom, but it is a rather different notion of freedom; where liberal citizenship sees freedom as being about a lack of interference, for republicans, liberty consists in a freedom from domination, which involves self-government.

A republican criticism of liberal theories of freedom is that they ignore relations of domination. Pettit draws a distinction between domination and interference. It is possible to exert domination without interfering. He cites the examples of the wife in fear of being beaten by her husband, the employee subject to the arbitrary decisions of the employer, and the welfare recipient dependent upon the caprice of an administrator. In these relationships, the 'master' may not actually do anything; he or she may not actually interfere. Yet, whether they do so or not, they remain dominant and the other party remains dominated. Such a situation is akin to that of the benign dictator. 'Under an older, republican way of thinking about freedom, individuals in such a dominated position are straightforwardly unfree' (Pettit 1997: 5). Therefore, for republicans, the absence of interference does not necessarily promote freedom. Equally, Pettit argues, the presence of interference does not necessarily represent a constraint on liberty.

How is this the case? How can we be free, but also subject to restraint from laws? The republican answer to these questions is based on classical republican ideals of civic virtue and public participation. Skinner argues that Machiavelli saw that the preservation of liberty depended upon the prevention of one group or class assuming dominance. Thus, for Machiavelli, it is necessary that the different social groups be active in pressing for their concerns, for in so doing, they create a kind of equilibrium which prevents one group from dominating the other (Skinner 1983). Law which ensures the freedom of the citizenry is dependent upon the participation of the citizenry. Whilst such civic virtue is necessary, it is not sufficient. There is also a need for a mixed system of government; a separation of powers, to ensure that power does not become concentrated in the hands of the few (see Madison, Hamilton and Jay [1788] 2003). Under such a system of government law is just, and obedience to just laws, which the citizen has played a role in authoring, represents self-government. This conception of liberty is what Benjamin Constant referred to as the liberty of the ancients. The liberty of the ancients, Constant argued, lay in their active participation in public life, self-government. The liberty of the moderns, which is perhaps most akin to liberalism, lies in the unfettered pursuit of goals in the private sphere (Constant [1816] 1988).

Civic virtue

Freedom, conceived as self-government, is central for republicans, as it is only when we are free in the respect of being self-governing, that other freedoms are secure. Rawls, a liberal, phrases the position thus:

> The idea is that without widespread participation in democratic politics by a vigorous and informed citizen body, and certainly with a general retreat into private life, even the most well defined political institutions will fall

into the hands of those who seek to dominate and impose their will through the state apparatus either for the sake of power and military glory or for reasons of class and economic interest, not to mention expansionist religious fervour and nationalist fanaticism. The safety of democratic liberties requires the active participation of citizens who possess the political virtues needed to maintain a constitutional regime. (Rawls 1988: 272)

Rawls goes on to argue that there is nothing inherent in this idea which clashes with liberalism, as civic virtues are encouraged in order to promote individual liberties. Yet, there is another strand of republican thought, sometimes referred to as Aristotelian republicanism (see Kymlicka 2000), which stresses civic virtues and civic participation because it is through political participation and public engagement that we realise our inner natures. For this conception of republicanism, participation is not an instrumental good, something which ensures our freedom, but rather a good in itself – and further, the highest good. Such a conception is inimical to liberalism.

Republican citizenship appears to oscillate between these two poles, between participation as a good in itself and participation as a means to an end. Yet, some have tried to straddle this divide. Skinner, in particular, has sought to defend a conception of republicanism where civic virtue and individual liberty are compatible and, actually, mutually constitutive.

We can only hope to enjoy a maximum of our own individual liberty if we do not place that value above the pursuit of the common good. To insist on doing so is [...] to be a corrupt as opposed to a virtuous citizen. (Skinner 1992: 221)

The question then becomes, how are we to ensure that citizens do carry out these roles? The first, liberal, answer is that in a plural society, the common good is promoted by everyone pursuing their own self interest. The right of an individual to choose and to be free from interference is maintained. This idea does not seem strong enough for republicans as it must allow for that fact that some citizens will choose not to participate. Rejecting it, Skinner argues, means that it is likely to lead to corruption as some people ignore or forfeit their civic obligations and power becomes concentrated (Skinner 1984). In many ways, the question of how to encourage or create civic virtue remains one of the most difficult for modern republican thinking. For example, the literature on social capital extols at lengths the benefits of social capital, that is, of people joining together in face-to-face activities, or participating in public and civic affairs (Putnam 2000). What it is less good at doing is answering the question as to how social capital is created (although see Kumlin 2004; Herreros 2004).

There seem to be three distinct republican answers to the question as to how civic participation can be encouraged and sustained. The first answer, to the question of how civic participation is to be fostered, stems from Rousseau ([1762] 1987). It argues that individual citizens need to be coerced out of selfish ways and forced into performing their civic duties and responsibilities. This is a position that Skinner seems to endorse in places, arguing that certain civic duties must be upheld in order to ensure the survival of the free state and the maintenance of our individual liberties (Skinner 1984; for a review see Shaw 2003). Shaw argues that in other places Skinner seems to place the emphasis on law; that individuals pursue their own self interest, but that the law modifies the worst excesses of these and thus promotes the public interest (Skinner 1983; Shaw 2003). These arguments, echoing Rousseau's invocation that citizens should be forced to be free, are abhorrent to liberals and seem to carry vaguely totalitarian connotations. Yet, there are many examples of this kind of policy. Citizens are 'forced' to vote in some countries, such as Australia, as if they do not, they incur a fine. In most countries, citizens are compelled to conduct jury service. These, and others, are examples of policies where citizens are required to perform their civic duties, which are seen as necessary to the continuation of the wider socio-political system which guarantees freedoms. The argument goes that we must accept the imposition of voting so that the democratic system, which protects our individual freedoms, continues to function. Yet, the idea that individuals should be forced to perform their civic duties is one that frequently attracts criticism. It is also something that, as Kymlicka notes, seems to fly in the face of prevailing liberal ideas. 'This is one of those cases [...] where liberalism has simply won the historical debate, and all subsequent debate occurs in a sense, within the boundaries of basic liberal commitments' (Kymlicka 2000: 297).

The second position adopted by modern republicans seems to be based around the idea that public and political discourse has become impoverished and distant from most people. The underlying assumption behind this is that individuals are by nature interested in politics and public and civic participation, and that the reason individuals increasingly choose not to participate in public affairs is that they lack substantive content (see Barber 1984). Deliberative democrats argue for more small-scale political forums where individuals can meet face-to-face and deliberate on political and civic matters (see Dryzek 2000). The idea is that in representative democracies citizens have little opportunity to participate and these opportunities do not engage people in public affairs, and that if people were given the opportunities to be active, participatory citizens, they would take them. Kymlicka finds such arguments lacking. The problem, he suggests, is one of transition. How do we get from a situation of low-frequency, low-intensity participation to one of high-frequency, high-intensity participation? It would require that citizens mobilise and demand these kinds of political spaces, but they would have to do so within the existing political spaces which do not inspire citizens to participate. Also, he suggests that the attachment that many, if not most, feel to the private sphere, is not solely because of the impoverishment of public life, but also because of the enrichment of private life. He goes on to argue that in plural, heterogeneous societies, 'we cannot expect a consensus on the intrinsic value of political activities, or the relative importance of political activities as compared to activities in the social or personal sphere' (Kymlicka 2000: 297–9).

The final way in which civic virtues might be encouraged is through the education system. This can be done implicitly (as described in liberal virtue theory above), or explicitly, through citizenship education. Bernard Crick (1999), the author of a report which introduced formal citizenship education classes, describes citizenship education as a necessity for a free society. The aim of such education varies from country to country, but there is a general consensus that it should go beyond simple civic knowledge, such that it aims at the creation of civic virtue. However, some have argued that such education in practice may be ineffective, counter productive and potentially, anathema to wider educational goals, as the promotion of a civic agenda can run counter to wider educational goals of questioning and critical thought (Murphy 2007).

Participation: integrative and educative

For republicans, public and civic participation, however encouraged and fostered, is the foundation of freedom. It is also the foundation of membership, of citizenship. For liberal citizenship, membership of the community is engendered through the granting of equal rights. For communitarians, membership is based around pre-existing cultural communities and citizenship rights are granted to members of that community who, in identifying with the community, will fulfil the responsibilities and duties of citizenship. For republican citizenship, participation is the cornerstone of membership, as it is seen to have integrative and educative effects (Dagger 2002: 150).

When we participate in public affairs, we leave behind our private concerns and engage with others and adopt a public position on affairs. (Again, this reflects the Rousseauian ideal that when we are active in public affairs we should reflect the 'general will' of the citizenry.) The idea that through the process of participation we become more likely to trust and cooperate with others is a central contention of social capital litera- ture. Putnam, with whom the concept is most closely associated, defines social capital as 'connections among individuals – social networks and the norms of reciprocity and trustworthiness that arise from them' (Putnam 2000: 19). For social capital theorists, these connections are forged through face-to-face interactions with one another, through civic engage- ment. Putnam establishes that other things being equal, people who are more active in civic life are generally more trusting of one another. The reason for this is simply that we are more likely to be trusting towards people we have had dealings with before; we have a basis on which to trust people. Participation, both civic and political, means that we encounter one another more often and in so doing, are more trusting of each other. A more trusting citizenry essentially means that the society functions more effectively as when cooperation is more effective, then society is more efficient. This goes for politics, economics and the social sphere generally. Putnam's earlier work, *Making Democracy Work*, found that the variance in the effectiveness of government institutions in Italy was related to the level of social capital. Where social capital was higher, local government functioned more effectively (Putnam 1993). Whilst some have criticised the seemingly tautological nature of social capital (in order to create social capital, individuals must participate – but don't they need social capital in order to participate in the first place?) and whether participation in social clubs and bird watching societies really can provide the necessary support for democratic societies (see Levi 1993 and Skocpol 2004), it represents a clear republican statement that participation in political or civic affairs integrates citizens, bringing them closer together and in so doing, allows for societies to function more effectively.

In addition to the integrative effects of participation, for republicans, participation also has educative effects. The educative effect of participa- tion is clearly linked to the integrative aspect. The argument is that when we participate in public affairs we make use of talents and abilities that may otherwise lie dormant. These flourish whilst we are active in public affairs but may then prove to be useful in other aspects of citizens' lives (Dagger 2002: 151).

In this way, republican citizenship is, in Oldfield's (1994) term, a prac- tice; it is not a set of rights, as in liberal citizenship, or something we bear by virtue of our identity and community, as in communitarian citizenship, but something that we do. In being active citizens, we become more closely integrated and cooperative with our fellow citizens, and are enriched as individuals. Participation is, therefore, for republican citizenship, the means by which we become citizens as well as a core feature of citizenship: 'Participation in public life thus seems to be a pathway to, as well as a defining feature of, republican citizenship' (Dagger 2002: 152). As discussed above, participation is also the key means by which we experience and protect liberty. Thus, republican citizenship prioritises participation as the means by which we secure our freedom, develop our relationships with our fellow citizens and enhance our individual capacities and skills.

Criticisms of republican citizenship

Republican citizenship is criticised from a number of different perspectives. We have already considered some of these, such as the claim that the republican conception of citizenship is unrealistic, as modern people derive their sense of worth and identity primarily from their interactions in the private sphere and not the public. Related to this, another criticism we have pointed to is the problem of how to encourage or foster such civic participation and whether citizens must be coerced into participation. One criticism that we have not yet examined is one that anticipates some of the debates that we will examine in the next chapter. The point is that the emphasis on the public and the common good may tend to marginalise or ignore those who are different. As the civic public has traditionally, historically been made up of able-bodied white men, the public or common good is frequently constructed in such terms. The imposition that we adopt the position of the common good thus means that some groups – women, ethnic and religious minorities – have to abandon or suppress their identity, their difference. We shall consider these arguments more fully in the next chapter, but briefly consider the republican rejoinder. Dagger makes two points; firstly, that any consideration of and respect for difference cannot rule out the possibility of trying to find common ground, for, without it, political debate, discourse and decision becomes impossible. The second point is that republicanism does not ask that we ignore our particular circumstances, but only that we seek to find common ground as different people, 'to find unity in the midst of diversity' (Dagger 2002: 155).

CONCLUSION

We began by citing Delanty's (2000) observation that citizenship involves a relationship between four different elements: rights, duties, participation and identity. The three theories of citizenship we have discussed in this chapter each privilege a different one of those elements. Liberal citizenship privileges rights; it seeks to provide individual rights which allow the individual to pursue their own conception of the good life, free from intrusion or coercion. It is through the granting of individual rights that membership of the political community is secured. The work of T. H. Marshall is particularly important in describing how citizenship evolves to try to create an equality of status which brings about sufficient inclusion in the society to allow individuals to follow their own different lifestyles and choices. The political community is the product of individuals' pursuit of different conceptions of the good.

Communitarian theories of citizenship reject some of liberalism's core claims. Most particularly, communitarians reject the idea that the individual is prior to society. For communitarians, society is constitutive of the individual. As such, liberal citizenship's emphasis on rights is misguided, as it does not pay sufficient attention to duties and identity. Communitarians are hostile to liberal citizenship's emphasis on rights. This is because they see that the community is prior to the individual and, as such, see that the interests of the community must be prioritised above individual rights. We identified three key elements of communitarian citizenship: a call for a rebalancing between rights and responsibilities, the importance of identity and membership, and a rejection of state neutrality and an assertion that the community needs to project a moral identity, rather than, as in liberal conceptions, the state being neutral on ethical and moral issues.

Republican citizenship shares some aspects of the communitarian unease with the prioritisation of individual rights. Republicans see freedom in terms of active participation in public affairs and self-government. As such, it criticises the liberal emphasis on privatism and a denigration of the public sphere. Therefore, republican citizenship prioritises participation. It is only by participating in civic and public life that we can be free. There are different ideas as to how this civic virtue can be promoted, but it remains the core of republican citizenship. It is seen as bringing about integrative and educative effects to the political community. As such, membership, for republican citizenship, is created through participation, rather than being presented through the provision of rights, as in liberal citizenship, or a pre-requisite for such rights, as in communitarianism.

Whilst emphasising the key differences between the main three theories of citizenship, it is important to recognise that the idea of three rigid positions is somewhat stylised, and that there is, to greater and lesser degrees, blurring of the boundaries between them. There are liberal communitarians (see Delanty 2000), liberal republicans (see Dagger

2000), and also overlaps between republicanism and communitarianism (Kymlicka 2000). These hybrid positions attempt to balance the emphasis on the different elements of citizenship, such that liberal republicanism seeks to encourage and stimulate public and civic participation whilst protecting the rights of the individual. Debates about citizenship, about rights, obligations, identity and participation are live, vibrant and ongoing.

CHAPTER 2

Theories of citizenship: feminism and multiculturalism

INTRODUCTION

The theories of citizenship discussed in the previous chapter, despite their differences, share a view that citizenship is a universal category. This means that for the classical theories of citizenship, no matter how we define citizenship, it should be the same for all citizens, for all members of the community. Whatever rights, responsibilities and duties that the status confers upon one, should be the rights, duties and responsibilities that all share. However, this is a position that has come under some scrutiny and criticism. The foundation of these criticisms might be broadly summed up as a concern with difference. There is a concern that citizenship excludes women and minority groups. Of course, historically speaking, this is an undisputed part of the historical record. Women and ethnic minorities were, in most 'advanced' western societies, simply denied the rights of citizenship. In many ways, both have been seen as property, either as slaves, or as the domestic property of husbands. Over time, the rights of citizenship have been extended to include women and ethnic minorities. However, it is argued that, whilst many of those formally excluded from citizenship are now included, they are not included in the same way and continue to suffer inequalities and oppression, that they are second class citizens. Feminist authors have articulated their concerns regarding citizenship and seek to develop a more gender equal conception of citizenship, whilst multi-cultural theorists stress that citizenship which is truly egalitarian needs to take account of people's different socio-cultural identities. We will consider each of these arguments in detail.

FEMINISM

Feminism contends that whilst the classical theories of citizenship may appear to be gender neutral, it is, in practice and in theory, a deeply gendered concept. Women have been excluded from citizenship in ancient and modern times, but, more than this, they argue that the concept of citizenship is one imbued with patriarchal and discriminatory tones.

Historically, women have been excluded from citizenship. From its inception in Ancient Greece, women were simply, along with slaves, not considered as citizens. The political thought of Aristotle and others held that women were apolitical, domestic beings. Women inhabited an apolitical private sphere, whilst citizenship was the domain of men, and the public sphere. This exclusion has been maintained for thousands of years, and it is arguably only in the twentieth century that women have acquired the basic rights of citizenship. Women were denied political rights, such as the right to vote and the right to stand for election, until the early twentieth century. Also, until the Married Women's Property Acts of the mid- to late nineteenth century in the US and UK respectively, a woman was not permitted to own property or make contracts without her husband's consent. This was a result of the doctrine of coverture, under which a married women lost her separate existence from her husband.

> By marriage, the husband and wife are one person in law: that is, the very being or legal existence of the woman is suspended during the marriage, or at least is incorporated and consolidated into that of the husband, under whose wing, protection and cover, she performs everything; and is therefore called in our law-french, a *feme covert* [sic] [lit. a covered woman]. (Blackstone, cited in Dolan 2003: 256)

In addition to depriving married women of the basic civil rights or property and contract, coverture also gave a husband unconditional conjugal rights to his wife's body (Lister 2003: 69). It was not until 1994 in the UK that rape within marriage was recognised formally by the law. Across Europe nearly all countries now have laws against rape within marriage, the exceptions being Romania and Malta (Hagemann-White 2007). However, for most countries it is only in the last ten to twenty years that such legislation has been introduced.

Whilst women have, by the early twenty-first century, secured many of the rights hitherto denied to them, it is difficult to maintain the proposition that women enjoy equal citizenship with men. Whilst many of the more obvious imbalances have been attenuated and there has been an equalisation of rights, this formal equality is not matched in substantive terms. Women's earnings are consistently lower than those of men. Rubery,

Grimshaw and Figueiredo (2005: 189) suggest that in Europe the gender pay ratio (that is women's earnings as a percentage of men's earnings) ranges from 93 per cent in Portugal to 76 per cent in the UK. In other words, in the UK for example, women's average earnings are three-fourths of those for men. For those only in full time work, the gap in the UK is 17 per cent (Women and Work Commission 2006: 1). The gender pay gap for the EU15 (the number of member countries in the EU before 1 May 2004) is 16 per cent. In terms of labour market segregation, only 31 per cent of managers are women; and 30.4 per cent of women work part-time compared to 6.6 per cent of men (Commission of the European Communities 2005: 4). These figures show that whilst women are formally included in the labour market, their participation is substantively different to that of men.

Women are consistently underrepresented in politics. Table 2.1 shows that women are persistently underrepresented in national assemblies. Whilst there is considerable debate about how important the proportion of women in national assemblies is, in terms of furthering gender equality (Childs and Krook 2006) the gender imbalance is striking. The fact that there is evidence that the gender gap in terms of turnout is narrowing (perhaps to the point where it does not exist – see IDEA (2006); Norris (1999)) raises complex questions about participation and representation. It seems that women are increasingly participating in formal politics whilst lacking formal representation.

Women do enjoy social citizenship rights, but as many forms of social policy are insurance-based, and thus dependent upon full-time participation in the labour force and women are disproportionately likely to be either out of work or in part-time work, they do so on a different, disadvantaged, basis to men.

The success of liberal feminist arguments, in removing many of the legal and formal barriers which excluded women from citizenship rights, has led some to consider that gender discrimination in terms of citizenship is a historical artefact, something to be regretted, but also something in the past. As Lister sums up, 'It is usual to treat the history of women's exclusion from citizenship as no more than an historical aberration or mistake, now more or less effectively remedied' (Lister 2003: 70). Essentially, for this view, citizenship is a neutral concept and was only discriminatory because of the prevailing social norms of the time. Given different, more enlightened and egalitarian societies, all that is required is that the same rights be extended to those previously marginalised.

Feminist authors, however, argue that this is mistaken and that citizenship is 'profoundly gendered' (Lister 2003: 71). It is not simply the case

Table 2.1 Percentage of women in national assemblies

Sweden	45.3	Luxembourg	23.3
Finland	37.5	Portugal	21.3
Denmark	36.9	UK	19.7
Netherlands	36.7	Italy	17.3
Spain	36.0	Ireland	13.3
Belgium	34.7	Greece	13.0
Austria	33.9	France	12.2
Germany	31.8	EU 15	27.5

(Data from Inter-Parliamentary Union: 2006)

that previous exclusions from citizenship can be overcome and rendered historical aberrations by extending (formal) citizenship rights to women, because, for feminists, the very category of citizenship is constructed in masculine tones. Lister suggests that central to this 'quintessentially male' (Lister 2001: 323) construction of citizenship are two intertwined elements: first, the abstract conception of the citizen and second, the public–private divide. The public, male, citizen is taken to be rational, abstract, impartial, concerned with the public interest, active, independent and inhabiting and maintaining the realm of individual freedom. The private, female, non-citizen, is by contrast constructed as irrational, particular, partial, concerned with private/domestic concerns, passive, dependent and inhabiting and maintaining the realm of the necessary (Lister 2003: 71). Thus, the qualities of a citizen are 'male' qualities.

> Men possess the capacities required for citizenship, in particular they are able to use their reason to sublimate their passions, develop a sense of justice and so uphold the universal, civil law. Women, we learn from the classic texts of contract theory, cannot transcend their bodily natures and sexual passions; women cannot develop such a political morality. (Pateman 1989: 4)

Citizenship is also constructed in terms of the public domain; to be a citizen is to be active in public affairs. Women lack the qualities of a citizen (which have been constructed in the image of men) and also inhabit the private realm, which is, in classic liberal thought, separate from politics and hence, citizenship. Therefore, as Lister points out, women are doubly excluded from citizenship.

> In a classic double bind, women are banished to the private realm of the family, either physically or figuratively, because they do not display such qualities and because of their association with that realm, they are deemed incapable of developing them. (Lister 2003: 72)

Thinking about the theories of citizenship outlined in Chapter One, gender biases might be identified in all. For liberal citizenship, the issue is around the emphasis placed on the public–private divide. This has long been a target of analysis and criticism for feminist authors, who argue that this division essentially excludes women from political affairs. As such, liberal citizenship is conceived in terms of being the public face of the private individual. Yet, this is a masculine conception of citizenship as women have been historically, and still are in many situations, denied that public face.

For republican citizenship, the gender bias initially seems more acute. The idea that military service and the defence of the public through force of arms is a central quality and feature of citizenship has a long history, from classical Rome through to the writings of Machiavelli, in particular, but also Rousseau and others (see Pocock 1975; Oldfield 1990; Burk 2000). Military service is seen as the ultimate form of political participation, defending the political community. Such a militaristic view of citizenship has a clear masculine bias. Whilst it is perhaps a commonsense assumption that women are excluded from such a conception of citizenship because they are not able to provide such military service, the issue is a little more complex. It is perhaps more the case that women are excluded from such service (there are many cases of sexual discrimination and abuse, which seem to indicate a hostility towards women participating in this masculine world, see Yuval-Davis 1997). Some have further argued that the notion which supports the above position, that women are peaceful, loving and weak (and thus, inherently unsuitable for military service) whereas men are bellicose, angry and strong, is simply a gender stereotype (Elshtain 1987). This absence of military service, whether real or constructed has been a genuine source of exclusion from citizenship.

Yet, even for less militaristic versions of republicanism, gender biases remain. The classical republican ideal relied upon non-citizens (women and slaves) attending to the domestic realm in order to provide sufficient time for citizens to concern themselves with the public good. In other words, the demands of contemplation of the public realm in republican citizenship requires that citizens are free from the mundane occupations of necessity in the private realm (Held 2006). Yet, this tenor remains in contemporary republican positions. As Lister points out, the demands that participation place upon individuals means that it is those who have more leisure time who will more easily be able to fulfil the requirements of republican citizenship. 'Given the sexual division of labour and of time, this minority is more likely to be predominantly male' (Lister 2003: 33–4).

Communitarian citizenship, it might be argued, is similarly gendered.

At one level, there are some elements of the communitarian critique of liberal citizenship that feminists might agree with: the rejection of the abstract (male) individual; the language of responsibilities and particularly family obligations (see Fraser and Lacey 1993). As Franklin argues, 'Their aim is to strengthen the moral basis of community life, to ensure that fairness and responsibility form the basis of relationships between individuals whatever their class, gender, sexuality or ethnicity' (Franklin 2000: 139). However, despite such initially promising tones, there are two distinct ways in which communitarian citizenship might be seen as gendered. Firstly, the forms of community which communitarians seek to promote are traditional communities with strict separation of gender roles. In valorising the past, communitarians celebrate communities which have oppressed women (Feder Kittay 2001: 523–4). Communitarian citizenship is based upon the idea that morality is derived from existing communities (see Chapter One). This means that what is seen as moral and right in existing communities should not be challenged. As Franklin (2000: 140) notes, this latent conservatism clashes with the more radical impulse for change, which lies at the core of feminism. For communitarians, such demands for radical social change (on gender issues) is profoundly destabilising and should be reigned in, in the interests of the community.

The second area where communitarian citizenship exhibits a gender bias is in terms of obligations. Communitarian citizenship argues for a reassertion of responsibilities or obligations. In and of itself, there is perhaps nothing gendered about this. But the responsibilities which are emphasised clearly place women in a subordinate position. Generally, the most important obligations are those concerning work (and, perhaps, military service, discussed above). Indeed, Pateman argues that work has now supplanted military service as 'the key to citizenship' (Pateman 1989: 186). Women, though, face barriers to their participation in the labour force because they are expected to carry out duties of child-bearing and care (of both children and the elderly). By placing such centrality on paid work, the role of the (female) carer and the value of care is unrecognised and downplayed. In some countries, there has been progress on maternity and paternity rights and child-care services (particularly in Scandinavia). Women, however, remain underrepresented in the labour market. In this, they lack the key to citizenship and are second class, or in Voet's terms, 'second sex citizens' (Voet 1998: 11).

Citizenship, classically conceived, seems irrevocably gendered. Liberal citizenship is premised upon a gendered distinction between public and private. Republican citizenship, originally based around military service and now around an ethic of participation which favours men, and

Communitarian citizenship, which stresses traditional family structures, gender roles and social formations, and paid work above all else, both seem to be based on gendered assumptions and foundations. This may lead to an argument that citizenship is a concept that is of little use to feminists. Yet, as Lister (2001: 325) points out, this is a route that few feminist authors have taken, instead preferring to embark on the task of reclaiming, and perhaps regendering citizenship. The key question has thus become what should a feminist conception of citizenship look like? The answers to this question at one time seemed to revolve around a debate about whether a feminist conception of citizenship should seek gender neutrality or should be based around women's distinct qualities. More recently, feminist authors have sought to move beyond this towards a synthesis.

Many feminist conceptions of citizenship revolve around the question as to whether women should seek a model of citizenship which emphasises their difference(s) to men, or whether citizenship should be based upon a gender neutral model. The former would acknowledge and recognise women's distinctive contributions, and particularly value their accomplishments/duties in the private sphere. The latter, on the other hand, would accord equal rights and responsibilities, enabling women to participate as equals in the public sphere (Lister 2003: 94). This dilemma is often summed up as the equality vs difference debate; is feminism's goal to achieve equality with men based on being treated the same as men, or equality by acknowledging the ways in which women are different to men? Pateman refers to this as 'Wollstonecraft's dilemma':

> On the one hand they have demanded that the ideal of citizenship be extended to them, and the liberal feminist agenda for a 'gender neutral' social world is the logical conclusion of one form of this demand. On the other hand, women have also insisted, often simultaneously, as did Mary Wollstonecraft, that *as women* they have specific capacities, talents, needs and concerns, so that the expression of their citizenship will be differentiated from that of men. Their unpaid work providing welfare could be seen, as Wollstonecraft saw women's tasks as mothers, as women's work *as citizens*, just as their husbands' paid work is central to men's citizenship [...] Either women become (like) men, and so full citizens; or they continue at women's work, which is of no value for citizenship. (Pateman 1989: 197)

In many ways, this debate is based on an ontological question – are men and women fundamentally different, such that there are real gender differences; or are the differences between gender (roles), social constructions, such that men and women are fundamentally the same, but inscribed with and along different socially constructed gender roles?

Equal or different? Feminist conceptions of citizenship

A leading advocate of a feminist conception of citizenship based on difference is Jean Bethke Elshtain. She argues that the distinctive qualities that women possess should not be quickly sacrificed in the rush for equality. She notes that feminist arguments for equality and equal incorporation into the public sphere assume a rather one-sided view of the issue. The public world is one marked by excitement, fulfilment and success, whereas the private sphere that women inhabit is referred to by Betty Friedan as a 'comfortable concentration camp' (Freidan, cited in Elshtain 1998: 364). This, Elshtain argues, is a rather misguided and potentially dangerous view. Elshtain harbours a profound suspicion towards the state and the public sphere and of some feminists' agenda to 'go public'. The public sphere, she argues, is one marked 'by bureaucracy and rationalisation culminating in the state's monopoly of authority in even the most vital fields of human activity' (Elshtain 1998: 367). The public sphere is one inherently marked by the state with its concerns for monopolising power, hierarchies, overriding civil liberties and eroding traditional and local identities and cultures (Elshtain 1998: 363).

For women to be fully integrated into this sphere would involve adopting 'impersonal, rational and abstract standards' (Elshtain 1998: 367) and the suppression and extirpation of an alternative identity. This alternative identity is one marked by 'the concrete, the particular, the bodily' (Smith, cited by Elshtain 1998: 368). Elshtain draws on the role of women as mothers to articulate what this alternative identity is. In being mothers, Elshtain argues, women have developed a whole range of characteristics and attitudes. Drawing on the work of Sara Ruddick, Elshtain argues that maternal thinking can be characterised as an interest in the 'the preservation, the growth and the social acceptability of her child' (Elshtain 1998: 375). These maternal characteristics and ways of thinking, it is argued, lie in sharp opposition to the bureaucratic and technological public sphere. This disposition, and this opposition to the prevailing norms of the public sphere, is a vital bulwark and critical tool for opposing a particular mode of domination that Elshtain identifies with the public sphere.

> Maternal achievement requires paying a special sort of attention to the concrete specificity of each child; it turns on a special kind of knowledge of this child, this situation, without the notion of seizure, appropriation control or judgement by impersonal standards. What maternal thinking could lead to, though this will always be problematic as long as mothers are socially subordinated, is the wider diffusion of what attentive love to all children is

about and how it might become a wider social imperative [...] *Maternal thinking [...] is a rejection of amoral statecraft and an affirmation of the dignity of the human person.* (Elshtain 1998: 375–6 emphasis added)

It is important to note that Elshtain is not claiming maternalism as an ontological feature of women. She argues that this maternal aspect is not some innate quality of women, that such a maternal disposition defines women in the abstract, but rather 'a series of overlapping imitations of a subject in the process of defining herself both within and against the available identities, public and private, of her epoch' (Elshtain 1998: 369).

Essentially, Elshtain is questioning what kind of emancipation or freedom that women and feminists are seeking with and through the concept of citizenship. She questions the simple assumption that the private sphere is one marked by drudgery and imprisonment and that the public sphere is marked by freedom, dynamism and importance. Instead, Elshtain argues that for better and for worse, women in the particular roles that they have adopted, socially and historically, have developed particular qualities and attributes that are of value. Moreover, she argues that the public sphere is not one of emancipation, but one of bureaucratic control and that the dispositions and attitudes of women are a valuable and important opposition and corrective to the impersonal and totalising narratives of the impersonal, bureaucratic public sphere. If it is genuine freedom that women seek, then, Elshtain is warning, equal enmeshment in the public sphere may not be the answer, and women risk losing part of what may be the solution.

Elshtain's position has been subject to some criticism, however. Whilst noting that maternalist feminist thinking on citizenship has made a number of contributions, including criticising the liberal emphasis on rights and equal access, authors such as Dietz argue that there are a number of problems with its position.

Firstly, Dietz argues that whilst maternalist feminists may not be making any ontological claims that women are, in some way, essentially defined by maternal virtues, and rather argue that women have *historically* fulfilled these roles (and as such developed particular qualities and virtues), in valorising such qualities they do risk turning them into universal characteristics. '[T]he maternalists stand in danger of committing precisely the same mistake they find in the liberal view. They threaten to turn historically distinctive women into ahistorical, universalised entities' (Dietz 1998: 389). Dietz is effectively arguing that whilst maternal qualities may not be seen as essential characteristics of women, in giving them such regard and prominence they come very close to suggesting that these qualities, developed in particular circumstances and historical periods, *are* the core attributes and characteristics of women, thus universalising the experience or condition of motherhood.

An additional and, for Dietz, more problematic issue is whether such maternal characteristics are indeed appropriate for citizenship. She argues that the relationship between a mother and a child is a very particular one and one that may not be an appropriate model on which to found relations between citizens.

> When we look to mothering for a vision of feminist citizenship, however, we look in the wrong place [...] At the centre of the mothering activity is not the distinctive political bond among equal citizens but the intimate bond between mother and child. (Dietz 1998: 389)

Further to this, Dietz suggests that emphasising maternal virtues, far from transcending the liberal paradigm, is actually beholden to it, for it maintains a public/private distinction. Maternalist thinking, Dietz argues, forces a choice between a masculine, competitive, statist public realm and a loving, virtuous, private sphere.

> But the maternalist would offer us no choice in the matter: we must turn to the 'intimate private' because the 'statist public' is corrupt. This choice is a specious one, however. Indeed, by equating the public with statist politics and the private with the virtue of intimacy, maternalist feminism reveals itself to be closer to the liberal view than we might at first suppose. (Dietz 1998: 389)

Dietz's conception of a feminist citizenship is one which seeks not to give up on the public sphere and fall back to feminine characteristics (be they essential characteristics, or historically conditioned), but rather one that pushes for a renewal of the political. Placing her arguments in a long line of republican thinking, Dietz argues that it is not the ends of political engagement that are the vital element, but the means. A feminist citizenship for Dietz is not one where particular goals are advanced, but one where women, *as citizens*, are politically engaged in the decision-making process.

> My basic point is a straightforward one: for a vision of citizenship, feminists should turn to the virtues, relations and practices that are expressly political and, more exactly, participatory and democratic. What this requires, among other things, is a willingness to perceive politics in a way neither liberals or maternalists do: as a human activity that is not necessarily or historically reducible to represen-tative government or 'the arrogant, male, public realm'. (Dietz 1998: 390)

Part of Dietz's argument is a belief that democratic participation has a transformative capacity, such that individuals who may have very different identities and roles can come together and deliberate and participate in the democratic process *as citizens*. 'Democracy offers us an identity that neither liberalism, with its propensity to view the citizen as an individual bearer of rights, nor maternalism with its attentiveness to mothering, provides' (Dietz 1998: 390). This notion is again, squarely within the republican tradition. Dietz takes up the same question as the maternalists; namely, what does an emancipatory conception of citizenship look like, but instead of arguing for the valorisation of particular qualities and ethics which women embody, posits a reassertion of participatory democracy. Realising that some may see this as a simple equation of feminism with democracy, Dietz argues that feminism is uniquely placed to resuscitate political, democratic, life. The activities of the feminist movement, she argues, embody 'forms of freedom that are far more compatible with the "democratic body" of the American experience, than with the liberal capitalist one' (Dietz 1998: 393).

At this point, one might mischievously suggest that this argument seems perilously close to being stuck on the horns of a dilemma. Either, it seems, Dietz's argument is a variant of the position of Elshtain and other maternal feminists, that the particular behaviours and attitudes of women offer an alternative to the narrow liberal paradigm, and in so doing, potential for emancipation. (There are differences, the main one being that Dietz argues for a very *political*, participatory form of feminine characteristics. But the point would be that there is something distinctive about female participation.) Alternatively, it seems that Dietz is arguing that the characteristics which are 'compatible with the democratic body' are not exclusively female characteristics at all. Indeed, to suggest that participatory, democratic norms are the exclusive preserve of the feminist movement (as opposed to any other social movement) seems difficult to maintain. This position is one that suggests that what Dietz offers may well be participatory and democratic, but that it is not clearly feminist. Other authors have pointed out that Dietz may underestimate the constraints that women's situation, in terms of the gendered division of domestic labour, places upon many women's participation (see Phillips 1993: 110–11). As noted above, when discussing republicanism, participation is easier for those who have more leisure time, an excess of which is something that many women lack.

Beyond equality–difference

A more recent development in feminist thinking about citizenship is one which seeks to problematise the category of 'woman' (and indeed, 'man'). Lister identifies two rather different sources of this development. The first is the theoretical arguments which stem from poststructuralist positions and the second comes from black and other 'minority' women. Lister notes that, although these positions have different origins, they are 'mutually reinforcing' (Lister 2003: 75). Poststructuralism draws upon a range of philosophical currents (including Freud, Lacan, Wittgenstein, Derrida, and Foucault) to argue that identity is not fixed and constant (see Belsey 2002 for an introduction to poststructuralist thought). If individual subjectivity and identity is not fixed, then larger identity categories, such as 'woman' and 'man' can have no meaning whatsoever. In other words, the label 'woman' does not represent some coherent set of characteristics that all women embody. In a different way, this is something that black feminists and women from other marginalised groups, such as the disabled, argue. Simply stated, the argument is that the interests of black feminists and white feminists do not automatically coincide (see hooks 1981; 1984; Mansbridge 1999). This line of argument has been extended further to question whether all black women share the same concerns and interests (Aziz 1992).

This deconstruction of the category 'woman' has left some with cause for concern. 'If woman is simply deconstructed and left in fragments, there is no woman left to be a citizen' (Lister 2003: 78). A number of feminist authors seek to grapple with the implications (see Lister 2003; Prokhovnik 1998). However, Chantal Mouffe, in some sense, argues that such deconstruction of essential identities is a 'necessary condition' in order to 'theorize the multiplicity of relations of subordination' (Mouffe 1993: 77). Mouffe goes on to consider the implications of abandoning such universalising categories. Firstly, she notes that it ends the equality–difference debate.

> The whole false dilemma of equality-versus-difference is exploded since we no longer have a homogenous entity 'woman' facing another homogenous entity 'man', but a multiplicity of social relations in which sexual difference is always constructed in very diverse ways and where the struggle against subordination has to be visualised in specific and differential forms. To ask whether women should become identical to men in order to be recognised as equal, or whether they should assert their difference at the cost of equality, appears meaningless once essential identities are put into question. (Mouffe 1993: 78)

What, then, does a feminist conception of citizenship, which rejects such essentialist categories, look like? Mouffe argues that the goal of a feminist conception of citizenship should be to render sexual differences meaningless in terms of citizenship (Mouffe 1993: 82). Drawing upon her wider work on radical and plural democracy, she argues that citizenship should be seen as a political identity which holds to the ideals of liberty and equality for all. In this way, citizenship is a democratic demand for equality and liberty to be extended. It encompasses many different groups, not just women. (This collective political identification, however, does not obliterate differences and these differences are overcome only to the extent that they are opposed to the same subordinating force (Mouffe 1993: 84). Indeed, Mouffe goes on to argue that, in a contingent way, partial and precarious forms of identification around the term 'woman' can act as a basis for a feminist struggle.) Effectively, Mouffe's conception of citizenship is one which seeks to understand and transform the various ways in which women are constructed as subordinates and that 'an approach that permits us to understand how the subject is constructed through different discourses and subject positions, is certainly more adequate than one that reduces our identity to one single position – be it class, race or gender' (Mouffe 1993: 88).

Most feminist conceptions of citizenship have moved away from what is increasingly seen as a sterile equality–difference debate. In many ways, the central challenge for feminist citizenship has become to reconcile the universalist thrust of citizenship as a concept with the 'different and shifting identities that women hold' (Lister 2003: 88).

MULTICULTURALISM

The challenge of diversity of multicultural societies has become a topic of contemporary debate in modern society. Cultural diversity is evident as many societies include different ethnic, religious, cultural and other communities, with more or less distinct ways of life. Contrary to experiences of past societies where marginalised groups were fully assimilated by the dominant ones or led a 'quiet' way of life, for the past two decades cultural and ethnic minorities have articulated their needs in the form of demands for recognition and equality. A complex set of factors has contributed to this change. The intensified flow of capital, post-Fordist modes of production, a global spread of Western consumer culture, the end of Cold war and bipolar international order, the emergence of transnational migrant networks, forces of secularisation and moral individualism, create cultural diversification in various societies. What is common for the individuals and groups, whether based on ethnicity, language, religion, or sexual identity, is that they demand full and equal inclusion in society and recognition of their particularistic identities. They oppose the idea of cultural homogeneity, a characteristic of the classic model of the nation-state, and press for specific institutional reforms.

Multiculturalism comes as a comprehensive response to cultural and ethnic diversity that aims to accommodate the competing cultural options in a society. It provides a wide range of public policies as well as potential processes for minority collectivities that want to gain recognition, protection and rights. The literature on multiculturalism is immense. It has been celebrated as a truly emancipatory project for the oppressed and the have-nots, but equally it has been criticised as a threat to national unity. The following section focuses on key themes and arguments in multiculturalism as presented in the work of Kymlicka, Young, Taylor and Parekh.

Multiculturalism and its proponents

Will Kymlicka has made major contributions in developing a theory that incorporates liberalism and recognition for cultural minorities. In his book, *Multicultural Citizenship: A Liberal Theory of Minority Rights* (1995), Kymlicka analyses the nature of group rights, the importance of culture for a community and he criticises effectively the supposed neutrality of the liberal state.

A description of his conceptual distinctions will facilitate our understanding of group rights. He distinguishes two kinds of cultural minorities, nations and ethnicities. A nation is 'a historical community, more or less institutionally complete, occupying a given territory or homeland, sharing a distinct language or culture' (Kymlicka 1995: 11). Common culture is the basic characteristic for an ethnic group but it is not territorially concentrated. Regarding multicultural societies, they can be multinational when they combine two or more nations, or polyethnic when people from different nations have emigrated to form a new society. Kymlicka then makes a very powerful distinction between national minorities, whose members should have a right to full cultural membership respected by the majority community, and ethnic minorities, whose members chose to voluntarily uproot themselves and relinquish their original culture.

Next, Kymlicka distinguishes three kinds of group-differentiated rights: self-government rights, polyethnic rights and special representation rights. We shall analyse each category in turn. Self-government rights are only for a national minority and involve the exercise of authority over the group by members of the group. By granting self-government rights to a national minority, a liberal state can redress past injustice, control and equalise power, as well as preserve the distinctness of a people. For Kymlicka, a truly liberal state should not impose its values on its national minorities as liberal institutions 'can only really work if liberal beliefs have been internalised' (1995: 167) by them, a process which takes time and should be voluntary. Successful examples of the above can be seen in federal states like Belgium, Canada and Switzerland.

Polyethnic rights refer to special recognition of cultural practices of a minority. The use of these rights can compensate and integrate a cultural minority that otherwise would be disadvantaged. This includes funding for heritage language programmes, exemptions from Sunday closing laws for Jews and Muslims, bilingual education, translations of public documentation into the native language of the recipients, and school food preparations according to dietary norms. It should be mentioned here that the term polyethnic has created tensions as these rights can be enjoyed by religious groups or even national minorities (Carens 1997). Thus, Kymlicka in later writings calls them 'accommodation rights' (1997: 73). But, more importantly, the difference between self-government rights and 'polyethnic' rights is that the former requires institutional and legislative changes that give control to the members of a national minority while the latter allows for the maintenance of specific cultural practices as they are integrated into common institutions.

Special representation rights refer to the adjustments that can be made for better group participation in political institutions. This set of rights can provide systemic corrections in order to avoid a group's misrepresentation in political selection processes. Representation rights are related to affirmative action, they can take a temporary character, as long as the disadvantages are eliminated, or a permanent one, as a necessary measure to ensure proportionate institutional participation. Kymlicka uses the example of the Canadian constitutional guarantee where three out of the nine judges for the Supreme Court have to be from Quebec (1995: 143).

Additionally, Kymlicka argues that there is much confusion between individual and collective rights. He draws a distinction between external protections (tropes that could protect a minority cultural group from an over-powerful majority) and internal restrictions (tropes of limiting the freedom of members of a group for overarching solidarity). Coming from a liberal tradition, he acknowledges only the second condition to be problematic as the first protects the minority from a disadvantageous position as a result of the economic measures or the political decisions of the majority. Group-rights are enjoyed by individual members of the group on many occasions; the important question is if the group-differentiated rights that were presented above are morally justified and required.

There are a number of examples from Canada and other liberal democratic states that show differentiated-group rights in practice. This allows Kymlicka to put forward a strong case for differentiated citizenship as the basis for fulfilling the major requirements of liberalism; equality and autonomy. In order to understand the above argument better, it is important to see how the state and culture are inexorably linked.

> Modern states invariably develop and consolidate what I call a 'societal culture' – that is, a set of institutions, covering both public and private life, with a common language, which has historically developed over time on a given territory, which provides people with a wide range of choices about how to live their lives. The emergence of a societal culture – which requires the standardisation and diffusion of a common language, and the creation and the diffusion of common educational, political, and legal institutions – is a feature of modernisation, but is also actively supported by the state. Indeed, the state is the leading force behind linguistic standardisation and institutional integration. (1997: 75)

Thus, if liberalism is to be taken seriously, it should allow differentiated citizenship to enable national minorities to protect their cultural interests. Another important advocate of differentiated citizenship is Iris Marion Young, who problematises the notion of universality of citizenship and stands for the inclusion and participation of oppressed and marginalised groups of the society. Young reveals the tensions and the silences behind the uniformity and homogeneity of universal citizenship that promote ideals of assimilation, perpetuate oppression and ignore differences in culture, values and behavioural styles that exist among groups. The following analysis will examine the philosophical and political aspects of the above argument in detail.

Young criticises the notion of a civic public life deriving from modern political thought. She argues that:

> Nothing in this understanding as universal as opposed to particular, common as opposed to differentiated, implies extending full citizenship status to all groups. Indeed, at least some modern republicans thought just the contrary. While they extolled the virtues of citizenship as expressing the universality of humanity, they consciously excluded some people from citizenship on the grounds that they could not adopt the general point of view, or that their inclusion would disperse and divide the public. The ideal of a common good, a general will, a shared public life leads to pressures for a homogeneous citizenry. (1995: 178–9)

For example, thinkers like Machiavelli and Rousseau excluded women from the public realm of citizenship because they identified masculinity with reason and femininity with sentiment. Thus, they championed a clear distinction between a public realm, characterised by dispassionate rationality, and a private one where 'disruptive' emotions and desires can take place.

In the quest for the common good and homogeneity, more groups were excluded: poor people and wage workers, 'on the grounds that they were too motivated by need to adopt a general perspective' (Young 1995: 180), blacks, Indians, and, later, the Mexicans and the Chinese in America, were perceived as a threat to the unity of the polity and left outside. Similarly, in Europe the Jews were targeted as a dangerous disruption to the cohesion and harmony of commonness. As Young observes:

> These republican exclusions were not accidental, nor were they inconsistent with the ideal of universal citizenship as understood by these theorists. They were a direct consequence of a dichotomy between public and private that defined the public as a realm of generality in which all particularities are left behind, and defined the private as the particular, the realm of affectivity, affiliation, need and the body. As long as that dichotomy is in place, the inclusion of the formerly excluded in the definition of citizenship – women, workers, Jews, blacks, Asians, Indians, Mexicans – imposes a homogeneity that suppresses group differences in the public and in practice forces the formerly excluded groups to be measured according to norms derived from and defined by privileged groups. (1995: 181)

Today, political thinkers recognise the importance of an inclusive and participatory citizenship; however, an emphasis on the pursuit of a shared sense of what community is reaffirms and suppresses differences among citizens. In order to promote a democratic public, social groups should be able to express their particular affiliations, interests and identities. This can be done by providing an institutionalised recognition and representation of oppressed groups. But when a group is oppressed? The conditions that constitute an oppressed group, according to Young, are divided into five categories: exploitation, marginalisation, powerlessness, cultural imperialism and violence. We analyse them in turn.

Exploitation is the transfer of the results of the labour of one social group to benefit the other. For example, women's work is unpaid or under-paid and results in the transfer of energies to please and comfort men. Also, there is racial exploitation, when the history of racial discrimination has reserved menial labour for people of colour and formal and informal tracking systems in public schools push students of colour into non-college preparatory classes and eventually into menial, low-paying jobs. Margin-alisation is the process by which a whole category of people is expelled from useful participation in social life. Powerlessness is the experience of a lack of authority or powering relations to others. These are the people over whom power is exercised without their exercising it, they take orders but rarely have the right to give them. Moreover, powerlessness includes incompetence where the opportunity for development and the exercise of skills is limited and one's capacities are restricted. Cultural imperialism is when the dominant meanings of a society render the particular perspective of one's group invisible and at the same time stereotypes for this group mark it as the Other. Finally, the last face of oppression is violence, which can be systematic or random and is directed against members of a group out of hate or fear. Groups that have been systematically oppressed in one or more of these ways are: women, blacks, gay men, lesbians, poor people, old people and mentally and physically disabled people (Young 1988: 337–45).

Because of the historical and social conditions that have advanced exclusion and oppression of disadvantaged groups, Young asserts that a democratic public should provide the mechanisms for their effective representation and recognition. Similar to Kymlicka's affirmation for self-organisation rights, Young argues for special rights for groups as a positive assertion of specificity in different forms of life.

Proponents of a multicultural understanding of citizenship are concerned with the power of the state and majority groups to undermine identity groups. In his essay, 'The Politics of Recognition', Charles Taylor argues that Kantian liberalism ignores the fundamentally dialogical character of human life. From this perspective, culture is not just the lens we use to understand the world but, much more importantly, it is also a part of us (1994: 32). In contemporary society, 'the understanding that identities are formed in open dialogue, unshaped by a predefined social script has made the politics of equal recognition more central and stressful' (1994: 36). Thus equal recognition is more than appropriate, it is essential: 'The projection of an inferior demeaning image on another can actually distort and oppress, to the extent that the image is internalised' (1994: 36).

It is important to have a fuller account of Taylor's arguments in order to understand better the basic concepts of multiculturalism. Taylor highlights the conflict between two approaches to identity that have emerged in modern age. One is found in the 'politics of universalism' in which every individual is entitled to the same rights and opportunities as every other. It emphasises the equal dignity, where no one has a natural right to exercise power over others, and the separation of the citizenry into first and second classes is unacceptable. However, according to Taylor, this politics of universalism is too often conducted at the exclusion of a 'politics of difference'. An inherent universal ethic emphasises the sameness of all citizens and it comes to conflict with their need to be recognised in their particularities. As Taylor says,

> With the politics of equal of dignity, what is established is meant to be universally the same, an identical basket of rights and immunities; with the politics of difference, what we asked to recognise is the unique identity of this individual or group, its distinctness from everybody else. (1994: 38)

In his analysis, the politics of recognition is perceived as a further development of the traditional liberal promise of universal freedom, equality and respect for the individual. Thus,

> the politics of difference grows organically out of the politics of universal dignity through one of those shifts with which we are long familiar, where a new understanding of the human social condition imparts a radically new meaning to an old principle. (1994: 38)

The problem between the two approaches arises because 'where politics of universal dignity fought for forms of nondiscrimination that were quite "blind" to the ways in which citizens differ, the politics of difference often redefines nondiscrimination as requiring that we make these distinctions the basis of differential treatment' (1994: 40). Liberal thought is viewed as problematic in this respect because equal respect to the equal potential inherent in all human beings does not mean equal recognition of the accomplishments of human beings, either as individuals or groups. Actually, for Taylor, liberalism's dedication to 'difference-blind' politics 'negates identity by forcing people into a homogeneous mould that is untrue to them' (1994: 43). Moreover, claims by the proponents of universal dignity on neutrality are in fact a reflection of the standards of the hegemonic culture. In short, the politics of difference criticises the notion that universal equality is violated if the expectation is conformity to a single model of public personhood and the failure of liberalism to recognise its shortcomings as a particular discourse masquerading as universal.

Taylor's presentation of his exemplary case of francophone Quebeckers (who form a minority in mostly English-speaking Canada) makes his analysis especially clear. In Quebec, where French-speakers are the majority, the preservation and the continuation of the French culture is perceived as a priority. In disagreement with Kymlicka's solution, who maintains a position of liberal neutrality with a provision of certain groups' differential rights that enables the minority to maintain its cultural integrity, Taylor argues for policies that aim at survival actively and seek to create members of the community. Accordingly, the former proposition works only 'for existing people who find themselves trapped within a culture under pressure, and can flourish within it or not at all. But it doesn't justify measures designed to ensure survival through indefinite generations' (1994: 41).

Furthermore, for Taylor 'liberalism is not a possible meeting ground for all cultures, but is the political expression of one range of cultures, and quite incompatible with other ranges [...] liberalism can't and shouldn't claim complete cultural neutrality' (1994: 62). By rejecting the liberal norm of neutrality that prioritises right over good because it presupposes actors who are able to make a certain number of distinctions between the public and private domain and by exposing the construction of the right within the particularist framework of values and ideas about the good, Taylor calls for a liberalism that accommodates a wide variety of ways of life without attempting to bring a deep social and political unity.

In order to problematise the specific preconceptions that cultural groups have and how it is possible to consider them in opening-up the political terrain, it is useful to consider the work of Bhikhu Parekh. The starting point for Parekh is the definition of culture as:

> A historical created system of meaning and significance, or [...] a system of beliefs and practices in terms of which a group of human beings understand regulate and structure their individual and collective lives. It is a way of understanding and organising human life. The understanding it seeks has a particular thrust [...] and the way it organises human life is not ad hoc and instrumental but grounded in a particular manner of conceptualising and understanding it. (2000: 143)

Then, in a multicultural society which consists of different cultures with their own distinct belief system and worldviews, any political doctrine formulated from within one particular cultural perspective is biased and can't do justice to others. For this reason, a multicultural society has to devise political structures that can deal with these conflictual demands effectively and impartially. According to Parekh, on the one hand, it has to 'foster a strong sense of unity and common belonging among citizens, as otherwise it cannot act as a united community able to take [...] collectively binding decisions and regulate and resolve conflicts', yet, on the other hand, 'it cannot ignore the demands of diversity [...] Diversity is an inescapable fact of collective life' (2000: 196). But, for Parekh, there is no assumption that gives legitimacy or adequacy to the norms and values of the political behaviour, structure and processes that are embodied in the dominant cultural group. Rather, he suggests that 'multiculturalism is about the proper terms of relationship between different cultural communities. The norms governing their respective claims [...] cannot be derived from one culture alone but through an open and equal dialogue between them' (2000: 13).

In cases where policies and structures are imposed from above, from a monocultural perspective that does not consider the dynamics found in the cultural minorities, tensions and conflict can be created. Parekh has studied societies characterised by these tensions among various cultural and religious groups like Israelis and Palestinians, Muslims, Hindus and Sikhs, where the exercise of power by one group threatens the others. But even in societies that are not characterised by overt conflict, issues of miscommunication can breed mistrust and a feeling of threat. Based on the above, Parekh understands multiculturalism in the way that

> cultures constantly encounter one another both formally and informally and in private and public spaces. Guided by curiosity, incomprehension or admiration, they interrogate each other, challenge each other's assumptions, consciously or unconsciously borrow from each other, widen their horizons and undergo small and large changes. (2000: 220)

Thus, it is possible for a society that is characterised by cultural differences to constitute new beliefs, values and norms that emerge from relating and communicating with the Other. This cultural change has to be open-ended, multifaceted and polymorphic with respect to, and recognition for, differences in order to accommodate the evolving nature of multicultural-ism. In order to capture the dynamism of multiculturalism in designing governance and policy structures, one should be aware of its processual character and offer the appropriate solutions analogously. Two additional features are essential in this development: the way multiculturalism is supported by decentralisation of power and the interaction between the public and the private realm. For Parekh,

> Decentralisation of power has a particular important role to play in ensuring justice in multicultural societies. Since different communities regularly encounter each other in the normal course of life at local or regional levels, respect for their differences at these levels matters to them greatly and shapes their perceptions of each other and the state. It is also easier for the local and regional bodies to accommodate differences than it is for the central government, because the adjustment required is more readily iden-tified, limited in scale, not too costly, and is generally free from the glare of publicity. There is also greater room for experimentation, mistakes are more easily corrected and different areas can learn from each other's good practices. (2000: 212)

The problem with the above proposition is that the formalistic nature even of local government and an 'obsession' with acceptable outcomes doesn't leave much room for experimentation and dynamic evolution for multicultural projects. Local and regional governance should be able to foster a vibrant civic culture because 'intercommunal tensions are less frequent and more easily managed when there is an extensive local network of formal and informal cross-communal linkages nurturing the vital social capital of mutual trust and cooperation' (2000: 212). By promoting cross-cultural collaboration and communication, people learn to acknowledge their differences and are more likely to overcome incomprehension and mistrust. For this reason the funding of programmes that are designed to encourage multicultural interaction in local environments can enhance co-ordination and transform conflict within a multicultural society.

Moreover, Parekh argues that as the public realm is the cradle for the flourishing of the civil society, aspects and manifestations of different cultures should be incorporated visibly into the 'high culture' of the society and throughout all its institutional spaces. By failing to do so, there is a danger of reproducing a monocultural public realm and a multicultural private one. Political activities should be characterised by an openness and facilitate the participation of those who are excluded by the official culture. It is important for the political realm to:

> welcome new conceptual languages, modes of deliberation, forms of speech and political sensibilities and create conditions in which their creative interplay could over time lead to a plural public realm and a broadbased political culture. Even established political values should not be treated as nonnegotiable. If they can be shown to be unfairly biased against certain cultures or to exclude other equally worthwhile political values, a critical dialogue on them should be welcomed as a step towards a richer moral culture enjoying a broad cross-cultural consensus. (Parekh 2000: 223)

Thus, the development of multicultural projects within local and regional governance should be complemented by a wider acceptance and interaction in the wider public realm. This pluralist approach affirms and encourages multiculturalism in both the public and the private realm. It adopts policies for the development of particular groups, acknowledges their legitimacy and fosters a political community around the benefits accruing to a diverse mix of cultures.

Multicultural policies in Europe

Theories of multiculturalism redefine citizenship in an effort to create a more participatory framework for fostering greater group involvement. In order to advance effective participation, though, there is a need for the analogous structures and processes as well as access and information. During the period of post-war immigration, on national and local levels across Europe, policy responses in administrative, legislative and judicial terms have been carried out in a piecemeal way, following a widespread condition which was termed, after Mark J. Miller, as 'policy ad-hocracy' (1986). This resulted in a variety of institutions and policies which were concerned with the incorporation and participation of ethnic minorities and immigrant populations within the different nation-states.

Miller (1989) identifies five types of activity and institutions that enable ethnic minorities and immigrants to participate politically and make known their interests to decision-making agents of the state. These are: (1) homeland organisations, (2) consultative bodies designed to represent foreigners' interests, (3) unions and workplace councils, (4) political parties or religious and civic organisations, and (5) confrontational means. In Table 2.2 we present some of the consultative bodies that are established on a national or local level in a range of European countries in order to examine closer how the state tries to incorporate ethnic/migrant demands. Anderson classifies the possible kinds of consultative structures as: (1) contact and co-ordination groups (inclusion of all majority and minority groups with a broad mandate to improve relations); (2) working and co-ordination groups (comprised mainly of government departments dealing with immigrants and ethnic minorities, with very few actual members of the latter groups, for the purpose of sharing information and co-coordinating programmes and activities); (3) parliaments of migrant workers (made up of representatives of immigrant groups only, in order to articulate their interests and press for the implementation of policies); (4) advisory councils (perhaps the most common type of institution, including representatives of both immigrant/ethnic minority groups and members of government, with broad scope for sharing information, expressing concerns, distributing resources, and lobbying for interests); and (5) committees on migrant affairs (established by government, with variable makeup but sometimes with decision-making powers). Cross-fertilisation and better communication is difficult to be established as the 'consultative institutions at the local, regional and national levels are not linked closely together' (Anderson, 1990: 118).

The diversity of multi-ethnic states in their institutional structures,

Table 2.2 Ethnic/migrant consultative bodies established
in six European countries

Belgium	Regional advisory councils since the late 1960s, and municipal migrant councils or immigrants' communal consultative councils.
Germany	Mostly local advisory councils for foreigners, municipal commissioners for foreigners' affairs, municipal social service sectors and offices of semi-public welfare agencies (such as churches, trade unions).
France	A variety of consultative institutions have existed among most prefectures and municipalities since 1971; in provinces immigrant issues are dealt with by employment offices and the Regional Commission of the Insertion of Migrant Populations (CRIPI) while in municipalities there are immigrant councils, social service bureaux and local offices of the Association of Social Assistance for Migrants (SSAE).
United Kingdom	(where 75 per cent of ethnic minorities are naturalized with full voting privileges): Race Equality Counsils – which replaced earlier Community Relations Councils – with close ties to the national Commission for Racial Equality (CRE), race relations units or committees or advisory groups (sometimes incorprating or incorporated by broader equal opportunity boards) of city councils, city-supported forums and umbrella groups for ethnic associations, municipal social services department, community centres funded by local government.
The Netherlands	(where immigrants and ethic minorities can vote in local elections): Municipal bureaux for ethnic minority affairs, councils for foreigners, foreign workers assistance units and municipal employment offices and social services.
Sweden	(where although local and regional voting rights have been granted to foreign residents, consultative procedures are still widely used and are seen as necessary supplement to voting rights, rather than as an alternative form of political participation): Immigration boards or councils and municipal employment offices and social services.

(Source: Andersen 1990: 119)

patterns of ethnic relations and their constituent ethnic groupings ensures that the forms of policy debates, and their outcomes, are highly varied. Policy issues which arise include opportunities to express, and to maintain distinctive elements of the ethnic culture, especially language and religion where these are associated with ethnic distinctiveness; the absence of ethnically linked social and economic disadvantage; opportunities to participate in political decision-making and the avoidance of racism and discrimination. An important symbolic issue is the involvement of minority groups in the formulation and expression of the national identity. Where a minority group has a distinctive territorial base the issue of the extent of its political independence may become an important issue. A list of issues that concerns ethnic minorities includes the following:

- The teaching and use of the ethnic minority language in the public sector.
- Freedom of worship and ability to observe religious rituals and practices.
- Access to nationality of the country of permanent residence.
- Availability of dual nationality.
- Freedom of cultural expression.
- Access to appropriate housing without discrimination.
- An absence of racism and discriminatory practices.
- The opportunity for the minority to take responsibility for making decisions relevant to its concerns.

As a result of the political, economic and demographic changes which have occurred over the last fifty years, diversity in patterns of ethnic relations and in the range of ethnic identities is a hallmark of the majority of societies in the world. Multiculturalism does not consist of one specific type of solution or strategy. Nevertheless, its important contribution lies on a re-conceptualisation of how to ensure cultural diversity by replacing often paternalistic provision of services to minorities in a more participatory and representational process.

Conclusion

We began this chapter by noting that the 'classical' conceptions of citizenship that we examined in Chapter One, whilst disagreeing on many points, all hold that the rights and responsibilities for citizens, whatever they may be, should be the same for all members of the community. As we have seen, both feminism and multiculturalism reject this idea. They, in different ways, both argue that such universalism serves to oppress certain groups. The positions here point to oppression around gender and ethnicity, but others have argued that sexuality (Richardson 1998) and disability (Beckett 2005) are also sources of exclusion and oppression. Both feminism and multiculturalism argue for a conception of citizenship which is sensitive to people's different identities. As we shall see in later chapters, particularly Chapter Six dealing with migration in Europe, such calls have proved to be controversial and have come under attack from a variety of perspectives (for a critique of multiculturalism see Barry 2001). Yet, they both raise important questions as to how societies go about seeking to include and foster membership between individuals of differing identities. In a somewhat different way, this theme is taken up again in the next chapter.

CHAPTER 3

Postnational citizenship

INTRODUCTION

The concept of postnational citizenship has gained momentum in the last two decades. The emergence of transnational political structures and the proliferation of transnational political activity, coupled with the internationalisation of human rights in the era of globalisation, have led some academics to argue for a postnational citizenship. The invocation of postnational citizenship raises questions about the nation-state based approach to citizenship and takes into account a multiplication of non-formal political participation and the deterritorialisation of citizenship practices and identities.

The assertion that citizenship is framed within national boundaries is maybe mostly celebrated in the work of Hannah Arendt, who argues that a citizen 'is by definition a citizen among citizens of a country among countries. His rights and duties must be defined and limited not only by those of his fellow citizens, but also by the boundaries of a territory' (1968: 81). There are, however, many scholars and activists that have expressed their discontent with an exclusively nation-based idea of citizenship. As Bauböck puts it, 'the new challenge for political theory is to go beyond a narrow state-centered approach by considering political communities and systems of rights that emerge at levels of governance above or below those of independent states or that cut across international borders' (2003: 704). The terms 'postnational citizenship', 'transnational citizenship', 'global citizenship', have been introduced in academic discourse as nuanced efforts that try to capture processes of cross-border inclusions, allegiances and affinities that have occurred in the context of globalisation. The following analysis will examine and assess the various efforts by scholars of political and social theory to approach 'postnational citizenship' descriptively and empirically. The criteria that someone addresses to citizenship vary; it can be seen as a legal status, a system of rights, a form of political activity, or a form of identity. In this respect, we will regard the manifestations of postnational citizenship in each of these usages and argue that within each, citizenship takes non-national forms.

What is postnational/transnational/global citizenship?

When somebody tries to describe the form that a postnational/national/ global citizenship could take, he or she generally speaks of the meaning and the plausibility of denationalisation. As Yasemin Soysal has argued, citizenship is 'no longer unequivocally anchored in national political collectivities' (1997: 512). But the problem with recent literature on the issue lies in the fact that there is no systematic theory of postnational/ transnational/global citizenship and the terms are often used casually. An attempt to provide an exegesis stumbles on the contested issues that are associated with the term citizenship itself. On the one hand, there are approaches that are defining citizenship primarily in reference to the state. On the other hand, different communitarian understandings of citizenship are grounded in membership in a political community, as we saw in Chapter One. Yet, these definitions have stirred great disagreement. For some, citizenship takes a legal form between individual and polity while for others, it denotes active political participation. Also, others confirm its importance to achieve individual justice, while yet others insist that it takes upon issues of collective identity.

Many theorists have tried to bring all these different conceptualisations of citizenship under one organising scheme that advances understanding and furthers analysis (Kymlicka and Norman 1994; Kratochwil 1994; Fox 2005). Usually, the distinct categories are the following: citizenship as a legal status, citizenship as rights, citizenship as political activity and citizenship as collective identity. In this chapter we will examine each of these categories in turn, to examine and analyse developments towards postnational/transnational/global citizenship. These conceptual choices can be perceived as incommensurable or complimentary and the following analysis will problematise the focus on determining citizenship according to a given set of assumptions and identify a plethora of discourses that render postnational/transnational/global citizenship plausible.

Citizenship as a legal status

One definition of citizenship stresses the legal relationship between the individual and the polity. Thus, the legal status refers to whom the state recognises as a citizen, and the formal basis for the rights and responsibilities of the individual in relation to the state. In this respect nationality becomes a precious good and a dividing line between citizens and aliens. It is the state that decides on the processes of naturalisation, admission criteria or acceptance of dual/multiple nationalities. The locus of citizenship status is the territorially-bounded nation-state. A relationship with a political community is the necessary condition of citizenship and allegiance to the state is essential. As Sassen argues,

> Many of the dynamics that built economies, polities and societies in the nineteenth and twentieth centuries contained an articulation between the national scale and the growth of entitlements for citizens. During industrialisation, class formation, class struggles [...] the advantages of both employers and workers tended to scale at the national level, and became identified with state-produced legislation and regulations, entitlements and obligations. (2003: 46)

Once in place, national citizenship came to be the main structuring framework for action; the legitimate collective good was defined in national terms and citizenship actions were directed towards this collective good. Even if people enjoy formal legal membership in subnational entities, it is the national citizenship that is regarded as legally and politically paramount.

It is interesting to see how the linkage between nationality and citizenship is affirmed in international law. Thus nationality is important in a variety of contexts, including:

1. Entitlement to diplomatic protection.
2. State responsibility to another state for failing in its duty to prevent certain wrongful acts committed by one of its nationals extraterritorially.
3. State receipt of its own nationals.
4. Nationality is said to import allegiance, and one of the principal incidents of allegiance is the duty to perform military service for the state to which allegiance is owed.
5. A state has a general right, in the absence of a specific treaty binding it to do so, to refuse to extradite its own nationals to another state requesting surrender.
6. Enemy status in time of war may be determined by the nationality of the person concerned.
7. States may frequently exercise criminal or other jurisdiction on basis of nationality. (Shearer 1994)

It seems that nationality secures rights for the individual by linking him to the state and it is perceived as a central dynamic in international law. However, recent political transformations, like the emergence of a European citizenship, the enjoyment of membership rights by long-term residents and the growing incidence of dual or multiple citizenships, have led many analysts to argue for the denationalisation of citizenship. We now turn to examine these.

The Treaty of the European Union states that an objective of the Union is 'to strengthen the protection of the rights and the interests of the nationals of its members States through the introduction of a citizenship of the Union' (CEC 1992). Although access to the status of European citizen is granted by national states, since it is open to the persons holding a nationality of a member state, it is nevertheless an institution of rights that offers new structures of representation and appeal beyond the national level. As Elisabeth Meehan points out, 'the rights associated with citizenship are no longer regulated or guaranteed exclusively by the institutions of nations-states but have, in addition, an increasingly significant European dimension' (1997: 67). Thus, European citizenship, according to Soysal, 'clearly embodies postnational membership in its most elaborate form' (1994: 148). The case of European citizenship will be covered and analysed extensively in Chapter Seven, but for the time being it is as important to assess its possibility as postnational membership.

For many commentators, EU citizenship is 'thin' and fundamentally grounded in national citizenship. For example, Bauböck (2003) suggests that the EU is better understood instead as 'supranational', meaning that individual membership requires citizenship in an EU nation-state and Bellamy and Warleigh insist that 'the scope and character of the equality conferred by EU citizenship is more akin to that of the subjects of a common ruler than of citizens capable of being both rulers and ruled in turn' (2001: 3). But maybe it would be more fruitful to understand EU citizenship as an evolving process that welcomes different positionings and expanded inclusion. Moreover, regarding Community law and its constraints upon state legislation, Hall argues that

> the power of States to make dispositions of nationality is an expression of their sovereignty in international law. Membership of the Community, however, involves the transfer of part of their sovereignty to the Community. To the extent that the exercise of State power to make dispositions of nationality impacts upon the rights and obligations arising under Community law, there is reason to believe that in principle State sovereignty in this area is subject to limits. (1995: 43)

Another important aspect of the denationalisation of citizenship status is the inclusion of non-nationals within the national sphere of social, civic and political rights. This latter postulation is associated with Soysal. Her definition of postnational citizenship refers to a regime that 'confers upon every person the right and duty of participation in the authority structures and public life of a polity, regardless of their historical or cultural ties to that community' (1994: 3). Through the extension of rights to aliens, Soysal sees the postnationalisation of citizenship as 'a new model which [...] reflects a different logic and praxis: what were previously defined as national rights become entitlements legitimised on the basis of person hood' (1994: 3). In other words, the overarching principle of membership in contemporary societies has shifted from the logic of national citizenship to the logic of personhood. The importance of Soysal's work resides in accepting and celebrating the international human rights regime as the legitimate and normative framework for granting rights to aliens. The emergence of supranational human rights institutions, such as the United Nations (UN), United Nations High Commissioner for Refugees (UNHCR), European Court of Justice, International Labour Organisation (ILO), and such documents as the Universal Declaration of Human Rights and other international covenants and conventions, including the UN International Convention on the Protection of the Rights of All Migrant Workers and Members of their Families and the ILO Migrant Workers Convention, are cited as examples of this trend.

Jean Cohen contends that

> human rights discourses are now a pervasive feature of global public culture. Their effectiveness goes well beyond moralistic exhortation: they constitute an international symbolic order, a political-cultural framework, and an institutional set of norms and rules for the global system that orients and constrains states. (1999: 26)

However, it has to be stated here that although the increasing guarantee of human rights in international law manifests a tendency for a denationalisation of citizenship, it doesn't mean that the legal status of aliens has changed. If we are talking about formal legal membership of the polity, aliens are considered outsiders to citizenship. Even if they enjoy some legal access to some economic rights as extended to non-citizens residing in a national territory of sovereign nation-states, the exercise of these rights may be precluded by the denial of social membership in the national community to these non-citizens.

Dual citizenship is also considered by Soysal as an important manifestation of the emergence of postnational citizenship as it transcends the notion of loyalty to a single state. In the past, dual nationality was an intolerable affront to the absolute authority of the state with regard to its territory and its nationals. Spiro describes it thus:

> Dual nationals represented on the one hand a constant source of international tension where one state attempted to protect its citizen from mistreatment at the hands of another state claiming the same individual as its own. On the other hand, the presumptively divided loyalties of dual nationals represented a potential threat from within the polity in times of international conflict. (1997: 47)

More recently, due to the recent liberalisation of different national rules on naturalisation, expatriation and assignment of citizenship at birth, dual or multiple citizenships are in fact the norm and will be more accepted in the future (although compare policy development in this area in Germany and the Netherlands in Chapter Six). Thus as Soysal suggests 'dual nationality breaks with the logic and aims of prior national citizenship strategies; the parameters, conflicts, referents, and political agents are no longer simply congruent with the single state' (1997: 512).

To sum up, the legal aspect of citizenship has been affected by social realities like the emergence of European citizenship, the extension of membership rights to aliens and the worldwide increase of multiple citizenships. However, it is rather different to argue that national citizenship is declining in importance in a postnational world, from asserting the claim that citizenship *itself* is becoming postnational.

CITIZENSHIP AS RIGHTS

Citizenship is traditionally associated with the enjoyment of rights and entitlements. As we described in detail in Chapter One, the conceptualisation of citizenship as possession of rights was most influentially developed by T. H. Marshall in 'Citizenship and Social Class' (1963). According to Marshall, citizenship is the way to ensure that everybody is treated as a full and equal member of society; this is achieved by granting people an increasing number of citizenship rights. For this reason, Marshall believed that the fullest expression of citizenship occurs in the liberal-democratic welfare state. This way the state becomes the guarantor of civil, political and social rights for all and ensures that every member of the society enjoys full participation and enjoyment of the common life of society.

The enjoyment of rights is granted by a very specific institutional entity, that of the nation-state, and although Marshall uses the example of Britain for his analysis, he assumes that the evolution of citizenship rights will take place in other national, capitalist societies. It is apparent that, for many commentators, citizenship as rights takes place in the locus of the nation-state, in the words of David Held: 'in the modern times, rights have nearly everywhere been effectively enshrined within the institutions of nation-states' (1995: 223). But if we are going to consider the rise and the expansion of the human rights regime, we have to accept the fact that the state is no longer the only provider and guarantor of rights. Human rights law represents an alternative source of rights and supersedes the jurisdiction of individual nation-states. The development and expansion of the international human rights regime has led many scholars to argue for a citizenship beyond the nation. For example, Rainer Bauböck contends that 'human rights are the cornerstone as well as the most extended application of a transnational conception of citizenship' (Bauböck 1994: 247).

The following human rights case (*Beldjoudi* v *France*) will better illustrate the above argument. Mohamed Beldjoudi was born in France in the 1950s to Algerian parents. He lived and socialised in France but he did not attain French citizenship because his 'special civil status' was not converted to full citizenship. Because of a history of criminal convictions and time spent in prison, the relevant minister issued a deportation order. The case went to the European Court of Human Rights where the majority opinion found that the decision to deport Beldjoudi would be in breach of Article 8 of the European Convention on Human Rights. Article 8 states that: (1) Everyone has the right to respect for his private and family life, his home and his correspondence; (2) There shall be no interference by a public authority with the exercise of this right except such as in accordance with the law and is necessary in a democratic society in the interests of national security, public safety or the economic well-being of the country, for the prevention of disorder or crime, for the protection of health or morals, or for the protection of the rights and freedoms of others.

> The majority decided that the deportation of Beldjoudi from the country in which his family lives will contravene with 'the right to respect for family life afforded by Article 8' if it is not justified when weighed against what is regarded as necessary and thus allowable pursuant to Article 8(2). (*Beldjoudi* v *France*, European Court of Human Rights 1992: 41)

Thus, for an action to be within the bounds of the Convention, 'the interference must correspond to a pressing social need and, in particular, that it is proportionate to the legitimate aim pursued' (*Beldjoudi* v *France*, European Court of Human Rights 1992: 43). The Beldjoudi case shows that significant citizenship rights are protected within the European human rights regime and that the state has to acknowledge that the social facts of an individual's participation in the life of a community are as important as mere nationality.

Citizenship rights are thought to be entrenched within the framework of international law, but according to Sassen there is a danger that human rights will override 'potentially contesting state sovereignty and devaluing citizenship' (1996: 58). One has to remember, though, that the rights guaranteed by the various human rights treaties are to be enforced by states; it is the states that are the signatory parties and are expected to initiate the analogous legislation. Nevertheless, the European Court of Human Rights is a transnational body that can enforce compliance with the human rights norms. Moreover, the expanding discourse of human rights has generated a process of moral vocabulary. As Vincent points out 'Human rights have become a kind of lingua franca of ethics talk so that much of the discussion about ethics in international relations takes place using the vocabulary of rights' (1992: 267). The growing legitimacy of international human rights provides a framework that can bridge a disarray of developments like globalisation, growing inequality, environmental destruction and ethnic conflict by enabling actors to pursue their rights at both local and global level.

However, defining citizenship in terms of the possession of rights has been criticised as promoting 'passive' or 'private' citizenship where an obligation to participate in public life is completely absent. If we are to accept this criticism then a postnational citizenship that is based in the international human rights regime would only exacerbate the situation on a greater level. The rights-based approach to citizenship is inextricably linked to our conceptualisation of citizenship. But as the expansion of global human rights continues, and it is followed by institutional entities that can protect and guarantee those rights, then the possibilities for a postnational citizenship are multiplied.

CITIZENSHIP AS POLITICAL ACTIVITY

As we saw in our discussion of republican citizenship in Chapter One, citizenship conceived of as political participation has a long history in political theory. First, Aristotle explored what it means to be a citizen,

> The citizen in an unqualified sense is defined by no other thing so much as by sharing in decision and office. [...] Who ever is entitled to participate in an office involving deliberation or decision is [...] a citizen in this city; and the city is the multitude of such persons that is adequate with a view to a self-sufficient life. (1981: 87)

This notion of citizenship was later developed in the Italian city states of the eleventh century and it was epitomised in the work of Machiavelli, for whom citizenship was central to politics. Participation in public life becomes essential in the theory of Rousseau. Subsequently, it played a major role in French and American revolutionary thought, and in this century was the central idea of Arendt (1958) as well as in the work of Pocock (1975), Skinner (1978) and Oldfield (1990). Political participation is a dominant theme in Arendt's political philosophy as every human life must have a public dimension. Thus, human life is separated into two distinct spheres: the private and the public. We need the shelter of the private realm to give us depth of character (Arendt 1958: 71) but by mastering our private necessities we obtain freedom in the public realm (Arendt 1958: 31). The private realm is characterised by deprivation as those subjected to it are 'deprived of political rights' (Arendt 1967: 141).

> To live an entirely private life means to be deprived of all the things truly essential to the human life: to be deprived of the reality that comes from being seen and heard by others [...] to be deprived of the possibility of achieving something more permanent than life itself. (Arendt 1958: 58)

However, the public realm is the locus of the political and allows freedom through speech and action (Arendt 1958: 28). In political terms the public realm is of utmost importance because it allows individuals to create a common world through appearance (Arendt 1958: 50) and a space for interaction where our individual ideas can compete to be seen and heard through speech and persuasion. It is also the space where the actual event of coming together is a series of unfolding happenings that highlight 'the miracle contained in the fact that each of us is made as he is – single, unique and unchangeable' (Arendt 1967: 301). As such the public sphere is based on the laws of equality, which is not given to us 'but is the result of human organization' through action (Arendt 1967: 301). The public realm plays an important role in bringing people together to debate and act together and forge a common reality that is secured by our equality of difference. Action corresponds to the human condition of plurality (Arendt 1958: 7) and 'plurality is the condition of human action because we are all the same, that is, human, in such a way that nobody is ever the same as anyone else who ever lived, lives, or will live' (Arendt 1958: 8). As such, not only is 'plurality the condition [...] for that space of appearance which is the public realm' (Arendt 1958: 220), but plurality guarantees citizenship in the sense that it allows all citizens a free and equal position to appear in public.

The importance of political participation was re-emphasised in the work of Benjamin Barber, who argues for a vision of participatory democracy as the remedy for the depoliticisation of western societies. He argues that:

> The future of democracy lies with strong democracy – with the revitalisation of a form of community that is not collectivist, a form of public reasoning that is not conformist, and a set of civic institutions that is compatible with modern society. The crucial terms in this strong formulation of democracy are activity, process, self legislation, creation and transformation. Where weak democracy eliminates conflict (the anarchist disposition), represses it (the realist disposition), or tolerates it (the minimalist disposition), strong democracy transforms conflict. It turns it dissensus into an occasion for mutualism and private interest into an epistemological tool for public thinking. (1984: 150–1)

Civic republicans and participatory democrats employ the concept of citizenship to indicate the importance of political activity; this is done in descriptive but equally in normative terms as well. For example, as Oldfield notes, 'empowerment and opportunity is not sufficient for the practice of citizenship' (1990: 28). Individuals must be motivated because it is the individual motivations that make civic actions effective. Skinner writes,

> A self-governing republic can only be kept in being [...] if its citizens culti-vate that crucial quality which Cicero had described as *virtus*, which the Italian theorists later rendered as *virtù*, and which the English republicans translated as civic virtue or public-spiritedness. The term is thus used to denote the range of capacities that each one of us as a citizen most needs to possess: the capacities that enable us willingly to serve the common good, thereby to uphold the freedom of our community, and in consequence to ensure its rise to greatness as well as our individual liberty. (1986: 242)

According to civic republicans, the community is the arena where citizens' involvement takes place, but for participatory democrats, political activity aims for an overall transformation of state and society and occurs in various social movements. Civic republicanism, similar to liberalism, accepts the status quo, looking for a more active kind of citizenship within it. Participatory democracy, owing to the influence of debates around the new social movements, aims at social change by transforming politics (Keane 1984; Laclau and Mouffe 1985). As Mouffe has eloquently argued, in radical democracy 'citizenship is not just one identity among others, as it is in Liberalism, nor is it the dominant identity that overrides all others, as it is in Civic Republicanism' (1992a: 378). Therefore, according to Mouffe,

> the political community should be conceived as a discursive surface and not as an empirical referent. Politics is about the constitution of the political

community, not something that takes place inside the political community. The political community, as a surface of inscription of a multiplicity of demands where a 'we' is constituted, requires the correlative idea of the common good, but a common good conceived as a vanishing point, something to which we must constantly refer but that can never be reached. (1992b: 30)

For Ancient Greeks, citizenship was located within the polis, for the Romans, it was the empire, and in modernity the exemplary political community is to be found in the nation-state. For some theorists, the state is the appropriate locus of citizenship (Kelly 1979), but many analysts today insist that citizenship increasingly takes place beyond national boundaries. This form of political participation has been characterised as transnational activism and it is defined as the activities of 'social movements and other civil-society organisation and individuals across state borders' (Piper and Uhlin 2004: 40–5). This definition was further refined by della Porta and Tarrow (2005: 7) who referred to transnational collective action as 'the coordinated international campaigns on the part of networks of activists against international actors, other states, or international institutions'. Recent works on transnational collective action, notably the works of della Porta and Tarrow (2005), Tarrow (2005), and Risse-Kappen (1995; 2002), suggest that three variables explain the rise and outcomes of transnational activism: the current complex internationalisation (growing density of international institutions, regimes, and contacts among state officials and non-state actors), and multiplication of linkages between local, national, and international issues (Tarrow 2005: 8); the multilevel political opportunities created by the interaction between complex internationalisation and domestic structures (i.e. 'institutional features of the state, society, and state-society relations' (Risse-Kappen 1995: 20)); and the emergence of a stratum of activists best described as *rooted cosmopolitans* ('a fluid, cosmopolitan, but rooted layer of activists and advocates' (Tarrow 2005: 34)).

The emergence and rise of transnational activism in the form of non-governmental organisations, grassroots social movements and other cross-border networks of advocacy are inextricably linked with the turn to postmodernity. In relation to citizenship, according to Bryan Turner,

it is possible to combine the claims of citizenship status with a postmodernist critique, if postmodernism can be regarded as a form of pluralism. That is, we must avoid the equation of citizenship with sameness. In citizenship, it may be possible to reconcile the claims for pluralism, the need for solidarity and the contingent vagaries of historical change. If citizenship can develop in a context with difference, differentiation and pluralism are tolerated, then citizenship need not assume a repressive character as a political instrument of the state. (1993: 15)

The term 'postmodernity' is highly contested in social sciences. For this analysis, we will follow a lose definition of the term which refers broadly to the changes in the features of modernity and not to a distinctive new epoch. For example, postmodern theorists like Baudrillard (1983) claim that changes such as transformations in capitalism from mass industrial production to services based on new forms of information technology; the 'globalisation' of economy that these transformations bring; the decline of 'class politics'; the rise of 'new social movements' and ethno-nationalism; a growing disenchantment with 'grand narratives' of history and reason, and the reduced ability of the nation-state to regulate national economics and social conflict, have all produced dramatic fragmentation of societies and a consequent intense interest in the political. Modernity is characterised by the separation of politics from society, which now is changing to a growing politicisation of social and cultural norms. Consequently, the political has come to be considered less separated from the social. This is evident in the emergence of new social movements that articulate demands over issues like lesbian and gay rights, feminism, the environment and so on. Likewise new social movements are linked to new forms of subjectivity and to new forms of political agency. Melluci (1985) believes that social movements could realise their interests beyond the state more effectively than through it. According to his point of view, new social movements try to escape from the intrusion of the state and the market into social life by requesting the individual identity, and the right to determine private life, against the suffocating omnipresence of the system. The significant element for new actors is the effort to seek and secure personal autonomy and not an increase of state intervention to provide security and well being. For Melluci, contemporary social movements do not operate along conventional political lines but are concerned instead with the democratisation of everyday life which requires them to organise as networks inhabiting an intermediate public space between state and civil society.

> A new political space is designed beyond the traditional distinction between state and 'civil society': an intermediate public space, whose function is not to institutionalise the movements nor to translate them into parties, but to make society hear their messages into political decision making, while the movements maintain their autonomy. (1985: 815)

New social movement theory emphasises the cultural plurality in expressive mobilisations. It also brings forward the importance of formal and informal communication networks that cross national boundaries. For example, internet communication between non-governmental organisations (NGOs) and their members, advocacy web sites and chat lists organised by NGOs and governance organisations are seen as a potential for developing democracy and citizenship beyond the nation-state (Ward 1995; Warketin and Mingst 2000).

Transnational social movements 'involve people in active citizenship and thus lay claim to a political space that may or may not conform to the spaces allowed by the existing system of government' (Magnusson 1994: 9–10). This form of political participation has been characterised as a mode of 'global citizenship' (Falk 1993). According to Falk, global citizenship comes as the answer from below to the oppression that is created by globalisation from above. He argues that business elites and interests, which increasingly share more in common with each other than with members of their own civil societies, are increasingly unconstrained in their activities (Falk 1994: 134–5). Similarly, Tully (2005: 11) refers to a 'continuation and intensification of Western imperial rule in a new informal mode' which overrides the peoples and processes of citizenship traditionally conceived.

By presenting the findings of Oxfam, he concludes that:

The majority of the world's population in the (informally) imperialized states is now more impoverished than under earlier formal colonial rule, after three successive waves of modernization and democratization policies since Decolonization. 840 million people are malnourished. 6,000,000 children under the age of 5 die each year as a consequence of malnutrition. 1.2 billion people live on less than $1 a day and half the world's population lives on less than $2 a day. 91 out of every 1,000 children in the developing world die before 5 years old. 12 million die annually from lack of water. 1.1 billion people have no access to clean water. 2.4 billion people live without proper sanitation. 40 million live with AIDS. 113 million children have no basic education. 1 in 5 does not survive past 40 years of age. There are one billion non-literate adults, two-thirds are women and 98% live in the developing world. In the least developed countries, 45% of the children do not attend school. In countries with literacy rate of less than 55% the per capita income is about $600. In contrast, the wealth of the richest 1% of the world is equal to that of the poorest 57%. The assets of the 200 richest people are worth more than the total income of 41% of the world's people. Three families alone have a combined wealth of $135 billion. This equals the annual income of 600 million people living in the world's poorest countries. The richest 20% of the world's population receive 150 times the wealth of the poorest 20%. In 1960, the share of the global income of the bottom 20% was 2.3%. By 1991, this had fallen to 1.4%. The richest fifth of the world's people consume 45% of the world's meat and fish, the poorest fifth consume 5%. The richest fifth consume 58% of total energy, the poorest fifth less than 4%. The richest fifth have 75% of all telephones, the poorest fifth 1.5%. The richest fifth own 87% of the world's vehicles, the poorest fifth less than 1%. (Tully 2005: 12)

These gross inequalities and oppression that are manifested in hegemonic forms of power create opportunities for informal networks to develop an opposition. Such networks, involving NGOs and civil society organizations (CSOs), take on the adage of think globally, act locally, connecting local groups into global networks which aim at confronting undemocratic power relations and try to force negotiations or action by national or global systems of governance. 'Here, the very relations of power that are employed to constrain them to adapt to a restrictive form of neoliberalglobal citizenship turn out to be able to be used to challenge and modify these relations' (Tully 2005: 14).

The participants in these networks are interested in transforming power relations and their activities take a diversity of forms like the Fair trade (in the interstices of free trade), the Landless Workers Movement, Food Sovereignty, Porto Alegre participatory democracy, the movements to democratize the UN, the Land Mines Convention, the International Forum on Globalization, the environmental movement, and countless others. A prominent example of transnational political activism in Europe is the European Social Forum, which is the regional expression of the World Social Forum in Europe. Based on its Charter of Principles,

> The European Social Forum is an open meeting space designed for in-depth reflection, democratic debate of ideas, formulation of proposals, free exchange of experiences and planning of effective action among entities and movements of civil society that are engaged in building a planetary society centred on the human being. (2002)

European integration and transnational activism

The process of European integration and European citizenship offers an opportunity to examine such transnational dynamics at work. An increasingly important question and issue concerning the EU is the role that its citizens play in the process of European integration. State-centric accounts of citizenship stress the importance of the territorially-based community that has a degree of sovereign self-governance. Similarly, the three theories of European integration (neofunctionalism, intergovernmentalism and federalism) have been influenced by these conventional conceptions of the political as sites of citizenship. As a theoretical perspective, neofunctionalism perceives integration as an elite-led self-sustaining process driven by the logic of spill-over. Whilst its early advocates Haas (1958) and Lindberg and Scheingold (1970) saw the importance of transnational, supranational processes, these were to be primarily elite-driven processes. Lindberg and Scheingold saw that the emergence of politically active supranational groups would endanger the 'legitimacy of the technocratic Community system' (1970: 269), thus denying political activism to the people.

The other two main approaches, intergovernmentalism and federalism, view the issue in quite different ways but both base their analysis on the model of the nation-state. The intergovernmentalist approach rests on the assumption that national states and national interests form the process of European integration. This perspective is closely related to the realist tradition, by advocating that European nation-states are both powerful and legitimate as they express popular sovereignty (Taylor 1996). From an intergovernmentalist point of view, a model of shared identification and central democratic institutions is closely bound up with the nation-state. The nation-state is legitimate because its central political institutions are formed through the consent of its citizens.

For Federalists, the EU should not be perceived as an agglomeration of sovereign nation-states, but as a super-state in the making (Williams 1991). Elements like common history, culture and political values can provide the basis for identification with the Union, and if the European institutions are responsive to the needs and the demands of its citizens, they will foster EU legitimacy (Wallace 1993). The scholars in this tradition argue that the lack of democratic and accountable European institutions endanger the project of integration as a whole. Although we agree with the above assumption, it seems problematic that change and legitimacy can only come from above, by modifying the operation of the institutions, and not from below, based on popular demands. Both inter-governmentalism and federalism draw assumptions from traditional statist approaches (Schmitter 1996). For intergovernmentalists, the model of shared identification and central democratic institutions is valid in the context of its original embodiment: the nation-state. For federalists, however, the same model is relevant in the context of an emerging super-state.

It is evident that the above theoretical approaches could not accommodate effectively the problem of legitimacy in terms appropriate to the EU. Increasingly, scholars understood that the above analysis was highly influenced and perceived through the experience of the nation-state, and it could not capture the dynamics of recognition and representation in the

EU. The now predominant view in the literature on European integration is to examine the EU as a new and complex form of multi-level polity, marked by the coexistence and interaction of European and national institutions. Within this new context, multiple and overlapping identities and institutions exist side by side and supersede any notion of an organisation of sovereign nation-states or a kind of supranational state.

In line with this view, the emergence of a European public sphere within the discourses and the actions of a plethora of NGOs, grassroots movements and other civil society organisations, manifests that politics is not confined to the domain of the state. Moreover, there is a tendency to conceptualise the notion of a European public sphere in a narrow way, implicitly or explicitly derived from an ideal-typical conception of the national public sphere. Taking the concept of the national public sphere as the basis for judging the public debate in the EU is problematic and hinders further engagement with a more flexible and dynamic understanding of European politics. Since language, culture and identity are regarded as being the key-elements that constitute the public sphere, and are considered to be deeply embedded in a population, then it is expected that the public sphere itself will be fairly stable. Deriving from the above position, a European public sphere would be too diverse and heterogeneous, as it has to bring forward diverse and conflictual opinions concerning the public debate of issues, whereas the national public sphere is seen as being unitary and homogeneous where consensus can be achieved. But, in order to link the theory of multi-level governance and the emergence of a European public sphere, one can consider the possibility of a vibrant and diverse public space, containing differences where the actors with plural constituted identities come together to debate on topics that are thought to be in the public interest of the European polity. Political participation in the European public sphere provides the locus for citizenship beyond the nation-state.

In November 2002 the Italian city of Florence hosted the first gathering of the European Social Forum (ESF) and 60,000 activists from all over Europe gathered to express their disagreement with the commitment of European governments to free market policies, growing militarism, and racism, as well as the degradation of environmental conditions. Preparatory meetings in Brussels, Vienna and Thessaloniki led to the involvement of more than 600 organisations in an effort to promote political and democratic participation from below. The thematic framework that was suggested for the actual forum was the following:

- The creation of a Citizen's Charter for Europe.
- An agenda of mobilisations against war, militarisation of politics, and the production of weapons in the European Union.
- Europe's role in the world with particular attention to Central Eastern Europe and the Mediterranean area.
- The organisation of cultural events and mass demonstrations in new forms.

The above choice of European issues as a focus for collective action shows that a significant portion of the public is not satisfied with the policies and the decisions that form the current process of European integration. Thus, the meetings of the ESF provide an international public arena for contestation and legitimation of the European polity from below. There is also an effort for

> different cultures, languages and experiences to meet together and express themselves, in a common framework provided by the Porto Alegre principles, aimed to include other experiences, which until now don't have a dialogue with the Porto Alegre process, even if they are part of the movement against neoliberism. Like in Porto Alegre, the European Forum has to provide a real citizenship for different subjects (women, youth, workers, students, migrants …), with particular attention to the involvement of the subjects of social exclusion (sans-papiers, homeless, unemployed …), and for different languages (not only political debates but also cultural events, for example). (ESF, Florence 2002)

CITIZENSHIP AS IDENTITY

Citizenship, as we have already analysed, is characterised by different dimensions. We looked at citizenship as a legal status, as a set of entitlements, and as a mode of political participation. Another very important aspect of citizenship is the feeling of belonging or the process of identification that it gives to people. Here we are dealing with the emotive side of citizenship and how people develop affective ties of solidarity with a group by experiencing feelings of belonging to a collectivity. It has to be mentioned, though, that this aspect of citizenship is inextricably linked with the dimensions of citizenship that we analysed previously, as collective identities and solidarities are constituted within these institutions.

The concept of collective identity has attracted scholars from many disciplines during the latter quarter of the past century. Although it is distinguished analytically from both personal and social identity, it is quite clear that all three types of identity overlap and interact. Social identities refer to the social roles that are attributed to individuals in an attempt to situate them in social space. They are grounded in established roles like 'mother', or 'nurse', or in more inclusive categories such as gender, ethnic or national categories, and are usually referred to as 'role identities' (Stryker 1980) and 'categorical identities' (Calhoun 1991). Regardless of a specific socio-cultural base that may hold, they provide points of orientation to alter or define other social objects.

Personal identities are traits and meanings attributed to oneself by the actor; they are self-designations and self-attributions regarded as personally distinctive. They are especially likely to be asserted during the course of interaction when other imputed social identities are regarded as contradictory, as when individuals are cast into social roles or categories that are insulting or demeaning (Cohen 1985). Thus personal identities may derive from role incumbency or category-based memberships, but they are not necessarily comparable since the relative salience of social roles or category membership, with respect to personal identity, can be quite variable.

As social and personal identities are different, yet typically overlapping and interacting constructs, so is the relationship between collective and social and personal identities. Providing a consensual definition of collective identity is a problematic task, as many scholars emphasise different traits. The majority of commentators suggest that it is a shared sense of 'one-ness', or 'we-ness', anchored in real or imagined shared attributes and experiences among those who form a collectivity and in relation, or contrast, to one or more actual or imagined sets of 'others' (della Porta and Dianni 1999). Embedded within the shared sense of 'we', a corresponding sense of collective agency suggests the possibility of collective action in pursuit of common interests as well as it invites such action.

When it comes to analysing the nature of collective identity in relation to citizenship, a great part of literature is dedicated to the development of identifications and solidarities that people sustain with the nation-state. In this way, the feeling of belonging is institutionalised in the form of citizenship, socialisation agencies, ethno-national narratives of historical memory, boundaries of sovereignty between us and them and a notion of familiarity within a specific territory. Thus, according to Miller, 'nationality and citizenship complement one-another. Without a common national identity, there is nothing to hold citizens together, no reason for extending the role just to these people and not to others' (Miller 1992: 94). For many people, this feeling of belonging is related with the notion of being at 'home'. Home, then, is where we belong, territorially and culturally, where 'our own' community is, where our family, friends and acquaintances reside, where we have our roots, and where we long to return to when we are elsewhere in the world. In this sense, belonging [...] is a notion replete with concreteness, sensuality, organicist meanings and romantic images. It is a foundational, existential, 'thick' notion. In the ways that it circumscribes feelings of 'homeness', it is also a significant determinant of individual 'identity', that elusive but still real psychological state of feeling 'in sync with' oneself under given external conditions. Most importantly, 'home' and 'belonging', thus conceived, carry affective rather cognitive meaning: the indicative and simplistic statement above, 'home is where we belong' really means 'home is where we feel we belong'. (Hedetoft 2002: 5)

But people often have multiple affinities and tropes of belonging, they may have several places and cultures they belong to which alter their identity as flexible, multiple, relational or fluid.

Several scholars have criticised the assumption that national identity defines people's sense of citizenship in liberal democratic nation-states. Some have argued that myths and imageries of a homogeneous identity have suppressed social and cultural difference. The multiculturalist position on citizenship calls for a 'differentiated citizenship' (Young 1989), but the granting of rights to groups and the protection of cultural difference takes place within the nation-state. Multicultural critics are interested in incorporating various social groups in the political community but they tend to use a concept of 'culture as synonymous with "a nation" or "a people" – that is, as an intergenerational community complete, occupying a given territory or homeland, sharing a distinct language and history' (Kymlicka 1995: 18). Thus, the presumption that collective identities and solidarities are formed in national civil society and they are bound up with nation-states still remains at large for cultural pluralists. As Torres notes, 'The multicultural paradigm in its first instance proposed a transformation of the public space within the confines of the nation-state, leaving unchallenged the notion of the nation-state itself' (1998: 161).

The state can be a powerful 'identifier' because it has the material and symbolic resources to provide classificatory schemes and categories. But, no state can monopolise the production and diffusion of identifications and categories. As Appadurai notes, 'the nation-state is not the only game in town as far as translocal loyalties are concerned' (1993: 423). The literature on social movements shows how alternative conceptualisations of identification can spring up and give rise to 'transnational identities'. Some scholars analyse global social movements which contest multilateral economic institutions (O'Brien et al. 2000), create conditions for a global civil society (Wapner 1996), and bring into existence a world polity (Boli and Thomas 1999).

The study of transnational politics within transnational social movements is diverse and creative. As Tarrow notes, it can be roughly divided in five categories with some overlap between them.

1. Some researchers examine the transnational activities of non-state actors.
2. Some are interested in particular issues like human rights and democratisation, the environment, immigrant rights, or indigenous peoples' movements.
3. Some investigate the structure and actions of organizations – either particular ones, or transnational networks of organizations.
4. Some explore the role of non-state actors in international treaties where they either played a constitutive role, or against which activists mobilized.
5. Some study contentious politics in the context of international agreements or institutions. (Tarrow 2001: 9)

The emergence and the rise of transnationalism activism can be perceived as a form of global citizenship where the identifications and the solidarities are formed due to the participation in cross-borders political actions. Similarly, Falk notes that

> Amnesty International and Greenpeace are emblematic of this transnational militancy with an identity [...] that can't really be tied very specifically to any one country or even a region [...] These networks of transnational activity conceived both as a project and as a preliminary reality, are producing a new orientation toward political identity and community. (1993: 47–8)

Thinking of the political in relation to the subject, especially within social movements, shows that our subjectivity is inherently unstable and it changes as the social and cultural forces which constitute us change. This understanding of forming identities could open up the possibilities for being and thinking. By accepting less rigid and fixed notions of the subject, we are able to explore ourselves and society in a myriad of ways. Even more importantly, it enables us to recognise and interact with a plethora of different subjectivities and open up dogmatic national identities that provide the foundation for oppression and conflict.

Another important aspect of transnational social and political identities focuses on the ways in which immigrants attempt to expand fields of social life beyond the nation-state. Specifically, this literature highlights the continued engagement of immigrants with their place of origin, facilitated by high-speed communications and transport technology (Cohen and Vertovec 1999; Vandenberg 2000). The main premise of this approach is that while transnational activity existed in the past, contemporary transnationalism is novel in scope and in its persistence, and reflects not simply immigrants' longing for home, but a new political geography structured between localities (Mandaville 1999; Itzigsohn 2000; Smith 2001). Immigrant groups (or diasporas and transmigrants) are said to exist in a new global market of political loyalties, engaging in a complex politics of 'here and there' and resisting attempts by the state to 'fix the parameters of political community and territory' (Mandaville 1999: 665; Appadurai 1991) and to assimilate newcomers into a national culture.

The blurring of once taken-for-granted boundaries differentiating states, ethnicities, and civil societies is producing new spaces of daily life, new sources of cultural meaning, and new forms of social and political agency that flow across national borders. The everyday practices of borderless people currently constitute transnational social spaces of survival, self-affirmation, and political practice. Thus, citizenship identity for transnational migrant communities moves beyond the nation-state and is more spatially fluid and territorially unbounded. The case of transnational migration, especially in the context of Europe, will be analysed in greater detail in Chapter Six.

Moreover, the transnationalised form of citizenship-identity can be found in the case of the EU's integration. As Turner notes: 'There is a growing cultural awareness of a "European identity" which challenges nationalistic conceptions of political citizenship' (1994: 157). Elizabeth Meehan's *Citizenship and the European Community* (1993) is the most significant attempt to date to explore the origins, nature and prospects of EU citizenship. As she argues, in the European Community what is emerging is 'a new kind of citizenship'. This new form is a complex one which is 'neither national nor cosmopolitan'. Rather it is a 'multiple' form which is expressed and institutionalised through 'an increasingly complex configuration of common Community institutions, states, national and transnational voluntary associations, regions and alliances of regions', 'a new legal order' which limits the sovereign rights of member states, and importantly, through 'the emergence of a new European-wide public space and civil society' (Meehan 1993: 1). This new multiple form of citizenship 'already offers us the opportunity to act on the fact that we have more identities than our nationality', and it allows us to develop forms of participation and politics concerning our interests and identity combining traditional 'vertical' channels relating to national governments with new 'horizontal' routes relating to transnational networks and common European Community institutions (Meehan 1993: 155). The development of European citizenship will be further analysed in Chapter Seven; for the time being, it is important to note that experiences within transnational politics can advance citizenship identity and solidarity.

CONCLUSION

By taking into account different claims of citizenship as identity in the European Union, the social formations of transmigrants and in transnational social movements, we see that there is a burgeoning literature that locates citizenship beyond the parameters of the nation-state. Advocates of the transnational or postnational citizenship have been criticised that extending the concept of citizenship beyond formal political communities runs the risk of it meaning little, but to their defence the opening up of the locus of citizenship can create more flexible and inclusionary sites of citizenship identity. Many scholars claim that citizenship increasingly takes a denationalised form that challenges its previous conventional statist conceptualisation. We have argued that there is a plethora of theoretical and empirical accounts of such processes within legal, political and social institutions and experiences to become a part of our political understandings. The nation-state cannot capture exclusively the needs and demands of the subject for identification and expression as it fails to grasp the importance of non-national collectivities. Postnational citizenship conveys the desire and aspiration for a multifaceted and pluralized understanding of citizenship identities and solidarities. Thus, it offers the possibility to open up our political references and accommodate our commitments of ethics and action in multiple political sites.

CHAPTER 4

Political participation

INTRODUCTION

The issue of political participation, or, more specifically, the perceived decline in political participation, has become of huge interest to both the academic community and political practitioners. As we shall see below, turnout at elections has been falling in most European countries. However, it is not only in electoral terms that a disengagement with politics is being noted. Figures for the membership of political parties and trade unions also seem to show secular decline. These trends have led many to question whether there is a crisis within the democratic system worldwide. Something, it seems, is wrong with democracy, if more people vote for candidates on reality television shows, than vote to decide who will govern the country. In some countries, such as the UK at the 2001 and 2005 elections, the numbers of people voting for the winning party are outnumbered by those who did not vote at all. A democracy requires people to participate; rule by the people cannot be said to function if the people do not get involved.

However, some studies have suggested that what is occurring is not a simple decline in political participation but a change in the nature of political engagement. As Norris argues:

> Indicators point more strongly towards evolution, transformation and reinvention of civic engagement rather than its premature death [...] Political Participation is evolving in terms of the 'who' (the agencies or collective organisations), 'what' (the repertoires of actions commonly used for political expression) and 'where' (the targets that participants seek to influence). (Norris 2002: 4)

An analysis of these trends in political participation will be one of the main areas of focus in this chapter. We will then go on to consider how we might explain this state of affairs. To do this we must consider the adequacies (and inadequacies) of theories which attempt to explain why people do or do not get involved in politics. Broadly, what we will find is that whilst some of these theories shed some light on this question, it is an area in which political scientists find themselves, surprisingly perhaps, a little short. The final section of this chapter will consider the issue of political participation from two of the theoretical perspectives from section one, republicanism and liberalism. We will examine how these two theories view the issue of political participation and the trends and developments outlined earlier in the chapter. On one level, as mentioned above, republican conceptions of citizenship would view any decline in political participation as problematic for the whole conception of citizenship. However, such positions might be rather less concerned if a decline in formal participation is counterbalanced by a rise in informal participation. For liberal citizenship, participation is not an essential feature. What is important is that people have the right to do so if they wish to participate. As such, liberalism, with what some have described/criticised as an 'anti-politics' position, might well see a decline in formal participation as a reflection of satisfaction or indifference to public life and a (reasonable) prioritising of the private sphere (although, as we shall see, liberals may become concerned if a lack of participation threatens liberty). However, before we engage in any of these activities, it is necessary to spend some time considering quite what we mean by political participation. If we are to assess the level, nature and significance of political participation, we must first define that activity. This is perhaps not as straightforward as we might assume.

WHAT IS POLITICAL PARTICIPATION?

Generally, there has been a tendency to define political participation from a 'top down' perspective. Parry, Moyser and Day (1992: 16) define political participation as 'taking part in the processes of formulation, passage and implementation of public policies' or 'action which seeks to shape the attitudes of decision-makers to matters yet to be decided, or [...] action in protest against the outcome of some decision'. There are a number of points to be made about this. Firstly, it is worth noting that Parry et al., in their study of participation in the UK, found that only 18 per cent of the actions which they characterised as political participation were seen as such by the respondents. This indicates something of a mismatch between academic or official views of political participation and the views of citizens themselves. Related to this, a second, crucial point, is that this disparity highlights the importance of how 'the political' is conceptualised.

How we conceive of political participation crucially depends upon ontological questions as to the nature of 'the political'. Ontological claims are inherent in political analysis.

> [T]he nature of the political [...] is, strictly, ontological, concerned as it is with the nature of the political world itself – its essence (if it might be said to possess one), its boundaries and the constituent units (if any) out of which it is comprised. (Hay 2002: 2)

Obviously a concept of 'the political' is central in constructing a notion of political participation. However, there are many different and contested notions of 'the political'. These distinctions, following Hay's analysis, might be said to be based around different ontological positions on the essence of politics, its constituent units and its boundaries. More 'scientific' or positivist conceptions of political analysis, that is those who adhere to a naturalist position and argue for a unity of method between the natural and the social sciences, tend to make narrower ontological claims. Such positivist positions posit an existing social world, independent of our perception, which is underpinned by law-like regularities, which can be uncovered given the correct method. For such positions, 'the political' is seen in terms of an arena definition which is concrete, and potentially, completely quantifiable. For positivist-type enquiries, 'the political' (and hence political participation) is in essence the business of government, made up of public, generally, state-actors and contained within the boundaries of the public sphere. Thus, for political analysts working within a positivist-type position, it is behaviour which takes place within or aimed at influencing, such an arena which is likely to be interpreted as political participation. An example of this is the work of Pattie, Seyd and Whiteley (2004). Whilst noting controversies about how one defines political participation, their study of citizen activity in the UK asked individuals whether they had partaken in a range of activities 'while attempting to "influence rules, laws or policies"' (Pattie, Seyd and Whiteley 2004: 76), reflecting the focus on the state arena.

This is not a conception shared by others making different ontological claims. Critical realist positions dispute the positivist assertion that social reality can be directly apprehended if the correct methods are applied. This scepticism is based on an ontological assertion that there are deep social structures which mediate our access to the given social reality. 'The political' may well be an arena, but given the existence of deep social structures mediating our access to knowledge of what 'the political' is, such a view of politics may be a distortion. This is certainly an argument that has been invoked by feminist authors who suggest that categories such as 'the political' have been gendered so as to reflect and protect the patriarchal system (Pateman 1989). As a result, there is seen to be a need to consider the role played by these structures, primarily involving power relations along with their interaction with such factors as gender, ethnicity, culture and ideas, all of which may be affecting the conception of 'the political' which is initially apparent to us. Hence, the essence of politics becomes *governance* (which invokes both governmental and state activity, but also goes beyond such an arena), consists of potentially all actors, but specifically, those enmeshed in relations of power, and its boundary is relationships between individuals and institutions where one 'redefine[s] the parameters of what is socially, politically and economically possible for others' (Hay 1997: 50). Consequently, this is a conception of the political which is much more clearly orientated to a process-based notion of 'the political'. A political context is one which involves relations of power.

> Politics is about power; about the forces which influence and reflect its distribution and use; and the effect of this on resource use and distribution, it is about the 'transformatory capacity of social agents, agencies and institutions; it is not about Government or government alone. (Held and Leftwich 1984: 144)

Thus, it is behaviour which takes place within the process of defining and redefining the scope of action of others which is likely to be observed and interpreted as political activity.

For constructivists, the ontological claim is quite different to that of positivism or critical realism. Constructivist-type positions hold that there is no social reality independent of our perceptions. As such, there is no pre-given object of 'the political'.

> What is the political? Does this mean that a definitional answer is necessary from the outset, or even that we have to look for such an answer? Or does it not rather mean that we must accept that any definition, any attempt to establish the essence of the political will hinder the free movement of thought, that its free movement requires us, on the contrary, not to prejudge the limits of the political, to agree to go on a journey of exploration without knowing our path in advance. (Lefort 1988: 1)

For constructivists, the tendency is to deny any objective status to any conception of 'the political'. There are only, rather, rival conceptions of 'a political' which lie in constant flux and tension, reflecting the ebb and flow of different interests. This has a clear tendency towards a more process-orientated conception of politics, denying a stability to 'the political' and instead pointing to a more fluid notion of politics. This type of conception can be seen in some aspects of feminist theory. Chantal Mouffe, for example, argues that politics is about conflict and antagonism and that, as identities are unstable, there always exists the possibility of conflict (Mouffe 1993: 77). Lyotard speaks of politics as 'a drive to act, understood as a necessity for life, itself interpreted as an unstable relation of feelings, desires and structures' (cited in Williams 2000: 2), which has no relation to institutional settings. Further, with particular reference to his work on the struggle in Algeria, he argues that politics can be and sometimes is a refusal to accept the traditional methods of political discourse and participation. He talks of the spontaneous, almost libidinal rejection of the discourse of the political mainstream which will not be understood as political because it is, in part, a rejection of such a conception of politics. 'Spontaneity, then, betokens a movement that cannot be recognised and understood from within the system it rises against' (cited in Williams 2000: 10). For constructivists, different conceptions of 'a political' are reflective of different discourses and the dominance of one conception of 'the political' reflects the pre-eminence of that discourse in power relations.

In many senses, the notion that there can be an essence of 'the political' is antipathetic to constructivist positions. The central ontological claim is a denial of objective essences of our conceptions and notions and an emphasis on their discursive basis. For approaches such as discourse analysis, 'the political' involves potentially all individuals and is contained within the boundaries of the discursive articulation and rearticulation, dominance and challenge of various conceptions of 'the political' and perhaps centrally, their relationship to questions of identity, which orders the nature of the social and political sphere.

> [D]iscourse analysis emphasises the construction of social identity in and through hegemonic processes of articulation, which partially fixes the meaning of social identities by inscribing them in the differential system of a certain discourse. (Torfing 1999: 41)

Hence, political participation is where discursive constructions compete and clash with one another over the inscriptions of social identities, and from this position it is behaviour which is engaged in this process which is likely to be observed and interpreted as political participation. Clearly, this raises a large number of activities and interactions as potential forms of political participation.

In the section that follows, the focus is on ascertaining the levels and trends of various forms of political participation. Much of this will involve analysis of arena-based activities, such as voting and membership of political parties. There will be, moreover, an attempt to consider a broader range of political activities. However, some of the less visible forms of what may legitimately be viewed as political participation may not be considered. In part, this is a methodological point. One of the aims of this chapter is to assess the broad picture of political participation in Europe. In this enterprise some activities are more visible than others and also, more easily compared to/with the situation in other countries. By including some and not others, we are making no claims or statements about what constitutes legitimate political participation. As we argue above, quite what constitutes political participation is, and should be, an open issue. This is merely one attempt to assess a complex and ever-changing picture.

POLITICAL PARTICIPATION IN EUROPE

In this section we will begin to address the issue of the level and pattern of political participation in Europe. In effect, we will be looking at whether there has been a decline in political participation. However, as stated above, any answer to this question must, in a sense, be partial. If, as argued in the preceding section, there is and can be no rigid conception of political participation, then we must accept that whatever activities we do look at and measure, may not be exhaustive of political participation, and as such, whatever empirical information is presented may not capture the entire picture. This said, what follows is an attempt to assess empirical information regarding a number of important political activities. In assessing the level and trends of such participation, we can begin to form an answer to the question as to whether there has been a decline in political participation in Europe. We will begin by examining formal participation, in elections and in terms of membership of political parties and trade unions. Then we will consider some evidence about citizens' stated levels of interest in politics. At this point we will note something of a paradox: electoral participation is, by and large, in decline yet, interest in politics is increasing. We will then go on to look at less conventional forms of participation and membership of political, civic and social organisations and movements. Here, we will note a general increase in political activity, with more and more citizens choosing to express themselves in and through organisations and protest activities.

Voting

Voting is clearly an important aspect of political participation. Whilst there are, as we shall see, a wide variety of ways for citizens of a country to influence political outcomes and decisions, elections occupy a particularly special place. Democracy relies on participation in elections. It is not a sufficient condition for democracy to exist for people to turn out and vote (a functioning democracy requires many more activities), but it is a necessary one. Without individual citizens' involvement in elections, democracy cannot function. Elections are also the main way individuals can express their political opinions, which are then aggregated.

> Citizens use various ways to influence politics, but the electoral connection through political parties is the primary basis of public influence in representative democracies. Elections are one of the few methods that enable a society to reach a collective decision based on individual preferences. The choice between (or among) parties aggregates the preferences of individual voters, thereby converting public opinion into specific political decisions. Other forms of citizen participation may exert substantial influence on government but they lack this representative quality. (Dalton 2006: 127)

Also, issues with electoral systems and boundaries to one side, elections are the only form of political participation where every citizen's voice counts equally. In protest politics, lobbying, demonstrations, or general political debate, the political context influences whose voice will be heard. In elections, with the above notable caveat aside (that in some electoral systems, particularly First Past the Post, voters in marginal seats have a disproportionate influence on electoral outcomes, and conversely, voters in safe seats, of any particular political persuasion, have relatively little influence), each vote counts equally. Another reason that elections are a particularly important form of political participation is that they are the only form of mass political involvement in politics in the modern representative democracies of Europe. In theory, if not in practice, everyone gets to have their say. Other forms of political participation are important, but only elections can claim such universality.

What, then, is the level of political participation at elections in Europe? Obviously, there are a number of different types of elections; national, presidential, local, federal and European. Here, for the sake of comparability, we will focus on national assembly elections and elections for the European Parliament. (For the former, it is important to note that we might expect turnout for these elections to be lower in countries such as France, where there is a directly elected President, as people may consider Presidential elections to be of greater importance, and thus be more likely to vote in them and perhaps less likely to vote in national assembly elections. However, the trend of turnout in such elections, if not the absolute level, is meaningful and important).

Figure 4.1 shows a graph of turnout in national assembly elections for

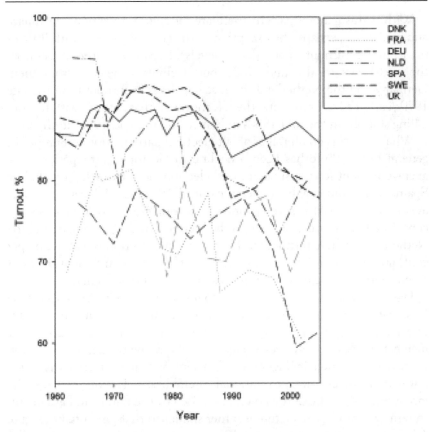

Figure 4.1 Turnout at national assembly elections in seven European countries 1960–2006. (Source: IDEA)

seven European countries: Denmark [DNK], France [FRA], Germany [DEU], Netherlands [NLD], Spain [SPA], Sweden [SWE] and UK. (Later analyses of political participation will also include Italy [ITA] and Belgium [BEL]. They are left out of this model as they have compulsory voting, and thus, generally higher and more stable levels of turnout. It is interesting to note, however, that despite voting being compulsory, turnout is still in decline for these countries.) There are a number of things to note in Figure 4.1. In simple terms, the countries with the highest turnout over the period are Denmark, Sweden and Germany. The countries with the lowest turnout are France and the UK. The main trend to be observed in Figure 4.1 is a general, if not pronounced, decline in turnout. In the early 1960s, the turnout figure is spread between a high of 95.1 per cent in the Netherlands and a low of 68.7 per cent in France. By the early 2000s, turnout is spread between 84.5 per cent in Denmark and 60.1 per cent in the UK.

Within this general pattern there are, of course, variations. Denmark and Spain are, perhaps, the exception to the general pattern, with little or no decline in turnout (if at different levels). In Sweden turnout rises from the mid-1960s to the mid-1980s, but declines somewhat from then. Germany and the Netherlands both see declines in turnout from the late 1970s/early 1980s. France and the UK show a similar pattern, with turnout falling sharply, in the mid-1980s in France and the mid-1990s in the UK.

What does this graph tell us about electoral participation in Europe? In general terms, there has been a decline in electoral participation. The average turnout for the six countries' election closest to 1960 (excluding Spain, which did not have elections until 1977) is 84.3 per cent. The average turnout for the seven countries' election closest to 2006 is 74.4 per cent. In addition, turnout seems to be high in Sweden, Denmark and the Netherlands (where turnout for the most recent election was above 80 per cent) and turnout is low in France and the UK (where turnout at the most recent national assembly election was just above 60 per cent).

Figure 4.2 shows data for the same countries' turnout at elections for the European Parliament. The European Parliament has 785 members and is directly elected by a potential electorate of 492 million citizens from 27 member states, every five years. Figure 4.2 shows the turnout for the seven countries examined in Figure 4.1. Turnout for these elections is much lower than for elections to national assemblies, reflecting, perhaps, the rather limited nature of the powers exercised by the European Parliament. In terms of trends, the picture is rather similar to that presented in Figure 4.1. The average turnout for the 1979 election for the five countries who were members of the EU in 1979 was 52.8 per cent. In 2004 the average for the seven countries was 42.1 per cent. There is, then, like elections to national assemblies, a drop of 10 percentage points in the average turnout.

The countries with the highest turnout are Denmark, as with national assembly elections, and Spain. The lowest turnout is in the UK and the Netherlands. Clearly, there are a range of factors particular to the EU and the process of European integration which influence turnout at these elections. Some have argued that low turnout at European elections indicates dissatisfaction with the EU, something that may be supported by the fact that turnout is lowest in those countries which are seen to be more sceptical of the process of European integration (although for an alternative account see Franklin 2001). The trend in turnout, though, is downwards; sharply so for Spain, Germany and the Netherlands, less sharply so for France and Sweden. Only Denmark and the UK (albeit from a very low level of turnout) seem to buck this downward trend.

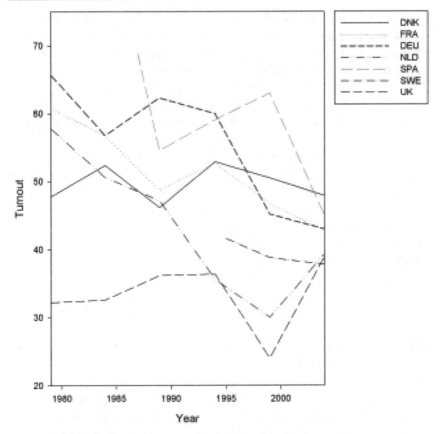

Figure 4.2 Election turnout for the European Parliament in seven
European countries 1979–2004. (Source: EurActive)

Political organisation membership

In addition to elections, another way in which citizens can influence
political decisions, procedures and outcomes is by joining a political organisation. Political parties are the main example of a political organisation,
but here we will also consider trade unions (which could also be considered
as social movements/organisations). Membership of a political party is
an important form of political participation for two reasons. Firstly, it is
members of political parties who undertake much of the mundane,
unglamorous work, without which parties, and ultimately democratic
elections, could not function as we know it. Secondly, although far from
complete, members of political parties do have influence over the policies,
personnel and direction of the party.

Data collected by Mair and Van Biezen shows that, taking aside the issue of trend for a moment, as of 2003, in the nine European countries considered here, being a member of a political party is decidedly a minority pursuit, with only between 2 and 6 per cent of citizens being members of political parties (average of 3.7 per cent) (Mair and Van Biezen 2001: 9–12). In terms of trends, membership of political parties is certainly in decline between 1979–2000, with only Spain seeing an increase in membership. This decline itself follows on from a fall from the 1960s, when an average of 15 per cent of the population were members of political parties (Mair and Van Biezen 2001: 9). Aggregating the figures (including the increase in members in Spain), political parties in these nine European countries have lost almost four million members in that twenty-one year period. The implications of this decline go beyond the scope of the present discussion, but such a drop clearly raises questions about the ability of political parties to function politically if their membership continues to whither away (Needham 2005).

Trade Unions are another form of mass political organisation. Aside from their partisan interests and concerns, trade unions have been seen as a positive mobilising force for participation (D'Art and Turner 2007). Higher trade union density is seen to be connected with higher levels of citizen participation with, it is argued, involvement in workplace decision-making fostering a sense of political efficacy, thus stimulating participation (Pateman 1970). Higher levels of trade union membership seems to be good for participation. What, then, has occurred to levels of trade union membership? The picture here is somewhat different to that seen in terms of political party membership. Union density is higher in the Scandinavian countries of Denmark and Sweden, with a union density of around 70 per cent, whereas trade union membership is lower in France, Germany, Spain and the Netherlands (Visser 2006: 45–6). In terms of trends, between 1970 and 2003 it seems that trade union membership has increased in Spain, Belgium, Denmark and Sweden (albeit that the latter two have experience a decline more recently). However, there have been sizeable falls in France, the UK, Germany and the Netherlands (Visser 2006: 45–6). The precise reasons for these differences go beyond the remit of this book (see Checci and Visser 2005), but include factors specific to the governing of the labour market and the economy. What is interesting to note here is that, unlike electoral participation and political party membership, there are differences in both the level and the trends in union membership.

'Informal' political participation

As stated at the beginning of this chapter, some have argued that we are not witnessing a decline in political participation, but a change in the ways citizens express themselves politically (Norris 2002). We have seen above that conventional forms of political participation, such as voting at elections and membership of political parties, seems to be in decline. It certainly seems that citizens are increasingly shying away from conventional forms of participation. Are these being replaced by other forms of political activity?

As discussed above, defining political participation is a fraught enterprise. If it is relatively straightforward to define formal political participation, it is more difficult to define informal, or unconventional participation. Yet, in this section we are seeking to provide some kind of empirical overview and are thus limited by what kinds of activities can and have been measured cross-nationally. The World Values Survey, a cross-national survey of social, political and economic behaviours and attitudes, is an invaluable aid in this enterprise. It collects cross-national data on a number of 'informal' acts of political participation. However, it should be noted that we by no means view these as exhaustive of the repertoire of political acts that citizens may choose to express themselves as political subjects. They do, however, allow us to gain some kind of picture of the levels and trends of these activities.

Before analysing the levels of and trends in these forms of activity, it is worth considering briefly some evidence of individuals' reported level of political interest. The 'common sense' explanation that is frequently propounded in the media for low turnout is that people simply are not interested in politics anymore. However, data from the World Values Survey suggests otherwise, as Figure 4.3 shows. In six of the nine countries (Sweden, Denmark, Belgium, Italy, Spain and the Netherlands), there is an increase in the number of people who say they are interested or very interested in politics. Only in France, Germany and the UK is there a decline. There seems to be scant evidence here, for the assertion that people are generally less interested in politics. (However, it should be noted that only in Sweden, Germany, Denmark and the Netherlands does the figure top 50 per cent, indicating it is only in these countries where the balance sheet is in the black for political interest. In the other countries, a majority of citizens say they are not interested in politics.) Although there is a lack of political interest in some countries, others appear to be experiencing a surge. This represents something of a paradox. Turnout at elections is, generally, in decline. Yet, in a number of countries, an increas-

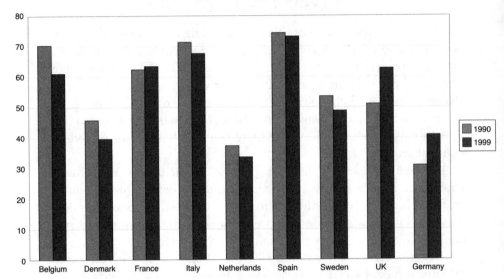

Figure 4.3 Comparing the percentage of people who report they are either
interested or very interested in politics in 1990 and 1999.
(Source: World Values Survey)

ing number of people say they are interested in politics. In this context
we might expect to see a rise in 'informal' political participation, as the
number of citizens interested in politics seems to be increasing and they
perhaps choose to express themselves beyond the ballot box.

The picture that emerges from the World Values Survey data is one of
rising citizen participation in these 'informal' political activities. Figure 4.4
presents the percentage change (the change between 1981 and 1999 levels
as a proportion of the original, 1981, level of activity) in these forms of
action (signing a petition, joining in a boycott, attending a lawful demonstration and occupying buildings), which in some cases is astronomical.
It also includes the same calculation for the same period for electoral
participation.

What Figure 4.3 shows is that for all nine countries, whilst turnout
at elections has decreased (between 1981 and 1999), 'informal' political
participation has increased massively (with the exception of Spain); in
some cases, by too much to be (sensibly) captured on a chart (Sweden saw
a 767 per cent increase in people participating in occupying buildings,
albeit from a low 0.3 per cent of the population to 2.6 per cent of the
population). In terms of the levels of engagement in these activities,
some interesting national variations emerge, which perhaps reflect (and

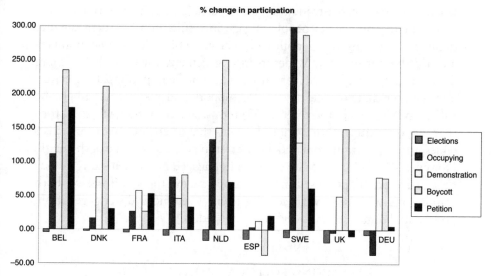

% change in participation

Legend:
- Elections
- Occupying
- Demonstration
- Boycott
- Petition

Figure 4.4 Percentage increase in 'informal' political participation activities 1981–99 in nine European countries. (Source: World Values Survey)

reinforce) different national political cultures. Sweden is the most participatory country in terms of boycotts and petitions, whereas France leads the way in terms of the more strident activities of demonstrating and occupying buildings. The World Values Survey also provides evidence that civic participation is increasing, with membership of and participation in civic organisations both seeing significant increases (particularly so for environmental and global justice groups). It seems that the claim that there has not been a general decline in citizens' political activity has some considerable purchase.

However, there is an important point to note. With the exception of signing petitions, the activities described above, are minority pursuits. In 1999 the number of people stating they had joined a boycott ranged from 5.6 per cent to 33 per cent. For demonstrations, the figures range between 13.3 per cent and 39.7 per cent; for occupations, 0.7 per cent to 9 per cent. Whilst there may be increases in such forms of political expression, they are not activities in which a majority of citizens engage. Electoral participation seems to be in decline, but 'informal' political participation is not sufficiently widespread to make up the shortfall. In making any assessment of the state of political participation in Europe, it seems that the activities and forms must be weighted. A small decline in a mass participation activity means that a large number of citizens do not participate politically, whereas a large, even astronomic, rise in participation in an activity that a much smaller number of people engage in results in a relatively smaller number of citizens being politically active. This said, simple numbers are not the entire story. Widespread engagement with politics in more demanding forms of participation (which 'informal' participation generally represents) may help to create, support and foster what might be called, in Almond and Verba's (1963) terms, a civic culture, which in turn may support citizen participation. It seems that assertions that there exists widespread alienation from and disinterest in politics are wide of the mark. However, the notion that citizens remain engaged in political activity may be equally presumptuous. Rather, Europe seems to be witnessing both trends simultaneously, with some citizens ever more dis-engaged from politics and some citizens ever more engaged.

EXPLAINING POLITICAL PARTICIPATION

Individuals and participation

At this stage, it seems appropriate to consider quite how and why this situation has come about. There are a number of theories that seek to explain why people do or do not participate in politics. These include the socio-economic resource, rational choice theory, and social capital approaches. What will be seen is that whilst these approaches do contribute to explanations of participation, they are all somewhat problematic and that these problems are in some way related to their difficulties in explaining spatial and temporal variation.

The first of these four approaches to explaining political participation is the socio-economic resources model, which explains participation in terms of individuals' resources, motivations and mobilisation, and posits that individuals with high levels of resources such as time, money and education are more likely to participate. As Verba and Nie (1972: 125) note when terming this approach the standard model, this generalisation is well born out by the data; 'Citizens of a higher social and economic status (SES) participate more in politics'. Yet, as Pattie et al. (2004: 145–6) note, in other ways, this theory does not compare well to established facts about participation. General levels of education have risen over the past fifty years, and yet, the trends in turnout point in the opposite direction. Equally, there is some evidence which suggests that it is not only individuals with lower levels of resources who do not participate. Further, Brady, Verba and Schlozman (1985: 281) suggest that a problem with the resource-based model is that the causal mechanism by which resources promote or discourage participation, is underspecified. By this, Verba et al. mean that whilst the theory may correspond with some empirical regularities, it offers little by way of explanation as to precisely why individuals who draw upon higher socio-economic resources are seemingly more likely to participate in politics.

Political participation, in rational choice theory, is explained as a product of utility maximisation. When benefits outweigh costs, then people will participate. Such a theory, however, leads to a paradox. Anthony Downs in his classic, *An Economic Theory of Democracy* (1959), argues that because the chance that one vote will have an impact upon the result of an election is almost nil, the potential voter is better off not voting. Although Downs' theory, and much subsequent rational choice work, is aimed at addressing electoral participation, the logic of the argument can and has been extended to participation in a more general sense. In this vein Mancur Olson's influential book, *The Logic of Collective Action* (1971), suggests that if individuals are rational, in the sense of maximising benefits and minimising costs, then individuals would not participate in collective endeavours. This has become to be known as the free rider problem, in that the rational course of action as regards public goods is to 'free ride', to let someone else expend the effort and yet, to reap the benefits.

However, as Uhlaner notes, 'Unfortunately for theory, people do vote' (cited in Green and Shapiro 1994: 50). This 'problem' has come to be known as the paradox of participation. In short, this paradox is simply that if people were rational, in the sense of minimising costs and maximising benefits, they would not vote or participate, yet, people do and frequently so in substantial numbers. Such is the nature of the problem, some authors have suggested that the voting paradox 'ate rational choice theory' (Fiorina cited in Mansbridge 1990: 9). There are a number of attempts to find a way out of this apparent paradox, none of which are entirely successful (see Downs 1957; Rider and Ordeshook 1968; Aldrich 1993; for a critical review, see Green and Shapiro 1994), leading Green and Shapiro (1994: 68) to conclude that 'readers interested in the determinants of voter turnout, in sum, will derive little insight from the empirical work in the rational choice tradition'.

An account and explanation of participation which has gained prominence recently centres around the concept of social capital. The concept is most closely associated with Robert Putnam's work on Italy and America (Putnam 1993; Putnam 2000). The central thrust of the social capital perspective is that individuals who engage in regular face-to-face activity in the form of memberships of associational groups generate social capital, by which is meant, networks of cooperation, social trust and norms of reciprocity. Higher levels of social capital, are, Putnam claims, associated with higher participation rates. In part, the social capital literature attempts to deal with the question posed by the rational choice literature as to why individuals should participate. With norms of reciprocity, social trust and established networks of cooperation, it is supposed that the free rider problem identified by Olson can be overcome. Yet, there are reasons to be sceptical as to the success or veracity of the social capital literature.

A key criticism identified by Levi (1996) is that the mechanism by which social capital is produced and/or maintained is not specified. Authors such as Putnam have derived an explanation from game theory which suggests that dense networks of horizontal (that is interactions of equals, rather than vertical interactions of dependence and inequality) interactions provide these networks of cooperation, norms of reciprocity, sanctions for defectors and information about others. Yet, Levi is sceptical about whether membership of football clubs and birdwatching societies can undergird and support higher levels of civic engagement (Levi 1996: 47). Or as Theda Skocpol (2003: 57) puts it: 'Can we imagine rates of voter participation and organised public activity sharply improving if people heed the call to hold more picnics and songfests?'.

A more fundamental problem with the social capital literature is that even if we accept that participation in social groups fosters certain characteristics which make one more likely to participate in other social activities, what makes one likely to participate in social groups in the first instance? In clichéd terms, this is a chicken and egg problem and it may seem to be a semantic point. Yet, it has serious implications. For, if individuals are motivated to join social groups by social capital factors, then the whole concept and argument becomes tautological. Individuals join groups because they have high degrees of social capital and this produces more social capital to encourage them to participate. However, if individuals join social groups in the first instance for reasons outside of social capital, then perhaps these factors become the more crucial and central ones deserving investigation. This point is developed by Rothstein, who argues that the reason social capital remains high in Sweden, in comparison to America, is because of the institutionalised, encompassing welfare state (Rothstein 2001). This effectively makes the argument that social capital is produced, at least in part, by state interventions. If social capital is fundamentally dependent upon institutional, or governmental, factors, then the pressing area for analysis becomes how government interventions change the climate and topography upon which citizens participate and how these interventions, or non-interventions, affect participation (for some examples of this kind of research see Kumlin 2004; Lister 2007; Soss 1999).

Aside from their individual problems, each of these explanations has significant problems in accounting for the variations in participation over time and space identified above. For the civic resources model, the problem seems quite clear. Over time, educational and economic standards in Europe have broadly risen, but, whilst some forms of 'unconventional' participation have increased, mass participation activities, like voting, have decreased. Furthermore, most of the countries considered above have similar levels of socio-economic and educational performance. Yet, as mentioned above, there are significant differences in the levels and trends of political participation. The social capital approach, we have already seen, has difficulties in accounting for change across time. Social capital seems to be self-reinforcing: when it's there it produces more; when it is absent it is difficult to create. It has already been noted that rational choice theory has difficulty with political participation, or more specifically, it has difficulty in explaining why people do participate, as according to rational self-interest people should not participate.

Institutions and participation

If we wish to understand why people participate or do not participate, it seems that to examine the question solely at an individual level is myopic. Looking at voter turnout, Franklin argues, 'the most striking message is that turnout varies much more from country to country than it does between different types of individuals' (Franklin 1996: 217–18). It is, therefore, vital to consider why participation varies so much between European countries which are, in many ways, broadly similar. Further, it seems that the main theories which seek to explain why *individuals* do or do not participate, are ill-equipped to deal with this question. If we are to understand why people participate, it seems that we must consider the variations across different countries and at different times, and that to do so we must go beyond the main theories of participation.

In terms of electoral participation, a number of authors from the rational choice perspective seek to explain why turnout varies so widely across different countries. They focus on how the institutional arrangements for different countries facilitate or inhibit participation. Stated simply, the argument is that different countries have different arrangements for the holding of elections and that these produce different incentive structures (Jackman 1987). Generally, nationally competitive electoral districts, a proportional voting system, a smaller number of parties, a unicameral system and compulsory voting, all provide institutional incentives to voting. In a significant way, much of this research and its findings marks an important contribution to the understanding of political participation.

Yet, it is not entirely unproblematic. This is a model of political participation premised upon a rational choice model. Such modes of enquiry suffer from the problems, outlined above, which afflict rational choice theory itself. If it is never rational to vote, then how can a more proportional voting system make any difference? The rational choice theory answer is that it does so by changing the incentive structure. This is, in simple terms, the argument of this literature; that certain institutional arrangements make it more or less 'irrational' to vote. A further problem with this argument is that it cannot explain why turnout varies across time. With the odd exception, electoral arrangements remain constant, but as noted above, electoral participation varies considerably over time. It seems we cannot look to these factors alone to explain changes in electoral participation (let alone political participation more generally).

An alternative explanation of political participation has been developed from an institutionalist perspective. As mentioned above, Rothstein (2001) argues that the reason that Sweden has not seen the same kind of decline in civic and political participation as America is due to the encompassing nature of Sweden's welfare institutions, which is not found in the United States. His focus is on how the nature of a country's institutions influences the way its citizens behave by encouraging (or discouraging) certain types of norms. Rothstein's argument is that institutions are not just the output of social relations and formations, but that institutions themselves are key factors in these social relations. The challenge becomes to identify by what ways and means (welfare) institutions create, support, challenge or influence social norms. Rothstein (1998) outlines such an approach. His central argument is that social norms can be explained 'by the manner in which political institutions structure the decision making situation faced by actors and influence trust' (Rothstein 1998: 134). His view is that institutions set the framework for individual decisions and behaviour and as such, are crucial in establishing social norms. He suggests that this view reverses the traditional direction of relations between norms and institutions, whereby institutional form is shaped by the prevailing norms of society, with interesting implications.

> The variation in norm governed behaviour, and the differences in norms between societies, can thus be traced to the design of political institutions. This idea has a politically interesting corollary, namely that a society's norms are not structurally given (by culture, history, the World Spirit, etc.). If

instead norms vary with the character of political institutions, then we as citizens have a critical role to play. We can, at least on some occasions, decide which norms shall prevail in the society we live in, *because we can choose how we design our political institutions* (Rothstein 1998: 134–5 original emphasis).

Rothstein goes on to argue that welfare institutions which are based on universalist lines, that is that welfare policies include everyone (rather than targeting specific sections of the population, as means testing does), create and promote solidarity by reducing inequality between citizens, and by being just forms of organisation. These twin aspects combine to engender social trust and solidarity between citizens. Such solidarity forms a social foundation for democratic participation. The flip side of the argument is that where such universalism is absent lack of trust, and a lack of solidarity, combine to weaken and corrode social norms of participation. This social foundation, clearly, is not the only factor which influences participation. But the argument here is that it is one, and one which may help to explain why participation varies over time and space as institutions change over time and space.

There is some empirical evidence to suggest that countries with more encompassing welfare state institutions have higher levels of political participation. Specifically, inequality seems to be negatively related to participation, such that where inequality is higher, participation is lower (Lister 2007). Considering the empirical information presented in the previous section one can see that, generally, participation is higher in those countries, such as Sweden and Denmark, where welfare institutions are most encompassing and inequality is lower. Interestingly, as we shall see in the next chapter, it is commonly held (although also hotly contested) that the welfare state is in decline, such that one might see a decline in political participation as coterminous with a decline in the welfare state. This is a position which, crucially, sees political participation within the context of citizenship. An argument can be derived from the work of T. H. Marshall that citizenship should be seen as a unified concept, such that the nature of citizenship in any one facet (civil, political and social) affects the other facets of citizenship (Lister 2005). For Marshall, social citizenship rights based around equality of status are central for a fully functioning conception of citizenship. Where social citizenship is more developed, supported by more encompassing welfare institutions, political citizenship, seen as citizens participating in political and social life, is more vibrant. It seems that less developed social citizenship rights negatively affects citizens' propensities to be politically active.

New social movements

The variation of (welfare) institutions and electoral arrangements within Europe may go some way to explaining variations and changes in electoral participation in Europe, and the former may contribute to an explanation of the variations and changes in 'informal' political participation. However, a little more can be said here. The 1960s and 1970s saw the rise of what many identified as 'new social movements'. These movements, orientated around environmental issues, feminism and peace issues, did not seem to correspond to class-based political mobilisations, in that the movements and the citizens participating in them were not making demands for economic or industrial gains but for recognition of new identities and lifestyles (Melluci 1985). Attempts to theorise and explain these movements, often referred to as New Social Movement theory (for an overview see Buechler 1995; Pichardo 1997), see the development of and participation in these movements as different to 'old' social movements such as trade unions. A key notion is the idea that contemporary society has shifted from an industrial society to a postindustrial society (Inglehart 1990). As such, new social movements reflect this shift in society and are concerned with 'postmaterialist' issues such as the environment, identity and lifestyle issues. Much of the activity by these movements is at the symbolic level at the level of civil society, rather than instrumental action at the political or state level. These movements, it is argued, resist co-option and may be as much about protecting and asserting autonomy as they are about gaining influence and power; in Jurgen Habermas' term, about resisting the colonisation of the lifeworld (Habermas 1987).

As such, New Social Movement theory arguably offers an interesting explanation for the pattern of political participation in Europe identified earlier in the chapter. It is not without problems, though (see Buechler 1995; Pichardo 1997). How shifts in material production have affected social movements is not particularly clear, and sometimes the explanations run close to a tautology as new social movements are taken to be both evidence and consequence of such changes (Cohen 1985). Yet, New Social Movement theory offers an interesting explanation for the patterns of participation identified above. The rise in 'informal' participation may be explained by citizens in Europe moving towards participation in forms of political action which reflect the priorities and themes of new social movements: concerned with lifestyle and identity issues, not orientated around class-based challenges to economic conditions, and orientated to symbolic protests in civil society rather than using instrumental actions to gain influence and power within the state and political sphere. In this context, more traditional organisations and movements, like political parties and trade unions, might engage fewer and fewer citizens.

> Political parties, together with other traditional and hierarchical organis-
> ations, appear to be suffering from the impact of the individualisation of
> social and political preferences, as well as from a more general unwillingness
> to rely on existing structures to represent and articulate what appear to be
> increasingly particularised demands. (Mair and Van Biezen 2001: 14)

(However, one should beware simple, monolithic explanations; other factors, such as the professionalisation of political parties (Katz and Mair 1994; 1995) and macro economic changes (Checchi and Visser 2005) respectively, play important roles.)

It appears that if we want to explain the patterns and variations of participation identified in the preceding section, we must look to a number of different theories and explanations. Variations in electoral participation may be due to differing electoral arrangements, but also due to the impact of state institutions on civic and participatory norms. These might also help to explain variations between countries in 'informal' participation. However, the shift from traditional collective organisations, such as political parties and trade unions, towards more 'informal' participation *may* be reflective of wider social trends. Rather than citizens' participation being a reflection of their class position or identity, participation may be a means by which postindustrial citizens define themselves as political actors and subjects. Yet, there may be a danger of overstating the case. The proportion of citizens actually engaging in informal political participation remains a minority. Whether the recent surge of participatory activism is a reason to be cheerful, or a chimera hiding deeper reasons for despair about citizenship in Europe, is something we now turn to.

THEORIES OF CITIZENSHIP AND POLITICAL PARTICIPATION

Thus far we have identified the basic outlines of what political partici-pation is, what is happening to it in Europe, and how we might explain these variations and patterns. Broadly, it seems that formal participation is declining (although not in all countries, or to the same extent in all), whilst most countries have experienced a surge of 'informal', activist based participation. What does this mean for citizenship? Is it a problem? Does a decline in formal participation mean that citizenship is in decline? Does a rise in 'informal' participation indicate a reinvigoration of citizenship in Europe? We will argue, in this section, that how we answer these sorts of questions is almost entirely dependent upon the theory of citizenship that one holds. To illustrate this, we will focus here mainly on liberal and republican theories of citizenship

Liberal citizenship and participation

In many ways, liberal citizenship is almost entirely unperturbed by declines in political participation. Some have suggested that apathy is a sensible expression of a liberal view that there is more to life than politics and that higher turnout suggests the dominance of a totalitarian mindset where: 'too many people have fallen into the error of believing in the efficiency of political solutions for the problems of ordinary lives' (Morris-Jones 1954). Providing that citizens have rights and opportunities to participate in politics, the actual act of doing so is an aspect of individual choice and freedom. This perspective has led some to depict contemporary declines in electoral participation as 'the politics of contentment', suggesting that people must be broadly happy with the public sphere; if they were not, surely they would vote and be active to change the situation. (However, a wide range of authors and studies have established that there is a clear socioeconomic bias to turnout (Lijphart 1997; Verba and Nie 1972; Parry, Moyser and Day 1992). To put it another way, it is poor, young, ethnic minorities who are least likely to vote. It seems perverse to suggest that these groups of people are experiencing the politics of contentment. Or, as Piven and Cloward (1989: 13) put it: 'Of course, no one has satisfactorily explained why "the politics of happiness" is so consistently concentrated among the least well off'.)

Liberal citizenship is sometimes seen as a passive concept, with individuals as the bearers of rights, but being required to do very little in return for such rights (Kymlicka and Norman 1994: 354). However, this position is something of a caricature of the liberal position, in two ways. Firstly, and simply, liberal citizenship is not entirely without a conception of responsibilities. The maintenance of individual liberty entails certain responsibilities; at a minimum, that one's own liberties are compatible with the same liberties for all. Yet, liberals are also concerned about protecting the liberty of the individual, and there is a recognition that a complete withdrawal into the private sphere runs the risk of political power falling into the hands of a concentrated elite and thus threatening individual liberty (Rawls 1988). In this way, liberal conceptions of citizenship are likely to be somewhat perturbed by current patterns of participation

Stated simply, then, liberal conceptions of citizenship might well be concerned about current patterns and trends of political participation *in some* European countries. If political participation becomes the preserve of a minority, as mass participation activities like voting decline and fewer people are involved in political organisations like political parties, then there is clearly the risk that political power becomes concentrated and this, in turn, may threaten individual liberties (one might even argue that a split between an increasingly passive majority and an increasingly politically active minority, would be of concern to liberals, as it runs the risk that the politically active minority begin to have disproportionate influence). This argument is effectively one that acknowledges the interconnection of citizenship rights; if political citizenship declines, there is a risk that civil citizenship, in the forms of civic freedoms, may also decline. Given some author's arguments (Korpi 1989; Esping-Andersen 1990; Hicks 1999) that political participation was and is crucial for the development of social citizenship, we may also argue that a decline in political participation may weaken social citizenship (although clearly, this is not a concern for classical liberals who do not support social rights)

Political participation is potentially, then, an instrumental problem for liberal citizenship. In and of itself, there is no great concern if people choose not to participate in politics, as long as people have the opportunities to do so. The concern arises if any decline is large enough such that there is a risk of political power being wielded by an elite (this is, of course, a position which is consistent with republican ideals). One might argue that such a state of affairs does not pertain to any European state at the moment, but if current trends continue such a situation may seem possible. Liberals would then have something of a dilemma; a (potential) problem without a clear means of rectifying it. If political participation does decline to such an extent, what can be done? Coercing people to participate (in the form of compulsory voting, for example) seems illegitimate, as does the promotion of political participation as a common good. Yet, there are various attempts to grapple with this. One suggestion has been the design of institutions which 'encourage broad participation in political decision making' (Hill 1993: 75; see also Rawls 1971); another, older, tradition is one which, using separation of powers (federalism, constitutional guarantees and judicial overview), produces institutional checks and balances which prevent concentration of power. Liberal virtue theory (Galston 1991; Macedo 1990) identifies questioning of authority and willingness to engage in public discourse as key liberal virtues, and argues for their development through the education system (although there are difficulties in doing so, such as limiting the impact of such measures on family and social structures (Kymlicka and Norman 1994: 367)).

Republican citizenship and political participation

If liberal conceptions of citizenship are perhaps a little more concerned about current trends in patterns of political participation than they might at first appear to be, what of republican citizenship? As we emphasised in Chapter One, participation is *the* central element of citizenship for republicans. Unlike liberals, who conceive of freedom largely in negative terms, republicans view freedom positively, as self-government. It is only by being involved in politics that one can be free, by being involved in the creation of laws that one must accord with. Furthermore, participation is also seen as something which helps promote belonging and integration. Participation is not only the means by which freedom is secured (a position not opposed to the liberal concern with maintaining freedom articulated above) and integration fostered, but also, for some strands of republicanism, a good in and of itself; the highest form of human activity (a position that is inimical to liberalism).

Straightforwardly, for republican conceptions of citizenship, a decline in political participation is problematic; indeed, the patterns of participation in Europe observed above might be viewed, from a republican perspective, as a decline in citizenship. Given the importance republicans attach to participation, and also given that declines in participation have been apparent for some years, this has not gone without comment. Benjamin Barber's *Strong Democracy* (1984) argues that contemporary liberal democracies are 'thin', as he puts it (citing Ambrose Bierce) 'the conduct of public affairs for private advantage' (Barber 1984: 4). The reason for the paucity of political participation is, for Barber, systemic and related to liberal principles which underpin contemporary liberal democracies. Strong democracy, which Barber proposes, means that 'all of the people govern themselves in at least some public matters some of the time' (Barber 1984: xiv), such that freedoms would be secure and common purpose created. He proposes a radical reinvigoration of civic and political institutions to give citizens the opportunities for meaningful participation. From such a position, there is much to be concerned about in contemporary European participation patterns. Instead of 'all of the people some of the time', it seems participation is coming closer to 'some of the people all of the time', as some sections of the population disengage from formal politics, whilst others engage ever more with informal politics. This is unlikely to produce freedom, in the republican sense, and also, perhaps most importantly, is unlikely to foster the common good and promote integration and common purpose.

Beginning, like Barber, with a critique of liberalism, the literature on deliberative democracy (Gutmann and Thompson 1996; Dryzek 2000) argues for greater depth and quality of political and civic engagement. The process of deliberation, which is conceived of as a communicative, social process, where the citizen is open to other ideas and opinions and is willing, in principle, to be persuaded of other points of view, is sharply in contrast to the simple aggregative mechanisms of representative democracy. This process of deliberation, it is argued, has transformative and integrative effects. Dryzek (2000; 1996) argues that such processes might be fostered more in civil society organisations *which maintain distance* from the state, as authentic deliberation may be distorted by power relations.

> But why should civil society often be more attractive than the state as a site for democratization? The answer is that it is relatively unconstrained. Discourse need not be suppressed in the interests of strategic advantage; goals and interests need not be compromised or subordinated to the pursuit of office or access; embarrassing troublemakers need not be repressed; the indeterminacy of outcome inherent in democracy need not be subordinated to state policy. (Dryzek 1996: 482)

Therefore, such deliberative democrats, whilst hardly welcoming declines in turnout and political party and trade union membership, may see reasons to be cheerful in an increase in 'informal' participation. It may represent a rejection of the impoverished political participation that is offered in formal channels, and an embracing (by some, at least) of a more deliberative, democratic, political participation. This may also reflect an embracing of political participation in non-instrumental terms; participation not simply to protect one's own private interests and freedoms, but participation as a good, perhaps *the* good, in and of itself.

CONCLUSION

In this chapter we have examined the nature of, levels of, and trends of political participation in Europe. We began by considering quite what we mean by political participation and found that this was a more complex category than it may first seem to be. Political participation may have formal and informal modes, but it may also involve an even wider set of practices and actions, or inactions. Many of these latter types of activity may be difficult, or impossible, to quantify, but it does not mean that we should not be aware of them. We then reviewed the levels and trends of the various forms of political participation in Europe that we can quantify. Generally, the pattern was for a decline in formal participation, with a sharp rise in informal participation (albeit that only small-ish minorities are involved in such pursuits). Explaining both the differences between countries, and the differences over time, is a complex process. Many of the standard theories of participation do not account well for change over time and space, particularly in Europe, where in socio-economic terms, the countries are relatively similar. We argued that looking to the different institutional configurations in different European countries, and the related effect on values, offers one potentially fruitful avenue to analyse and explain the patterns observed. Returning to what this means for citizenship, we took this question from the liberal and republican theoretical view. For both perspectives, the patterns observed, and particularly the trends observed, are causes for concern. Liberal citizenship, whilst, on the surface, unconcerned by individuals choosing not to participate in politics (providing the opportunities are in place), does have a concern with participation. If political power becomes concentrated, then individual freedoms are threatened; in an instrumental sense, a serious decline in participation is a threat to liberal citizenship. Republican citizenship is clearly concerned about any decline in political participation, given its centrality. It threatens individual freedom, conceived of as self-government, and the absence of participation mitigates against inclusion and common purpose. Yet, there are developments, such as the increase in informal participation, which is participation of a higher quality (in the sense of being a deeper engagement in political debate and issues than simply voting), which republicans may see in positive terms, offering the potential for democratic renewal, and as such a reinvigoration of citizenship.

CHAPTER 5

The welfare state

INTRODUCTION

The welfare state is an institution, or complex configuration of institutions, practices and policies, which seems to attract controversy. Indeed, it might be argued that considering the welfare state in a volume on citizenship is itself controversial, as some conceptions of citizenship, notably classical liberal conceptions, do not consider the welfare state, or the social rights of citizenship that it delivers (to varying degrees, as we shall see), to be part of citizenship. There is controversy about what the welfare state should or should not supply to its citizens, and amongst academics there is considerable controversy and debate as to whether the welfare state is undergoing retrenchment; whether, that is, the quality and extent of social rights is in decline.

The argument that the welfare state provides rights which are central to citizenship is a position which is most frequently seen to originate with T. H. Marshall's work on citizenship. In his famous essay, 'Citizenship and Social Class', Marshall argued that a full conception of citizenship was one with civil, political and social rights of citizenship. He defined social rights as 'a universal right to real income which is not proportionate to the market value of the claimant' (Marshall 1963: 100). Marshall's argument for social rights to be seen as a part of citizenship was twofold. Firstly, he claimed that the meaningful exercise of citizenship rights, in the civil and political spheres, required some basic level of social well-being; as he put it, 'the right to freedom of speech has little real substance if, from lack of education, you have nothing to say that is worth saying' (Marshall 1963: 91). There is a further, more theoretical, argument which suggests that citizenship is based upon a doctrine that citizens are of equal status and that social rights instantiate this principle, which underpins civil and political rights, in the social sphere (see also King and Waldron 1988; Lister 2005).

This conception of citizenship, which sees social citizenship rights as an integral element of citizenship, has been subject to criticism. The New Right have attacked social citizenship rights as being incompatible with civil rights (Nozick 1974). It has been argued that rather than enhancing freedom social citizenship rights, and the welfare state, induce passivity and dependency, and thus undermine citizenship (Mead 1986). Such authors have called for a re-emphasis of obligations and responsibilities (clearly echoing a more communitarian conception of citizenship). Others have argued that it is not the case that social rights *per se* create dependency and passivity, but that the way that social rights and policies are administered and structured does. Soss (1999) argues that where social rights are provided through means tested programmes, political efficacy is low (as individuals feel that they are at the whim of a powerful bureaucratic apparatus). This is also a finding of Kumlin's study of attitudinal effects of the Swedish welfare state. He, too, finds that institutions where citizens face a good deal of bureaucratic discretion have demobilising effects.

> Experiences with empowering institutions yield more political trust than do experiences with less empowering institutions. In fact [. . .] experiences with customer institutions increase both satisfaction with democracy and trust in politicians whereas client experiences tend to have negative effects. (Kumlin 2002: 40–1)

Contra Mead, it may be the case that rights and policies which emphasise responsibilities, and require citizens to prove they have fulfilled certain obligations to gain access to social benefits, contribute to feelings of passivity and dependency, whereas social policies and benefits which are based upon rights and entitlements, such as social insurance schemes, may induce more positive 'lessons' about government and contribute to citizen efficacy.

From a citizenship perspective, there is rather more controversy and disagreement than we observed in the previous chapter. Those theories, such as liberalism, which were most indifferent to political participation, did not really see political participation in negative terms. Yet, as we have already seen (and shall see later on), communitarians and some strands of liberalism argue for a change in the nature and extent of the welfare state, and may even see the welfare state as it exists, or has existed, as a drag on citizenship (an argument, that in a different context, has been made by feminist theorists of citizenship; see Pateman 1988). Other strands, including a more social liberal perspective, would see the social rights of citizenship as a necessary aspect of citizenship. It is also worth pointing out that whilst political participation is the prerogative of individual citizens, this is not the case (or certainly not to the same extent) with the welfare state. Political participation is not something the state can control. It certainly has an influence (and, as was argued in Chapter Four above, maybe a significant influence) in a number of ways, but it cannot determine the quality and depth of what we might call an individual's political citizenship. Yet, the state can, and does, to a significant degree, determine and control the quality and depth of an individual's social citizenship. The state makes and implements welfare policy, and whilst citizens may, and do, influence this policy, the relationship is rather different to that concerning political participation.

As such, the question of what has happened in regard to the welfare state is less a matter of what citizens have or have not done (although this is clearly relevant; policy does not exist in a vacuum) and more a matter of what the state has or has not done. This will be investigated in the second main section of this chapter, where we will examine arguments around the retrenchment of the welfare state. Discussion and debate about welfare state retrenchment began in the 1980s, prompted by the election of various 'new right' governments. What scholars observed, however, was that despite rhetoric about 'rolling back the state', these governments did not achieve significant welfare state retrenchment (Pierson 1994). In the 1990s this debate seemed to intermingle with a developing literature on globalisation, which questioned whether, given economic liberalisation, states could continue to afford extensive and generous welfare state institutions and policies and whether we might not be witnessing a convergence around a minimal, safety net, welfare state (Garrett 1998; Reich 1992; Ohmae 1990). There is a rich and voluminous literature questioning, critiquing and analysing this issue (for a sample of which see Pierson 2001a; Hay and Marsh 2000; Hay 2006a; 2006b; Boyer and Drache 1996). We will try to examine what precisely has happened to the welfare state in Europe; whether there has indeed been retrenchment of European welfare states. What we will broadly see is that there has indeed been some retrenchment of European welfare states since the 1980s, although for most countries the cuts seem to be relatively small ones. In the third section of the chapter, we will look to explaining these patterns, examining and evaluating explanations for welfare state retrenchment, including globalisation, Europeanisation, partisan politics and socio-demographic factors. The chapter will conclude by examining what these developments in the welfare state mean for citizenship. Primarily focusing on (social) liberal and communitarian conceptions of citizenship, we will see that retrenchment or reform of the welfare state is either a welcome development which supports and bolsters citizenship (in the case of communitarian conceptions of citizenship), or a potentially very damaging process which would weaken citizenship in Europe (for social liberals). However, as with political participation, we must begin with a consideration of quite what we mean by the welfare state. The discussion is somewhat different here, as it is not so much an issue of how we define the welfare state as it is about how we *measure* the welfare state. If we are to gauge whether the welfare state, and social citizenship, in Europe has experienced retrenchment in recent years, we must be able to say how we would know this. This can be seen as an empirical question, and is sometimes referred to as 'the dependent variable problem' (Pierson 1994; 1996; 2001a; Green-Pedersen 2004; Clasen and Siegel 2007) but it also contains theoretical elements; how would we measure change in the welfare state?

HOW DO WE MEASURE THE WELFARE STATE?

How one measures the welfare state is a deceptively simple question. Pierson (1994; 1996; 2001), in the context of discussing and evaluating contemporary changes to the welfare state, refers to this as the dependent variable problem (see also Green-Pedersen 2004; Clayton and Pontusson 1998). Pierson notes that this problem exists for three reasons (Pierson 2001b: 420). Firstly, the welfare state is an extremely complex set of institutions, covering a wide variety of areas. It is, therefore, inherently problematic to arrive at a single statistical proxy measure which covers all the various activities of the welfare state. This problem has been exacerbated by the trend amongst scholars to point to an ever wider range of activities and spheres which should be considered as important aspects of the welfare state. Whilst adding to the theoretical richness of studies of the welfare state, it makes the task of finding empirical indicators ever more difficult. It also means that researchers can be, in effect, talking past each other as they may be including or excluding aspects of the welfare state which others do not. The second issue Pierson identifies is one of data limitations. Even if an appropriate domain of what constituted the welfare state could be agreed upon, the practical problems in actually measuring it are immense. As Esping-Andersen (1990: 21) notes, summary measures of expenditure simply will not do: 'It is difficult to imagine anyone struggling for spending *per se*'. A simple example that Esping-Andersen cites illustrates the point. In the 1980s the Thatcher government made a number of cuts to welfare state programmes. Yet, spending on unemployment benefits rose over this period as the increase in unemployment meant that the higher number of people claiming benefits offset the cuts to the programmes. More people were claiming less expansive benefits. However, simply to look at spending levels could lead to the conclusion that the Thatcher government was expanding welfare state benefits. The third problem Pierson notes is how any notion of change in the welfare state is to be measured. He suggests that welfare reform or retrenchment does not operate on a simple more or less scale and that there are a number of processes at work which evade a simple additive function.

Green-Pedersen (2004), revisiting Esping-Andersen's arguments, makes an interesting point at this stage. He argues that the problem is not simply an empirical one of finding the most appropriate statistical measure, but also a theoretical problem. The welfare state is defined and conceptualised in different terms. Wincott (2001) suggests that there are three main definitions of the welfare state. The welfare state variously refers to the dominant characteristics of the post-war 'golden age' of the Keynesian Welfare State, a distinct ontology or form of that state that provides social citizenship rights and, thirdly, sectors of state activity, such as social security, health provision etc. Each of these definitions lends itself towards a different empirical measure. It may be therefore, that the dependent variable problem is not solely the search for an accurate and sophisticated measure, which encapsulates the multifaceted nature of the welfare state, but is, in part, the problem of how to properly align how one measures the welfare state with how one conceptualises the issue at hand. The task, then, is to find the statistical indicator which is aligned to the theoretical argument that one is seeking to assess.

In this book we are concerned with citizenship and our consideration of the welfare state is shaped in these terms. Our concern is orientated around how changes in the welfare state in Europe have affected citizenship. Social rights, or social citizenship, thus becomes a key concept. T. H. Marshall defines a social right as a 'universal right to real income which is not proportionate to the market value of the claimant' (Marshall 1963: 100). Korpi and Palme (2003), and others, argue that a useful indicator to assess the strength or status of social citizenship rights is the replacement rate of key social insurance programmes. Replacement rates calculate the proportion of income when employed which is 'replaced' by social security benefits. These have clear affinities with Marshall's conception of social citizenship rights; where more of a worker's income is replaced when they are unemployed or sick, they are less dependent upon market outcomes; they are less commodified, or decommodified. As Esping-Andersen puts it, higher replacement rates enable 'individuals and families to maintain a normal and socially acceptable standard of living regardless of their market performance' (Esping-Andersen, cited in Bambra 2006: 76).

Replacement rates, however, have also been subject to criticism. A key criticism that Whiteford (1995) makes is that there are difficulties in making precise cross-national comparisons. The standard method of calculating replacement rates is to divide the amount of benefit received by income when employed. The usual way this income when employed is calculated is by using the disposable income (that is net of tax and benefits) of the average production worker (APW). Whiteford argues that the average production worker data measures different things in different countries. Firstly, he suggests that the average production worker status varies in different economies. This, he argues, means that the APW occupies a different position in the earnings distribution in different countries. If two countries have different APW average wages, they can provide the same amount of income in benefits, yet, in replacement rate calculations, one will be seen as replacing more than the other. However, this problem is rather less pronounced if one uses replacement rates to assess change of benefit generosity over time, within each particular country, rather than comparing countries' generosities against each other.

A second problem noted is that replacement rates only assess the cash transfer aspect of welfare provision and ignore other aspects and services of welfare state policy. As Scruggs (2006: 351) notes, generosity is multi-dimensional; it entails not only the cash benefit, but also the duration for which one can receive the benefit and the conditions attached to the gaining of the benefit. A high cash benefit that has heavy qualifying conditions and a short duration, may be *less* generous than a medium level cash benefit which is more widely available and with a longer duration. These factors need to be considered, therefore, to the wider point that even if we look at the generosity, in a broad sense, of social insurance programmes, many other aspects of the welfare state are still ignored, so our response is Janus faced. This criticism is both valid and, at the same time, somewhat unfair. It is valid in that replacement rates clearly do not provide information on some important areas of welfare policy. It is unfair in the sense that, as noted above, seeking a single statistical indicator for the welfare state is probably an impossible task.

Given the lack of a single comprehensive measure of the welfare state, one strategy is to examine a number of different indicators. Beyond replacement rates and qualifying conditions, there are other ways in which the welfare state can be statistically measured. One might seek to measure how well-developed a welfare state is, how expansive are social citizenship rights, by measuring the level of poverty and equality in a given country. In effect, this is a measure of welfare state development which focuses on outcomes. Marshall refers to social citizenship rights as the whole range from the right to a modicum of economic welfare and security to the right to share to the full in the social heritage and to live the life of a civilised being according to the standards prevailing in the society. (Marshall 1963: 74)

Defining social rights as the right to live a life of a 'civilised' person relative to the standards in that society would seem to fairly clearly equate to an absence of relative poverty. Poverty in western countries is measured in relative, not absolute terms (for more on this distinction see Alcock 2006). Relative poverty is normally measured in terms of the percentage of people who have less than 50 per cent of the median income. In terms of measuring the extensivity of social citizenship rights, such a measure has much to commend it. Although there is no way of assessing what social rights are, or are not, in place, it can be argued that it is a good 'bottom line' assessment; where relative poverty is high(er), one might assume that social citizenship rights are either inadequate, or failing, as if one is living on less than 50 per cent of the median income, one is not able to participate fully in society as others do.

As well as poverty levels, one might use inequality figures to assess to what extent a given welfare state 'succeeds' in maintaining a low level of inequality. The theory would be that high levels of inequality indicate that social citizenship rights are lacking, and as such, that the welfare state, in some sense, does not deliver effective social citizenship rights. However, it is important to note that inequality is a complex factor, related to many different aspects of the socio-economic system, such as the labour market and household size and structure. Yet, as Goodin et al. (1999) note, pre-government inequality (that is, a measure in income inequality excepting government taxes and transfers) is higher in virtually every country than post-government inequality and, surprisingly, there seems to be some evidence that such pre-government measures of inequality are very similar. This is important as it suggests that whilst inequality has many causes, its base line, pre-government level, may be similar in advanced Organisation for Economic Cooperation and Development (OECD) countries. Yet, when government taxes and transfers are taken into consideration, inequality levels begin to vary significantly. This strongly suggests that a major determinant of income inequality is the nature of the welfare state. As such, whilst inequality is not solely about the welfare state, it is a good measure of how much the welfare state does to achieve equality and thus, a good measure of the strength of social citizenship rights. Further, inequality may be a particularly good indicator of the nature of social citizenship rights as inequality, like social citizenship rights, is not entirely dependent upon welfare transfers. Social citizenship rights, at heart, refer to the extent to which a citizen of a given state has a right to a social status which is roughly comparable to other citizens. This social status can be achieved in a number of ways, some of which may include social transfers, but it can also be achieved by ensuring that employment in the market is fair and safe. Inequality is not a measure of the gap between those on benefits and those who work. It is a measure of the gap between the richest and the poorest. To varying degrees, the poorest elements in any given country include the working poor. As such, inequality figures indicate, to an extent, how 'fair' labour market outcomes are, as well as how generous benefits are. To that extent, they may represent an important indicator of the nature of social citizenship rights.

Assessing and measuring the welfare state is a complex task. In this section we are seeking to analyse how the welfare state impacts upon citizenship in Europe. This involves a consideration of how generous social citizenship provision is. To this end, we will use two main indicators to assess the welfare state in Europe; the generosity of major social insurance programmes, and poverty and inequality figures. This data will enable us to assess both the differing levels of social citizenship provision in Europe, and to examine trends in that provision. Do different European states provide differing levels of social citizenship provision? Have we seen a reduction in social citizenship provision? Has this been universally experienced? It is to these questions that we now turn.

THE WELFARE STATE IN EUROPE

Following the above discussion, we can now examine the level of, and trends in, welfare state provision in Europe in the past thirty or so years. Although, as stated above, there is no 'perfect' indicator of welfare state provision, we will be able to begin to form an answer to the question as to whether welfare state provision in Europe has been in decline (the reasons for any such decline, or indeed, the lack of it, will be considered in the next section). We will begin by examining replacement rates for the main social insurance programmes, unemployment benefit, sickness benefit and public pensions. This will be supplemented by a consideration of the differing levels of and changes to, qualifying conditions for these programmes. Broadly, what we will see here is, firstly, that there are significant differences between European countries in social citizenship provision and secondly, that for the majority of the countries considered here, welfare state provision has declined since the 1980s – in some cases, quite dramatically. Following this examination of the major social insurance programmes of the welfare state, we will consider poverty and household inequality in Europe. Here, we will find a similar pattern; different levels of poverty and inequality in different European countries and a trend for higher poverty and inequality from the 1980s.

Unemployment insurance

The data for the main social insurance programmes comes from Scruggs' *Welfare State Entitlements Data Set* (2004). The replacement rate for the social insurance benefits data has been calculated in two ways; the first is the ratio of net unemployment insurance benefit to net income for an unmarried single person earning the average production worker (APW) wage and the second is the same ratio for a household with one APW worker, a dependent spouse and two dependent children (Scruggs 2004). For each benefit, these have been averaged, by taking the mean of the two values for each year. Figure 5.1 shows the data for eight European countries, Belgium, Denmark, France, Germany, Italy, the Netherlands, Sweden and the UK (data was not available for Spain). We can see that there are clear differences in the amount of income unemployment insurance replaces. The countries with the highest ratios in 2002 are the Netherlands, Sweden and France. The countries with the lowest replacement rates in 2002 are the UK and Italy. For many of the countries, there is a general pattern that sees a decline in the replacement rate beginning around the 1980s. Belgium sees a slight rise before, in 1988, a moderate decline; Denmark sees a decline from around 1983; the Netherlands from 1981; Sweden sees a slight rise until 1993, when the replacement rate drops; and the UK sees a very sharp decline from the end of the 1970s. Italy, France and Germany are the two countries which buck this trend, with the former two countries seeing rises in the replacement rate.

It seems, therefore, that in financial terms unemployment benefits from the 1980s have become slightly less generous in many European countries. The picture in terms of qualifying conditions and durations of benefits is less clear cut. There is some evidence of declining generosity. Between 1971 and 2002 three countries raised the number of weeks that need to be worked in order to qualify for unemployment benefit (Belgium, France and the Netherlands), with only one cutting the qualifying period (the UK), with the others holding the qualifying period steady. In terms of the duration of benefits, there is some evidence of cutbacks, as two countries (the UK and Denmark) have reduced the duration of benefits from the highs of the mid-1980s. However, the Netherlands and Belgium raised the duration entitlement, with the remaining countries making no changes (Scruggs 2004). For most European countries, unemployment insurance

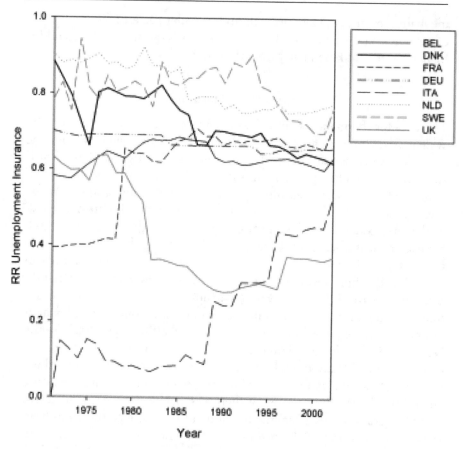

Figure 5.1 Average net replacement rates for unemployment benefits in
eight European countries 1971–2002. (Source: Scruggs 2004)

has become, since the mid-1980s, slightly less generous in a financial sense,
without much evidence for cuts in generosity in terms of qualification and
duration.

The two standout features of Figure 5.1 are the sharp decline in replacement rates in the UK that occurs at the end of the 1970s, and the sharp
rise in Italy in the late 1980s. Both these trends deserve a little more
attention. The sharp fall in replacement rates for unemployment benefits
coincides with the election of the Thatcher government in 1979, an
administration explicitly committed to cutting back the welfare state. As
many authors have noted, the rhetoric may have exceeded the reality
(Pierson 1994) but in the case of unemployment benefit real, significant
changes were made. The Social Security Act (No. 2) of 1980 phased out

the Earnings Related Supplement to unemployment benefit and made unemployment benefits liable to taxation (Atkinson and Micklewright 1989: 21). These changes, along with others introduced in the mid-1980s, produced the 'sizable cut in the generosity of Unemployment Benefit' (Pierson 1994: 107) that we see in Figure 5.1 (see also Dilnot and Morris 1983).

The situation with regard to Italy is a little different. On one level, the sharp rise in replacement rates is an artificial one. The replacement rates in Figure 5.1 are for the 'ordinary' unemployment benefits paid in Italy, which were very low. However, this benefit was little used as unemployed workers had the opportunity to claim a Wage Supplementary Fund (CIG), even though this was intended to cover only short lay-offs (Martin 1996: 13). In 1991 a new Mobility allowance was introduced on similar lines to CIG, and was linked to active labour market policies. The benefit paid was more generous than the 'ordinary' unemployment benefit, but it seems that the unemployed in Italy were not usually claiming this, but the higher CIG benefit. As such, the jump at the beginning of the 1990s is, in one sense, due to a raising of benefit levels, but at another level, is misleading, as many of the unemployed were receiving different, more generous benefits (OECD 1995: 127–30).

Sickness insurance

The same replacement rates for benefits paid for short-term illness, averaged for both a single person and a family (as above), are displayed in Figure 5.2. There are a number of features which are noteworthy. The highest levels of sickness benefit seem to be found in Germany, Belgium and Sweden, with the lowest in the UK and France. Probably the most striking feature of the graph is the sharp decline in the replacement rate for sickness benefit in the UK. Over the period 1971–2002 it more than halves, with a particularly steep drop around the late 1970s, coinciding with the election of the Thatcher government in 1979. The Thatcher government changed the basis for increasing sickness benefit from earnings to prices, and, as with unemployment benefit, made sick pay liable to taxation (Pierson 1994: 139–40). These measures over time, reduced the replacement rate. For the remaining countries, there is, again, evidence of a small decline in the financial generosity of benefits from the 1980s. Belgium, Denmark, the Netherlands and Sweden see some drop in the replacement rate in the 1980s, with Germany experiencing a drop in the 1990s. Only Italy and France avoid the trend, with small increases. In terms of the qualifying period and duration of sickness benefits, the

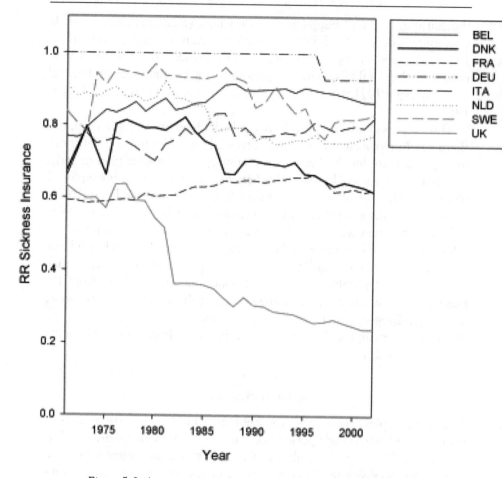

Figure 5.2 Average net replacement rates for sickness benefits in
eight European countries 1971–2002. (Source: Scruggs 2004)

trends are again, more ambiguous, with some cuts in Denmark and France
to the duration of benefits, with little change elsewhere. In terms of
the qualifying period, there is little change, and no evidence of greater
conditionality in the form of longer qualifying periods.

Pensions

The data for pensions is presented for both the minimum pension, for
which no work history is required, and also for the standard pension for
someone who has worked, earning the equivalent of the APW wage, for
every year of their working life. These are both calculated for single

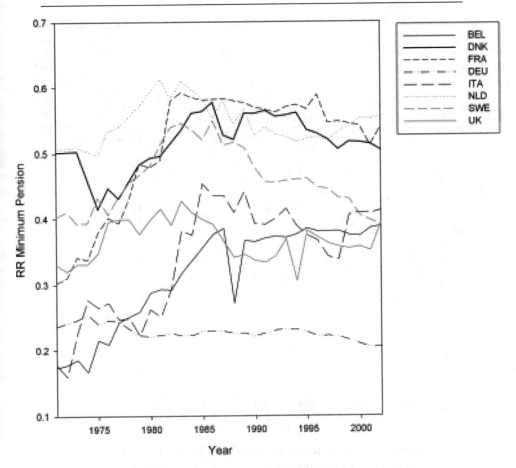

Figure 5.3 Average net replacement rates for minimum pension in eight European countries 1971–2002. (Source: Scruggs 2004)

persons and couples, but here are averaged to produce a replacement rate for the minimum pension, in Figure 5.3, and a replacement rate for the standard pension, in Figure 5.4.

In Figure 5.3 we can see that the countries with the highest level of minimum pension provision in 2002 are the Netherlands and France, with the lowest levels of provision in 2002 found in Germany and the UK. It is interesting that Figure 5.3 shares some commonalities with Figures 5.1 and 5.2 in terms of the trends in replacement rates. As in the first two graphs of unemployment and sickness benefit, we find that the replacement rates for pensions, for most of the countries considered here, rise until the mid-1980s, before declining. The exceptions to that pattern in Figure 5.3 are Germany, which exhibits a more secular decline in the replacement rate

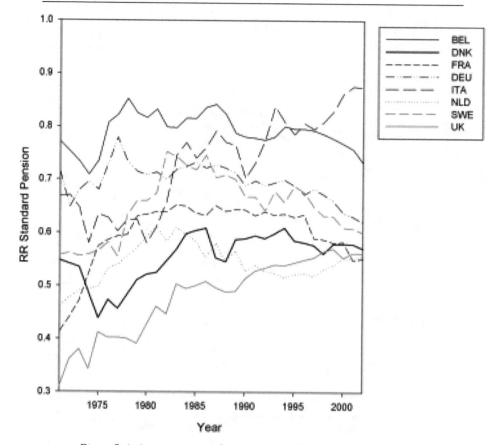

Figure 5.4 Average net replacement rates for standard pension in eight European countries 1971–2002. (Source: Scruggs 2004)

for the entire period, and Belgium, which sees an increase to the mid-1980s and then a period of little overall change. The declines for the remaining countries are mostly small ones, with the exception of Sweden, which sees a sharp decline from around 1986.

In Figure 5.4 the countries with the highest replacement rates for standard pensions in 2002 are Italy and Belgium, with the lowest replacement rates found in France, the Netherlands and the UK. The picture in terms of the trends in replacement rates for standard pensions are slightly different to those in Figures 5.1, 5.2 and 5.3. For some countries, such as Italy and the UK, there are increases rather than cuts in the replacement rate; in the case of the UK, there is a secular increase over the whole period, albeit from a low base (and despite the increase, by 2002 the UK has one of the lowest replacement rates for the standard pension). For the remaining six countries, the familiar story of increases until the mid-1980s, and cuts thereafter, seems to be in evidence once again. It must be noted that reforms of pensions are notoriously difficult to assess (see Ney 2000), with, as Korpi (2003) argues, the consequences of decisions made at a given point in time, only becoming fully apparent decades later. Pierson's analysis of pension reform in the UK suggests that changes introduced to earnings-related pension provision in the 1986 Social Security Act will have major effects many years hence.

> The changes introduced will make little difference in the short run because of transition arrangements. However, by 2021, SERPS [State Earnings Related Pensions Scheme] expenditures are expected to drop by well over 50 per cent compared with pre-reform estimates. (Pierson 1994: 63–4)

Therefore, it seems that levels and trends in pension provision, particularly standard pensions, may be somewhat misleading in terms of retrenchment. Significant changes, based on decisions made recently, may not be felt fully until many years into the future.

In terms of the conditions attached to pensions, there is some evidence of declining generosity. For four of the countries considered here, Denmark, Sweden, the UK and France, the number of years that a person has to work to be considered fully covered has increased (with no overall change for the other four countries). The retirement age has also been raised, although this is more the case for women than for men. Four countries, Denmark, Belgium, Germany and Italy, all raised the retirement age for women, with Italy also raising the age for men. This does point to lower generosity for pensions, as the entitlements to qualification have been raised in a number of countries. However, this must be balanced by an increase in the proportion of citizens in receipt of a public pension, in nearly all countries.

Conclusion: social insurance schemes

The above analyses of replacement rates (and qualifying conditions and benefit duration) for key social insurance programmes do seem to exhibit some generalities. Firstly, they do point towards declining generosity of the main welfare state social insurance programmes. Considering unemployment insurance, benefits are lower in 2002 than they were in 1971 for five of the countries, Sweden, the Netherlands, Denmark, Germany and the UK, higher for two, France and Italy, and about the same for Belgium. For sickness insurance, benefits are lower in 2002 than in 1971 for four countries, Germany, the Netherlands, Denmark and the UK, with increases for this period in Italy and Belgium, and about the same in France and Sweden. It is interesting to note that for all countries, both forms of pension are more generous in 2002 than they were in 1971.

The above snapshot tells us something about which countries have experienced retrenchment in key areas of the welfare state. However, these declines in replacement rates vary, with Sweden and Germany experiencing very modest cuts, slightly larger, although still relatively small, cuts in the Netherlands and Denmark, and with only significant cuts seen in the UK, where the replacement rates for sickness benefit and unemployment benefit have seen substantial reductions. Perhaps worryingly for citizens of the UK, these cuts were made to benefits that were already amongst the lowest in Europe. However, it is worth noting that amongst such cutbacks in some areas of social policy in the UK, there have also been social policy innovations, particularly around child care, which stand out as amongst the most progressive of any advanced industrial democracy. Wincott (2006) argues that this 'paradox' is due to the fact that welfare state settlements contain multiple elements and do not constitute the pure liberal, conservative or social democratic types which Esping-Andersen (1990) famously introduced. Similarly, there does not seem to be a 'market leader' in terms of which countries seem to have the most generous social insurance programmes. The same countries do not have the highest replacement rates for all programmes (Scruggs and Allan 2006: 68–9). (However, as noted above, due to the ways in which replacement rates are calculated, we should be more circumspect in making cross-national comparisons.)

The main theme to emerge from this presentation of the replacement rates for the main social insurance programmes between 1971 and 2002 is that there seems to be a general trend to slightly decreasing generosity of the welfare state, at least in the terms considered here. Whilst it would be incorrect to say that all countries have a similar experience, it would equally be remiss not to note the decline in replacement rates that a number of countries experienced for all social programmes, beginning around the 1980s. Yet, this observation should be tempered by the fact that for most countries, where the replacement rates for unemployment and sickness benefits had declined, they had not generally fallen much below the 1971 level (as mentioned above, the UK is the notable exception to this). Whilst not as pronounced as trends in the replacement rate, there is also some evidence of greater conditionality attached to these benefits. It certainly does seem to be the case that the European welfare states, and social citizenship rights, have experienced some retrenchment from the 1980s onwards, although for the most part, these are small declines.

Poverty and inequality

As stated above, poverty and inequality measures offer little insight into the mechanics of how social citizenship rights operate and are instantiated, but they do offer an effective output measure. Where poverty and/or inequality are higher, it can be argued that social citizenship rights are less extensive. In recent years, politicians have tended to be more concerned about poverty than inequality (Tony Blair famously declared that 'it is not a burning ambition for me to make David Beckham earn less money' (Blair, cited in Orton and Rowlingson 2007: 61)). This is generally because it is perceived that poverty is more debilitating and harmful to individuals than inequality; if citizens are poor, they are suffering hardship and deprivation, whereas inequality does not *per se* indicate deprivation. However, as argued above, inequality is important for citizenship. It matters on a theoretical level, as citizenship, in some fundamental sense, implies equality. Of concern to some is the fact that economic inequalities may reflect, or worse, cause, other forms of inequality (see Jacobs et al. 2004). Speaking about America, but with relevance to all countries, they note,

> The privileged participate more than others and are increasingly well organised to press their demands on government. Public officials, in turn, are much more responsive to the privileged than to average citizens and the least affluent. Citizens with lower or moderate incomes speak with a whisper that is lost on the ears of inattentive government officials, while the advantaged roar with a clarity and consistency that policy makers readily hear and routinely follow. (Jacobs et al. 2004: 1)

Debates exist around the effects of income inequality on health, crime and social cohesion (Wilkinson 1996). High levels of inequality, it seems, may act as a drag on the exercise of citizenship, as well as indicating less effective social citizenship provision.

Figure 5.5 shows poverty rates for the eight countries we have examined in this chapter. The poverty rate is calculated as the percentage of people whose disposable income is less than 50 per cent of the median income for that country. In terms of the levels of poverty around 2000, there seem to be two groupings. The first, including Belgium, Denmark, France, Germany, the Netherlands and Sweden, exhibits lower levels of poverty (5–8 per cent of the population) and, with the exceptions of Denmark and perhaps Belgium, also less volatility in their poverty rates. The second grouping, consisting of Italy and the UK, have higher levels of poverty, (12–13 per cent of the population) and a greater volatility in their poverty rate.

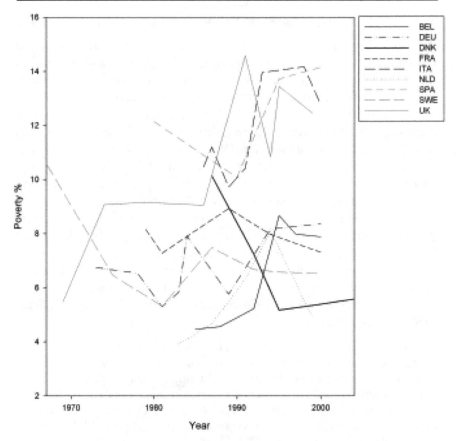

Figure 5.5 Relative poverty rates for eight European countries 1969–2004.
(Source: Luxembourg Income Study)

It is also worth noting that the UK, over the period considered in Figure 5.5, moved from being a country with quite low levels of poverty, to a much higher poverty rate. In 1969 the UK had a poverty rate which was comparable to that in Germany, around 5–6 per cent. Over the next thirty years, Germany did see an increase in its poverty rate, to around 8 per cent; but over the same period, the UK saw its poverty rate almost double. The pattern is almost identical for inequality figures (Luxembourg Income Study). From the mid- to late 1980s, The Netherlands and Denmark saw a slight decline in inequality. Belgium, France, Germany, and Sweden experienced no change or modest rises, Italy seeing a slightly larger rise in inequality, and the UK experiencing the largest increase, with the gini coefficient (a common measure for inequality, which varies between 0 and 1, with 0 indicating complete equality (everyone having the same income) and 1 complete inequality (one person holding all wealth)) rising by almost 40 per cent between 1979 and 2000, from 0.25 to 0.35 (Brewer et al. 2005: 22). Whilst any simple notions of causality should be resisted (poverty and inequality are complex, and involve many, interwoven, processes), it does seem to be the case that those countries with the lowest poverty and inequality rates tend to be those countries with more generous social insurances programmes (measured as replacement rates). In addition, the country where there have been significant cuts in social insurance programmes, the UK, is also the country which has experienced the largest increases in poverty and inequality. Hills points out that the changes in social security made in the 1980s, of linking benefits to prices rather than earnings, has played a role in rising inequality. 'When general living standards are rising, those dependent on price-linked benefits will inevitably fall behind the rest of the population, which increases inequality' (Hills 2004: 93). This feeds into a trenchant debate as to whether the welfare state does aid poverty reduction, which we will examine in a little more detail below.

The empirical information presented in this section suggests that social citizenship provision, for most European countries, remains robust and intact. There is evidence of some retrenchment, and tightening of qualifying conditions and benefit duration, but these do not constitute *at present* wholesale reduction of social citizenship entitlements. This is also the case when we look at output measures of the welfare state, poverty and inequality. Despite some small increases, most European countries considered here have low (relative) poverty and inequality rates. The exception to this rule is the UK, which has seen significant cuts in replacement rates for unemployment benefit and sickness benefit, as well as large increases in poverty and inequality. The two questions that the remainder of this chapter seek to grapple with are: how do we explain the patterns observed in this section and, secondly, what do they mean for citizenship in Europe?

Explaining the welfare state

In the preceding section we have examined data which suggests that there has been some retrenchment of the welfare state in Europe, although this has been differentially experienced, with most countries seeing some modest declines since the 1980s and some, notably the UK, much larger declines. We will now go on to consider some explanations for the trends observed above.

Globalisation

As we noted above, it is 'something of a popular truism that globalization spells if not quite the passing of the nation state itself, then the demise of inclusive social provision and with it the welfare state' (Hay 2006: 200). The argument is a relatively simple one; in the past, national economies were closed, with business and investments operating primarily in the national economy. Keynesian macro economic policies saw the welfare state as part of the means of achieving low inflation. Wage restraint was sought in return for social benefits. As business primarily operated in the national environment, all the competitors in an economy had to play by the same rules (Scharpf 1996). With increasing internationalisation of economic activity, both in terms of the liberalisation of financial markets and the globalisation of production, this ceased to be the case. Suddenly, the mechanisms which had seemed essential to continued social and economic well-being, appeared as fetters and threats to future prosperity. In a situation where business and capital can relocate if it so wishes, countries with higher levels of taxation and regulation become unattractive to business, as there are other countries which have lower levels of taxation and regulation, thus offering a larger return on investments. This induces governments to cut back social provision and regulation in order to be competitive and secure and maintain investment and economic activity. The 'race to the bottom' hypothesis argues that expensive welfare state regimes, even if desirable, are no longer affordable.

This argument has been subject to extensive review and criticism (Castles 2004; Hay 2006a). Castles argues that the race to the bottom argument is a 'crisis myth' (Castles 2004: 46) as there is no evidence of an overall, general and persistent downwards trend in social welfare effort amongst OECD countries. Others, who argue that there may well have been retrenchment in welfare policies point to empirical evidence that the welfare state enhances competitiveness rather than acting as a drag upon it (Hay 2006a; Hay 2006b; Garrett 1998), or (as we shall see below) point to rather different causes for cutbacks in provision (Pierson 2001c; Korpi 2003). Hay (2002; 2006a) argues that it is not the material processes and relations of globalisation itself which produce cuts to the welfare state, but ideas that political leaders hold about globalisation. If political elites believe the globalisation thesis, and cut back social provision accordingly, this doesn't 'prove' the globalisation thesis; it merely shows that it is influential. This point would seem to have some analytical purchase for the above data. There is little evidence of large-scale retrenchment in most European countries, with the exception of the UK, which, along with the US, is seen as the home of such liberal, low tax, low taxation, ideas. It may be that the fact that the welfare state in the UK has seen retrenchment, whilst other European welfare states have not, is due to the receptiveness of UK political elites to neo-liberal ideas.

Europeanisation

Hay, in his critique of the arguments surrounding globalisation and the welfare state, argues that there is little evidence that European economies are becoming more globalised. Instead, he argues, they are becoming Europeanised. For a globalised economy, Hay argues, we should see geography matter less in trading relations (distance becoming less of a factor in trading relations). However, he finds the opposite to be the case for most European countries, that proximity has become more important in trading relations, not less. The same trend is evident when considering Foreign Direct Investment (FDI), with the amount of FDI coming from distant countries falling over time (Hay 2006a: 13–17). In terms of economic pressures on the welfare state, Hay argues that these do not come from any processes of globalisation (which appear to be weak in Europe) but from the processes of European Integration and particularly the 'deflationary bias' (Hay 2006a: 20) of EMU and the Maastricht Convergence criteria (later the Growth and Stability Pact) (Hay 2004: 255–7; also Korpi 2003). The data presented above does afford this explanation some credence. Hay (2004) particularly emphasises how the costs of German reunification impacted upon Scandinavian economies, which were heavily dependent upon Germany as an export market. Unemployment rose in these countries, at a time when they were trying to reduce budget deficits in line with the Maastricht convergence criteria. Hay argues that this meant that 'cuts in public spending were inevitable' (Hay 2004: 256). Figures 5.1 and 5.2 show cuts in the replacement rates for unemployment benefit and sickness benefit for Sweden and Denmark around the early 1990s, in keeping with Hay's thesis. The implications of this argument are that some of the cuts in welfare state effort may be due to specific economic and political conditions in Europe, rather than any general problem with states providing generous welfare for their citizens.

Postindustrial strains

Pierson shares a scepticism of the simple globalisation thesis, but notes that its appeal is partly related to the fact that governments do seem to be under pressure to cut back welfare provision.

The correlation in timing between globalization, on the one hand, and both mounting demands for austerity and strong indications of lost policy making capacity, on the other, has lent credence to claims of a causal relationship between globalization and a weakening nation-state. (Pierson 2001c: 81)

However, rather than some catch all, globalisation explanation, Pierson points to several, related, aspects of postindustrial societies as the reasons for the 'austerity' of welfare states in Europe. He argues that there are four factors behind the increasing pressure on the welfare state: the shift to a more service-based economy, the expansion and maturation of government commitments, demographic changes and changes to household structures (Pierson 2001c: 81–99). The shift to a service sector economy has, it is argued, reduced economic growth as such sectors are less dynamic than manufacturing, which has negative consequences for the welfare state, particularly reducing the growth in wages, upon which the fiscal health of the welfare state rests. The costs of pension and health care commitments, established in the period of welfare state expansion, it is argued, place considerable strain on welfare budgets.

The third factor Pierson identifies is the demographic changes that have taken place in Europe and other advanced industrial democracies. As birth rates have fallen, and people live for longer, pressure on the welfare state grows as 'all welfare states are heavily tilted towards the elderly' (Pierson 2001c: 93). The costs associated with more elderly citizens claiming pensions (and fewer, younger, people working and paying into the system) are significant, with an increase of around 3.9 per cent of Gross Domestic Product (GDP) between 2000 and 2030 required to fund existing provisions (for more on pension reform see Pierson 2006: 212–21; Ney 2000; Taylor-Gooby 1999; World Bank 1994). The ageing population also raises health care costs, by around 1.7 per cent of GDP between 2000 and 2030 (Pierson 2001c: 94–5). In addition to changing demographics of populations in Europe, the structure of society and households has undergone profound changes, all of which pose challenges, Pierson argues, for the welfare state. The increase in female labour force participation is, for some feminists, an important source of independence and freedom (Orloff 1993; Orloff, O'Connor and Shaver 1999), and in one sense aids welfare state budgets, reducing the numbers of women who make claims on the welfare state and adding numbers who contribute to it. Yet, the movement of women into work, Pierson argues, also raises the need for different kinds of services; maternity and paternity leave, as well as providing care roles which might previously have been undertaken by women within the household. The final area of household structure Pierson identifies as increasing the pressures on the welfare state is the rise in single person households. Related to the above point concerning care roles, smaller households have fewer private resources for care roles to draw upon, placing a heavier responsibility on the state. These, primarily domestic in nature (although intersecting with wider economic changes) are the reasons Pierson identifies for the welfare state facing conditions of austerity.

Partisan politics

Pierson argues that the challenges he identifies are experienced differently in different countries (Pierson 2001c: 99–100). However, it is open to question as to whether Pierson's work explains the trends identified in the preceding section. For example, Pierson argues that conservative welfare states, such as Italy and Germany, will face particularly strong effects from demographic change and population ageing, whilst the UK will experience virtually none. Although this is only one area, and Pierson does not explicitly categorise which countries will face particularly strong austerity challenges, his work seems to be unable to explain why the UK, for example, exhibits the most severe retrenchment of the European countries examined here.

One factor that Pierson has dismissed as of importance is partisan politics; that is the political power of left (and right) forces within and without the state. He argues that there is little evidence that such forces matter (Pierson 1996: 150). Others (Korpi 2003; Korpi and Palme 2006; Scruggs and Allan 2004) contend that Pierson's downplaying of the political dimension is misjudged. Korpi (2003: 590) argues that Pierson's position is one where governments of all political persuasions are driven to cut back welfare provision. However, for Korpi and Palme (2003), politics matters, and particularly, the political persuasion of governments matters. They find that the partisan composition of the government in a particular country has a significant effect on retrenchment, with the risk for cuts much higher when right parties are in office, than when left parties hold office (Korpi and Palme 2003: 441). This is also a finding of Scruggs and Allan. Interestingly, their statistical analysis (controlling for macro economic factors) finds that before the mid-1980s, left governments are associated with increases in replacement rates (with no significant influences on replacement rates thereafter). For right governments, the situation is the reverse, with no association with replacement rates prior to the mid-1980s and after this a significant connection to cuts in replacement rates. (Scruggs and Allan 2004: 505–7). These two analyses suggest that the balance of political power does have a significant influence on welfare state provision. This also offers some analytical purchase on the data presented in the preceding section, as the UK, which exhibited the largest declines in unemployment and sickness replacement rates, is noteworthy for the eighteen years of unbroken, single party, right wing government.

Perhaps, as with the preceding chapter on political participation, explanations of changes to the welfare state elude a single, simple, explanation. These are, after all, complex processes, involving a plethora of actors and dynamics. What might be stated with some certitude is that inevitability is, and should be, absent from any adequate explanation of the changes that have occurred (and are occurring) with regard to European welfare states. There is no inexorable process which is driving a decline of welfare states. In this respect, any simple form of the globalisation thesis, seems to run aground on empirical details; its case simply isn't born out by available evidence. Changes with regard to the welfare state in Europe, then, are influenced by a range of converging and confluent factors. (We have, here, limited ourselves to a discussion of what might be termed common processes; those factors which might be said to affect all European countries. Yet, this should not obscure the fact that there are numerous endogenous processes at work which affect such matters. For example, see Ryner (2002) for an account of welfare state change in Sweden, which considers global, regional and local pressures.) The processes of European integration, economic changes, demographic trends and the ascendancy of neo-liberal ideas and political parties all seem, to varying degrees in varying contexts, to play a role. The welfare state does face pressure and challenges, yet, these are all subject to political mediation and debate.

THE WELFARE STATE AND CITIZENSHIP

Above, we have considered quite how we might go about conceptualising and measuring the welfare state, provided some evidence and data on the levels and trends of social provision through the welfare state and poverty and inequality levels, and considered some of the main explanations for these patterns. The picture is broadly, for most countries, one of limited retrenchment in key social security programmes, with little or no significant increases in poverty and inequality. Some countries, such as the UK, have experienced much larger cuts in their welfare programmes and also much larger rises in poverty and inequality. As stated above, there is not a single explanation for this picture, but it is rather, probably due to a confluence of factors involving macro social change, Europeanisation, and the ascendancy of neo-liberal politics and ideas.

How, then, is this complex set of processes and relationships to be understood? Are we to evaluate the contemporary situation with regard to the welfare state as worrying, or troublesome, for citizenship; or does it represent a much needed reinvigoration of citizenship? As we have argued in other chapters, how we understand and interpret contemporary developments in the welfare state depends upon which conception of citizenship one is operating with. Here we will focus on liberal, communitarian and feminist conceptions of citizenship.

Liberal citizenship and the welfare state

The view that liberal citizenship takes of the welfare state in contemporary Europe depends upon which strand of liberal citizenship one is looking at. Classical liberal citizenship, affirming and valorising civil rights of property and negative freedom, sees the welfare state as an illegitimate interference (Nozick 1974). As such, any cuts in welfare state provision and generosity are likely to be welcomed and seen as a reduction of such unwarranted violation of property rights. However, given that many European countries did not experience massive cutbacks in welfare provision, the situation of the welfare state in contemporary Europe is likely to still be seen in negative terms from such perspectives.

A more social liberal position, as classically espoused in the work of T. H. Marshall, sees social provision, or social citizenship, as an essential aspect of citizenship (Marshall 1963; see also King and Waldron 1988). For individuals to be free and equal, there is a need for social citizenship, which Marshall defines as a right to income, irrespective of their position with regard to the market (Marshall 1963: 100). The extent to which citizens are decommodified might be said to depend on the level of benefits, their coverage and eligibility criteria. Where benefits are higher, cover more people and have fewer eligibility criteria, social citizenship rights are more fully provided. As we have seen above, there have been some downward movements in each of the above elements. The UK has experienced the most pronounced cuts in the levels of benefits (and also some tightening of eligibility for and duration of benefits) and from relatively low initial levels, whereas for most of the other countries considered here, the cuts were generally smaller and from a higher start point. From this perspective, it appears that social citizenship provision in Europe is, to varying degrees, in decline. This is of concern to social liberals, who would see that such erosions would limit and constrain citizenship more generally. Yet, is it the case that the fact that these declines are of different magnitude and start from different levels, has an effect? It might be argued that cuts to already meagre programmes threaten social citizenship more than similar sized cuts to more generous programmes.

Communitarian citizenship and the welfare state

For communitarians, the emphasis on the individual and their rights is profoundly misjudged. The individual only exists as they do because of the community into which they are born; the community is prior to the individual. This also means that the interests of the community comes before individual interests. Communitarians thus assert the individuals' responsibilities to the community; as it is the community that gives us our identity and sustains us, the concerns of the community should be as weighty as those of individuals, if not more so. The emphasis on welfare rights has weakened communities and individuals. The rights-based welfare state is said to create citizens who are passive dependents, looking to the state to rescue them without looking to their own responsibilities. It is also seen to create perverse incentives which mitigate against work ethics and families (Murray 2006). For communitarians, the welfare state needs to be reconfigured so that it asserts citizens' own responsibilities to themselves and reduces the incentives to socially harmful behaviour. These ideas have flowed into the same tributary as neo-liberal economic ideas about freedom and 'rolling back the state'. Although not entirely congruent, in terms of the welfare state, communitarian and neo-liberal ideas share similar concerns and a similar focus of attack: individual (social) rights. Calabrese (2005: 304) refers to communitarianism as 'the rhetorical nursemaid of neo-liberalism'. Similarly, the Third Way (Blair and Schroeder 1999; Giddens 1998), which asserts the importance of rights being balanced by responsibilities, is sometimes seen, as White (2004: 26) notes, as 'a humanized version of neo-liberalism'.

Cuts in welfare generosity, both in terms of the levels of benefits (replacement rates) and duration, would be welcomed by communitarians, but it would be a strengthening of eligibility criteria and conditionality that would be particularly welcomed. As we have seen above, there is evidence of cuts in replacement rates, but not much evidence of large-scale cuts in the duration of benefits or increases in the qualification criteria. In some senses, the re-emphasising of obligations is nothing new. The more generous Scandinavian welfare states have been traditionally based upon full employment for at least two reasons. Firstly, as Korpi and Palme (2003: 428) point out, the right to work can be seen as a right, and one which empowers citizens. Secondly, the high level of spending in the Scandinavian states requires large numbers of people in work and few out of work and receiving generous benefits (Esping-Andersen 1990). This also places significant emphasis on citizens fulfilling work obligations. Therefore, emphasising responsibilities has been, certainly for Scandinavian countries, a key part of welfare state politics and policies for many years. Some authors argue that entitlements have been tightened in recent years (Gilbert 2004), and that countries have in recent years invested more in a shift from passive to active labour market policies (Martin 2000). This may be seen as both a defence of the right to work (in keeping with a social liberal perspective), or a growing contractualism and reassertion of responsibilities (a more communitarian one).

Communitarian conceptions of citizenship are, thus, likely to view positively the current trends in the welfare state in Europe. Communitarian ideas have been more influential in certain European countries, notably Germany (Pfau-Effinger 2005) and the UK (Heron and Dwyer 1999). As argued above, the emphasising of citizens' obligations is nothing new. Indeed, it may be that in Europe we can see two rather different forms of communitarian discourse; one, institutionalised in Scandinavian countries, which emphasises obligations as a way of maximising benefits to citizens; and a more minimal model of communitarianism, which is interwoven with neo-liberalism, which emphasises citizens' responsibilities, almost as a form of 'rugged individualism', such that the citizen should be responsible, primarily, for their own welfare. The evidence presented in this chapter suggests that both streams are alive and well.

Feminist citizenship and the welfare state

Just as we have noted above that there are not single, monolithic liberal and communitarian conceptions of citizenship, we must acknowledge the same for feminist conceptions of citizenship. Some feminist scholars have written that the welfare state enshrines and institutionalises patriarchy in its support for a male breadwinner–female carer family structure (Pateman 1988). Yet other scholars have discussed the extent to which the welfare state has the capacity to be, or become 'woman friendly' (Hernes 1997; Orloff 1993). Such authors have also pointed to the ways in which social citizenship provision impacts upon women's citizenship generally. In terms of the recent trends in the welfare state in Europe, feminist scholars find diverse and varied effects. Lewis (2002), in the context of the previous discussion about responsibilities, argues that alongside the change from passive, entitlements-based welfare, to active, responsibility-focused welfare, is its generalisation to women. This, she argues, begins to treat men and women equally (both are 'citizen workers') and offers the prospect of greater independence for women, but fails to consider the complexities around the gendered division of care work (Lewis 2002: 340). If public and social policies do not address or consider the fact that caring roles fall disproportionately upon women, the result will be that women are forced to do the so-called 'double shift' (Prokhovnik 1998), in the sense of combining employment and caring roles. The extent to which this gendered division of caring is addressed by public policies varies, and with it the impact of contemporary changes in the welfare state for feminist conceptions of citizenship varies too. Scandinavian states have been much more able to promote what Orloff (1993) calls 'defamilialisation', whereas the liberal welfare states, such as the UK, which are more reliant upon market provision, tend to be less strong in this area (Orloff, O'Connor and Shaver 1999). In a similar vein, others have pointed out that current changes in the welfare state are likely to have very different outcomes for women, depending upon the starting point. Emphasising the case of Italy, Trifiletti (1999) argues that any retrenchment is likely to have particularly adverse consequences for women. It seems that the extension of the work obligation to women, such that men and women both are citizen workers, offers potential gains for women, but the crucial mediating factor is how existing and future social policies seek to manage the (domestic) burdens associated with such change. Where public provision is lacking, some (affluent, middle class) women may be empowered, at the expense of other women, who are employed to fulfil domestic care responsibilities (poorer women, and increasingly, unskilled, migrant women). Such discussions resonate with the shift to considering the multiplicity of women's experiences and positions, discussed in Chapter Two. Women's experiences in terms of contemporary changes to the welfare state and citizenship depend on a number of cross-cutting factors; gender relations certainly, but also class and ethnicity.

CONCLUSION

In this chapter we have examined the levels and trends of welfare provision in contemporary Europe. We began by noting the difficulties in defining the welfare state precisely. Having settled on examining replacement rates as a measure of generosity, we saw that some countries have experienced some retrenchment in some areas of welfare state provision; others, such as the UK, have experienced sharp cuts, particularly in unemployment and sickness benefit. These trends are reflected in poverty and inequality levels, which for most countries show little change, but for the UK show marked increases. It seems that whilst many European countries have experienced some retrenchment of the welfare state, for most countries, *at the moment*, this is not of a significant scale. Therefore, whilst (social) liberal citizenship may be concerned about cuts in social citizenship provision, *at this moment*, it does not seem to represent a significant reduction, for most countries.

Communitarian conceptions of citizenship are likely to view the limited restructuring of the welfare state in Europe in positive terms. We argued that communitarian ideas can be seen in two different ways; one, in conjunction with neo-liberal ideas, where obligations are emphasised as part of a reduction in welfare provision, and another, more social democratic element, where citizens' obligations have always been important, as a part of maximising welfare effort. Feminist conceptions of citizenship have also pointed to the rather ambiguous implications of contemporary restructuring of the welfare state, with greater female labour market participation offering emancipatory potential, but only to the extent that the gendered division of care was addressed at the same time. It seems that in terms of citizenship in Europe, current trends and patterns in the welfare state offer reasons for hope and concern.

CHAPTER 6

Migration in Europe

INTRODUCTION

Migration (and the associated issues of citizenship and belonging) is one of the most controversial issues in contemporary politics. As we shall see, it is frequently linked to questions of terrorism, crime and disorder and, if left unattended, seen as something that will prompt a general collapse in European society. In this chapter we will examine migration and citizenship in Europe and try to analyse why migration is so controversial, and what it means for both existing and potential citizens of Europe, and our conceptions of citizenship. It is frequently argued, as we have seen in previous chapters, that migration (and associated developments in human rights discourses) prompts a move away from a conception of citizenship focused upon the national. Yet, although there may be such theoretical moves amongst scholars, the passion and the fury that migration generates in political debates suggests that the national continues to play an important role in contemporary citizenship politics.

We will begin the chapter by examining levels and trends in migration and asylum for European countries, before going on to consider in detail, how three European countries (the Netherlands, Germany and Italy) have responded to contemporary patterns of migration. Amongst the specifics of each country, we will see here that the EU has come to hold a prominent position in the politics of migration. In the fourth section of this chapter, we will argue that EU policy here has come to be dominated by a securitised understanding of migration, which we will examine in greater detail, before concluding by considering how migration impacts upon our understandings and conceptions of citizenship.

MIGRATION LEVELS AND TRENDS IN EUROPE

There is a widespread assumption that migration in Europe is increasing.

In order to assess this, we have to be clear about what we mean when we talk about migration. There are numerous forms and types of migration: permanent migration, temporary migration, labour migration, asylum seeking, legal and illegal migration. All of these contribute to the general pattern of migration and, as we have seen in previous chapters, measurement is no easy task. In what follows, we will consider OECD data on 'permanent-type legal migration' (OECD 2007: 33). By this is meant 'a person of foreign nationality who enters the permanently resident population either from outside the country or by changing from a temporary to a permanent status in the country' (OECD 2007: 34). This excludes temporary migrants, such as students and seasonal workers (although they are included if they change their status from a temporary migrant to a permanent one). It also excludes illegal migration, which means that such figures underestimate migration rates, particularly for southern European countries. Clearly, by definition, illegal migration is difficult to track and measure, although the OECD quotes 'semi official estimates' of around 1 per cent of the population for most European countries, rising to as high as 4 per cent of the population for southern European countries (OECD 2007: 47). We will begin by referring to some data on permanent migration and go on to consider data on asylum applications.

Permanent migration

The OECD notes that many European countries do not have systematic tools to calculate the inflows and outflows of foreign populations. The data is generally estimated from either populations surveys or residence permit data (although in the case of the UK the data is based on numbers of people entering or exiting the country by plane, boat or train; there seems to be some recognition that such data is not adequate as it was revised in the light of census data) (OECD 2007: 300). Figure 6.1 shows the absolute level (in thousands) of inflows of foreign populations into the nine European countries under consideration. Given that the figures are absolute and not relative to population size, too much should not be made of the differences between countries as we might expect larger countries to have larger levels of migration.

What are noticeable, immediately, are the sharp increases in such migration in Italy, the UK, and particularly Spain; and what becomes equally striking is, relative to that, the stability of migration flows in the other European countries. In Germany the inflow of migrants has actually slowed in the last ten years, albeit from a very high level initially. (Data is not available for all nine countries with regards to the outflow of

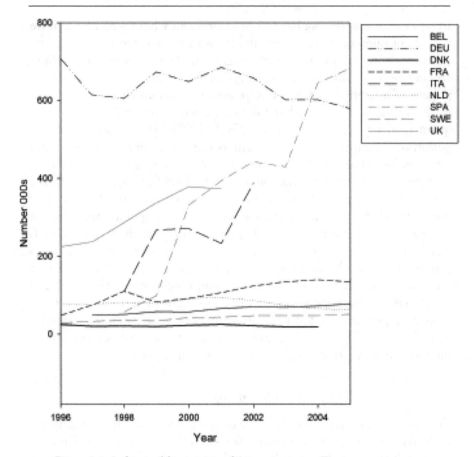

Figure 6.1 Inflows of foreign populations into nine European countries.
(Source: OECD 2007)

foreigners, but for those countries where data is available, the pattern is broadly the same in Figure 6.1.)

A significant factor in migration, and migration policy is demographics. The OECD suggest that if no migration were to occur and current demographic trends continued, the working population would decline in European countries by between 1 per cent (France) and 7 per cent (Italy) by 2020, as the birth rate in Europe is low and the large cohort of baby boomers move into retirement (OECD 2007: 32). Some countries, such as Italy, can address this trend, in part, through greater incorporation of women into the labour market. However, where this is well-developed, as in Sweden, where a 4 per cent decline in the working age population is predicted, increased migration seems likely to play an important role in addressing the issue.

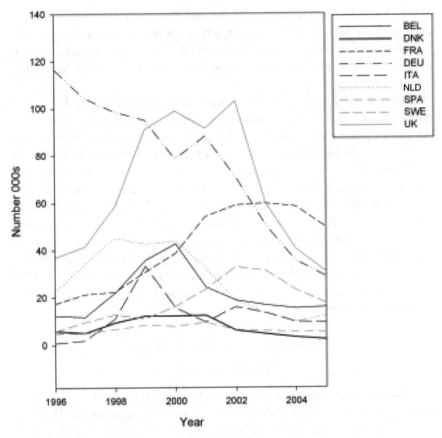

Figure 6.2 Inflows of asylum seekers into nine European countries.
(Source: OECD 2007)

Within the above patterns of migration, there are commonalities and variations. In the UK, Denmark, Belgium, Germany, Italy and Sweden, labour migration plays an important role in migratory patterns, accounting for 30–40 per cent of migration. Within this, it is estimated that half to three quarters of this movement is related to the free movement of EU citizens. In Italy, France and the Netherlands family migration (consisting of family reunification, families accompanying workers and family formation – i.e. marriage) plays an important role. Asylum seekers and refugees account for a relatively small proportion of migrants for most countries, the exception being the Netherlands, where they account for around 30 per cent of all migration, and to a lesser extent, the UK and Sweden (15–20 per cent) (OECD 2007: 35–8). Specific data on asylum is presented in Figure 6.2. The general pattern which can be observed here is one of a rise in asylum seekers in the mid- to late 1990s, followed by a decline. The exception to this pattern is Germany, (see below) which exhibits a secular decline over this period (the high water mark for asylum in Germany was reached in the early 1990s and it has been in decline since).

Whilst it is not possible to produce accurate estimations for illegal migration, it seems that in Europe migration is increasing, and that this is primarily made up of labour migration and family migration, with asylum playing a limited and decreasing role in the overall increase in migration in Europe. We will now go on to consider government migration and citizenship policies in the light of these overall trends and patterns. We will look at three crucial cases: Germany, as the European country with, traditionally, the highest levels of migration across its borders; the Netherlands, as it has been seen as having the most developed multicultural policies to deal with migration and citizenship (although this may not be the case any longer, as we will see); and Italy, as an example of a southern European country, which, as we have seen, seems to have experienced the highest growth in migration

Migration policies in Europe

The Netherlands

The Netherlands' migration policies and politics have traditionally been seen as a bastion of multiculturalism in Europe (Entzinger 2003). More recently, however, scholars have argued that the Netherlands has shifted, with Joppke (2004: 249) referring to the 'turn from multiculturalism [...] [that] reflects a seismic shift'. Others still argue that the notion of a rise and fall of Dutch multiculturalist policies on migration is a somewhat stylised and misleading view of policy development, arguing instead that multiculturalism was never as entrenched as it was commonly held to be (Vink 2007). We will examine briefly the major developments in migration policy in the Netherlands in order to assess in what ways it has changed.

In the post-war period, the Netherlands, like many post-imperial societies, experienced migration from its former colonies. In addition, guestworkers from the Mediterranean countries arrived. For most of the post-war period, there was little by way of systematic government policy to deal with such migration. It was assumed that those arriving from former colonies needed no integration and that guestworkers were temporary migrants, who would return to their country of origin. Around the late 1970s and early 1980s, this view changed. It was realised that migrants were not temporary and that without attention, migrants would be disadvantaged. The policy was one of social integration whilst preserving the language and culture of the immigrant groups.

The 1983 Minorities Memorandum was the first attempt to 'realize the equivalence and equal opportunities of all residents' (cited in Vink 2007: 340). Under the minorities policy, a whole raft of measures followed, including voting rights in local elections after five years of residence in 1985, a more generous naturalisation policy (1986 Nationality Act), a range of anti-discrimination measures (1994 Equal Treatment Act, 1998 Act for Stimulation of Labour Market Participation) and between 1992 and 1997, a tolerance of dual citizenship. There was also a recognition that minority groups, such as those of Surinamese and Antilean descent, guest-workers from Greece, Italy, Portugal, Morocco and various travellers groups, should be provided with the means by which to protect their cultural identities, such that they could, for example, claim government subsidies for broadcasting and education (Vink 2007: 341; Joppke 2007).

However, by the end of the 1990s, this 'multiculturalist haven' was under attack. Joppke (2004: 247–8) argues that this was for two main reasons. Firstly, the source of immigrants had diversified and no longer consisted solely of the groups identified earlier on, making it difficult to operate a policy that relied on singling out specific groups. Secondly, it was argued that the policy of emancipating these groups with parallel institutions had detrimental, segregational, effects, particularly in educational and economic terms. Unemployment for non-EU migrants in most European countries is double that of the native population; in the Netherlands it was three times as high and even as much as 5.4 times higher in 1999 (Joppke 2007: 6). It seemed that the policies pursued were creating, or at least abetting, social exclusion, rather than inclusion. It came to be felt in the Netherlands that multiculturalism was targeting migrants as in need of assistance, 'minorising' them. This creates significant problems, particularly in terms of social policy, as, if ethnic minorities are identified as a 'problem' and particularly one requiring social policy interventions, this creates a division between the needy migrant and the Dutch citizen (who pays for the assistance) (Geddes 2003: 115). As Rothstein (1998) has argued, the social consensus underpinning welfare and social policy is much harder to maintain with such divisions.

Vink (2007: 338) argues that the unease surrounding the Dutch multicultural model had a long gestation period and did not suddenly appear with the right wing politician Pim Fortuyn. He goes on to argue that the multiculturalism espoused in the Netherlands was of a descriptive kind, noting the increasing diversity of Dutch society, rather than a normative, prescriptive kind. As such, the shift from a more multiculturalist set of policies to one espousing obligations and integration is a gradual process.

In 1997 the Dutch senate vetoed the introduction of multiple citizenship and removed the toleration of dual citizenship. 1998 saw the introduction of a law on Civic Integration of Newcomers, which aimed at creating self sufficiency of migrants. Non-EU (and non-OECD country nationals) migrants were required to participate in a twelve-month integration course, consisting of 600 hours of Dutch language training, civic education and preparation for the labour market (Joppke 2007: 6). Public service and benefit entitlements became more closely linked to legal status and the 2000 Immigration Law tightened asylum policy. More recently, the Dutch government has distanced itself from multicultural policies. Vink argues that government discourse has changed with phrases like 'responsibility' and 'civic integration duty' prominent (Vink 2007: 17). The substance behind such rhetoric can be seen in the 2006 Civic Integration Abroad Act, which aims to restrict immigration through family reunion and requires those applying for a residence permit to sit a civic integration exam (at a Dutch embassy) as a precondition for even a temporary residence permit. Civic integration tests were also introduced for those already resident in the Netherlands. The 2006 Civic Integration Act meant that all non-Dutch/EU residents had a civic integration duty, in the form of a civic integration course and exam. One interesting aspect of this new Act is that responsibility is shifted to the individual. The 1998 Civic Integration Act made language training and civic education mandatory, and made the state responsible for its provision. Under the 2006 legislation, the individuals themselves have to pay for the tests (which costs approximately €350, with the resident permit a further €800) (Vink 2007: 346; Joppke 2007: 7). Joppke (2007: 1) argues that this is an attempt to urge migrants to accept Dutch norms and values and marks a shift from the previous policy of accepting different cultural values and norms.

Policy on migration and citizenship in the Netherlands has undoubtedly shifted from a more multiculturalist position towards a more civic integrationist approach (Joppke 2007: 6). It is backed up by strong coercive elements; civic integration is obliged, not requested. There is also a shift from focusing on groups to focusing upon the individual. Geddes (2003: 124) argues that a range of pressures have led to demands to close the doors to the Dutch welfare state and examining who is a legitimate receiver of welfare state benefits, which in turn leads to a range of questions about culture and identity and immigrant and host.

Germany

Germany officially viewed itself as *kein Einwanderungsland*, or not a country of immigration. But this view was rather at odds with the facts and patterns of migration in Germany. By 1999, 14 per cent of Germany's population had not been born in Germany (Geddes 2003: 79) and as Figure 6.1 shows, some 600,000–700,000 migrants arrived in Germany every year between 1996 and 2005, indicating that the idea of *kein Einwanderungsland* should be seen as a political, cultural norm (Brubaker 1992) rather than any kind of statement of fact. This paradox will be explored in greater detail below, but is related to the specificities of West Germany and its constitution.

Geddes (2003: 80–1) points out that there were four main sources of migration to Germany. The first was *Aussiedler*, or ethnic German, migration. Those who were of German descent were given automatic German citizenship, meaning that around 12 million people fled to Germany from Soviet countries between 1945 and 1955 (Geddes 2003: 80). The second source of migration was due to the recruitment of guestworkers, where workers from first Italy, Spain and Greece, and later Turkey, Portugal and Morrocco, were invited to fill gaps in the labour market. The numbers of such workers peaked at 1.3 million in 1966. The third source of migration was the family and dependents of guestworkers, and the final source of migration was asylum seekers who, under Article 16 of the German constitution, had a right to make such a claim.

Prior to 1973, migration was driven by economic imperatives, with large numbers of guestworkers invited to fill labour shortages. In 1973 the German government stopped guestworker migration, ostensibly due to the oil crisis and economic slowdown (Castles 2006: 743). Yet, large-scale immigration persisted. There were two significant factors in this, both of which were related to legal, constitutional provisions. The *Aussiedler* migration, which was initially intended as a short-term provision, allowed for hundreds of thousands of ethnic Germans to migrate to West Germany. During the Cold War this was relatively uncontroversial, as it was taken as evidence of West Germany's pre-eminence. The end of the Cold War changed this and the situation regarding *Aussiedler* migration became more debated and a desire emerged to limit the flows. The 1990 Ethnic German Reception Law meant that ethnic Germans wanting to move to Germany had to make an application in their country of origin. In 1992 a quota (of 225,000) was placed on *Aussiedler* born before 1993. Those arriving after 1992 were designated as *Spätaussiedler* (late resettlers) and subject to dispersal, and thus treated in a similar fashion to asylum seekers (Geddes 2003: 84–5).

The other source of continued migration growth was asylum seekers. Article 16 of the constitution enshrined the right to make an application for asylum for those enduring political persecution. This is somewhat different to other European countries where the state only has a responsibility to consider a claim (Geddes 2003: 85). This, along with the lengthy appeal and redress procedures guaranteed by Article 19, empowered asylum seekers, to the extent that Germany was seen as 'the destination of choice for most asylum seekers in Europe', with 1992 seeing a peak of 438,191 applications (Geddes 2003: 85). Article 16 effectively restricted the state's capacity to control its own borders. Part of the difficulty in dealing with this came from the rights granted to all individuals, irrespective of citizenship status, by the German constitution and the Constitutional Court's interpretation of this (Joppke 2001: 349). The route out of this problem for German policy makers was the EU. In 1993 the Asylum Compromise amended Article 16 and brought Germany into line with other EU states and the Dublin Convention (1990). It allowed for safe third countries and safe countries of origin, to which asylum seekers could be returned, which, along with the creation of a 'buffer zone' in central and eastern Europe, contributed to a reassertion of state territorial control and a decline in asylum applications (Geddes 2003: 88).

Castles (2006) notes that despite the moves to restrict migration in the 1990s, there have been recent shifts, particularly with regard to migrant workers. The Süssmuth Commission Report of 2001 stated that Germany was a migration country and would need migrant workers to fill both skilled and less-skilled vacancies in the future. Concern about shortages in key sectors, and particularly Information Technology (IT), had prompted the German government in 2000 to issue 20,000 five-year work visas to IT specialists. These did not allow family reunion or permanent settlement and take up was low, with only 5,000 taken up (Castles 2006: 749). The subsequent 2004 *Zuwanderungsgesetz* (Immigration Law) was designed to attract highly-skilled workers that were requested by employers, and for the first time such individuals could apply for permanent residence immediately. Lower-skilled labour policy is regulated under a series of foreign worker programmes. The largest of these, set up in 1991, is a seasonal worker programme, which, through bilateral agreements with central and eastern European countries, admits workers for up to three months for work in construction, agriculture or catering (Castles 2006: 750).

Just as Germany has not, until recently, had a system for the regulation of migration, so it also lacked a coherent policy on the integration of migrants. This has, in part, been based upon the distinctive nature of German citizenship. German citizenship is based upon *jus sanguinis*, such that citizenship is based on ethnic descent. This contrasts to *jus soli*, where citizenship is a territorial birth right (Brubaker 1992). As such, German citizenship is based on an ethno-cultural identity and places significant obstacles in the way of migrants becoming citizens. As Castles (2006: 742) notes in terms of the guestworker system, 'Germany [...] was trying to import labour, not people'. The difficulty for migrants to naturalise and become citizens is one of the reasons for the extensive protections granted to non-citizens in the German constitution; if migrants were granted far-reaching and substantial rights (although, generally, these did not include political participation rights – see Kurthen 1995: 931), it helped to justify their exclusion from full citizenship (Joppke 2001: 351). Accordingly, naturalisation was a difficult process and dual citizenship was not encouraged. The 1913 Nationality Law gave the authorities complete discretion. Guidelines from 1977 required spoken and written German, knowledge of the political system and ten years' residence; even then nationality was only granted if it was in the public interest. The result of these restrictive measures was a naturalisation rate of less than 0.5 per cent of the foreign population (Geddes 2003: 94).

Joppke (2001: 351) argues that the exclusive nature of German citizenship was based on the unresolved question of the German nation. West Germany understood itself as a temporary state designed to facilitate the reintegration of all German peoples. Once reunification was complete, Joppke (2001: 351) contends, 'there has been a steady trend to more inclusive citizenship. Once citizenship was divested from the national question, it could be seen as a tool of immigrant integration' (see also Hansen and Koehler 2005: 636). In addition to this, there was a recognition that around 70 per cent of the foreign population had lived in Germany for ten or more years and around 1.5 million people, officially designated as foreigners, had been born in Germany (Geddes 2003: 95). A revised Alien Law passed in 1990 and enacted in 1991 relaxed the naturalisation regulations somewhat. The children of labour migrants could become naturalised if they were between the ages of 16 and 23, if they had resided in Germany for eight years, been educated in Germany for six years and were willing to give up their previous citizenship. More stringent requirements existed for those over 23, such as fifteen years of residence and guarantees of subsistence (Kurthen 1995: 933). Further reforms were agreed in 1999, after heated political debate and contestation (see Joppke 2001: 351–3). These allowed for dual nationality of the children of migrants born in Germany up to the age of 23, when a decision had to be made. This combination of both *jus sanguinis* and *jus soli* marks a 'rupture with Germany's ethnocultural citizenship tradition' (Joppke 2001: 353).

In addition to somewhat relaxing the naturalisation criteria, integration has now become a concern of government policy in Germany. In the past there was little emphasis placed upon integration as Germany was *kein Einwanderungsland*, not a country of immigration. Integration was only to be encouraged for *Aussiedler*, who were provided language courses to prepare them for a status test which had to be passed to entitle them to emigrate to Germany, with a further six month package of language training and civic orientation on arrival. In 2004 this was extended to non-EU, non-ethnic migrants (although without the coercive element seen in the Dutch system) to encourage integration. It is also noteworthy that ethnic and non-ethnic migrants are enrolled in the same programme (Joppke 2007: 12).

German policy on migration has thus undergone some significant transformations in the past twenty years. There has been a tightening of some forms of migration, including asylum seeking, the *Aussiedler* and migrant workers systems. Yet, alongside this, there has been a shift in attitudes and a recognition that Germany is an immigration country. This has produced a liberalisation of German nationality and citizenship law, with a move away from the *jus sanguinis* principle, towards *jus soli*. Post-unification, Germany has shifted its policies on migration and citizenship, aiming to integrate existing migrants and restrict further migration.

Italy

For many years, Italy was a country of emigration. However, as Figure 6.1 shows, in recent years, this situation has changed and Italy has become a country of immigration. Part of this reflects a shift, over time, of Europe's migratory boundaries to the south and east (Geddes 2003: 149). This changing context makes the Italian experience an interesting one to examine, in terms of migration and citizenship policy.

As with a number of European countries, the colonial legacy has played an important part in migration to Italy, with post-war immigration from African colonies. Colombo and Sciortino (2004: 56–7) note that, although Italy lacked the systematic approach of a country like Germany to migrant labour, this does not mean that such flows did not exist, just that they were rather disorganised and fragmented. Migrants have come to Italy from Tunisia, Yugoslavia, East Africa, the Philippines, and the Middle East to fill various gaps in the labour market in sectors such as agriculture, domestic labour and industry. Much of this labour migration is linked to the informal nature of much economic activity in Italy (Geddes 2003: 152).

The numbers of asylum seekers were traditionally low in Italy compared to other European countries, and prior to 1980 Italy only recognised citizens from the Soviet bloc as potential legitimate asylum seekers. Geddes, however, argues that the low level of asylum seekers is in part a product of categorisation; migrants that might be considered asylum seekers in other countries are more often categorised as irregular immigrants (Geddes 2003: 156). A growth in such numbers began around 1998, with a related change in the areas from whence they came, with people coming from the Balkans, the Kurdish areas of Iran, Iraq and Turkey and Afghanistan (Colombo and Sciortino 2004: 59). Colombo and Sciortino (2004: 60) note that over time, the origins of migrants to Italy has shifted, with the 1970s seeing migratory flows not determined by geographical proximity, whilst twenty years later, the southern Mediterranean figured prominently, and the late 1990s saw Eastern Europe and the Balkans growing in significance.

Di Pascale (2002: 71) argues that prior to 1998, Italian immigration regulations were 'incomplete, not coordinated and often adopted in emergency procedures [...] [and] often confusing and contradictory'. Processes were focused on legalising and regularising migrant flows. A first attempt to regularise illegal immigrants was attempted in 1986, but failed as the requirements were too stringent (Veikou and Triandafyllidou 2001: 65). The Martelli law of 1990 was a mixture of liberal and repressive measures. The right to asylum was extended to people from non-Soviet bloc countries and it allowed around 250,000 previously illegal immigrants to gain residency (Geddes 2003: 154). Yet, it also attempted to limit migration through visas, deportations and strengthening borders. Some have argued that that irregular migration was not effectively dealt with. 'The result was that the law sent out the message that Italy was relatively open to illegal migration' (Geddes 2003: 158).

The 1998 Turco-Napolitano law was an attempt to create 'a unitary corpus of norms which regulates the rights and obligations of foreigners in Italy, their stay and work conditions and other matters regarding family reunion, social integration and cultural life in the host country' (Veikou and Triandafyllidou 2001: 65). As such, it attempted to deal with both immigration control and integration policies. In terms of controlling migration, the law introduced quotas in order to regulate entry, provided sanctions against irregular migrants and organisations or employers who facilitate illegal entry, and established centres of 'residence and assistance', where migrants can be detained (Di Pascale 2002; Veikou and Triandafyllidou 2001). More liberal elements can be seen in the rights regarding family unification, which is allowed for any migrant with a residence card or work permit and in normalisation procedures. Any migrant who has been resident in Italy for more than six years is entitled to a residence card, which entitles them and their families to permanent residence and a legal status close to that of Italian citizens (although without political participation rights, which were included in the first version of the bill, but were watered down to a declaration of principle due to political opposition. See Campani and De Bonis 2003). The law also extended rights to some services such as healthcare and education (for minors), to irregular as well as regular migrants. Anti-discrimination measures were also strengthened (Di Pascale 2002).

2001 saw the election of a right-wing government headed by Silvio Berlusconi. A new immigration law, the Bossa-Fini law, influenced by the Lega Nord and post-fascist party Alleanza Nazionale, was introduced. This legislation linked the length of a residence permit to the length of an employment contract and increased the length of time migrants could be held in detention centres from 30 to 60 days. If illegal migrants were arrested for a second time, under the new measures they could be imprisoned for between one and four years. The rules for family reunification were tightened and the length of time needed to qualify for permanent residence was increased (Geddes 2003: 158–9). 'The aim of the Bill, inspired by the functionalist and identitarian logic of the *gastarbeiter*, was to have immigrants act as a flexible production factor, not a current or potential part of the permanent population' (Zincone 2006: 361). In addition to this, the Italian government has increased spending on border controls, and stepped up cooperation with other states. Again, though, alongside such restrictive measures was a regularisation of domestic workers who fulfilled important caring responsibilities, which was the largest regularisation ever performed in Europe (Zincone 2006: 348; Geddes 2003: 159).

In terms of integration policy, results have been mixed. The 1998 Turco-Napolitano law met with little success (Campani and De Bonis 2003: 26; Solé 2004: 1216). Fearing being seen as too pro-migrant in a context of a right-wing coalition making heavy use of immigration as a political issue, the measures dealing with integration were not implemented. Integration through the granting of citizenship is made more difficult as Italy, like Germany, operates with a *jus sanguinis* conception of citizenship. Campani and De Bonis argue that citizenship serves a symbolic function linking Italian communities abroad with the mother country. 'In Italy the right of citizenship has always be aimed at maintaining political and economical ties with Italian migrants (exogenous effect) instead of as a measure to regulate inclusion/exclusion mechanism of foreigners living in the country (endogenous effect)' (Campani and De Bonis 2003: 6). A 1992 Italian citizenship law means that migrants must be resident for ten years before being eligible for citizenship and makes it easier for EU citizens to become Italian citizens, than those coming from outside the EU (Solé 2004: 1216). As such, a sort of denizenship exists for legal residents. The current policy of strengthening borders and regularising residents and paying relatively little attention to integration may pose problems in the future.

> This still leaves open the issue of internal controls and what Sciortino calls the 'Pandora's Box' of state-society relations that could be opened if Italian governments attempted to tackle high levels of economic informality that provide the context for the economic incorporation of irregular migrants. (Geddes 2003: 159)

Italian policy on immigration seems somewhat Janus faced. The focus of recent policy has been on restricting immigration. Yet, at the same time, the large informal economy almost depends on illegal and informal migration, meaning that the Italian economy, despite political rhetoric, tacitly encourages (illegal) migration. This is summed up, surreally, by the group of fifty Italian companies who, when 800 illegal migrants working for them were deported, formed the 'Pro Illegal Labour Committee' (Zincone 2006: 362). In addition, the nature of the Italian welfare state makes Italian society reliant upon migrant workers. The Italian welfare state places a large responsibility for welfare upon the family, and in this way is typical of southern European welfare states (Ferrera 1996). In a context of rising female participation in the labour market, there is a greater demand for migrant workers to fulfil caring and domestic responsibilities (Sciortino 2004). As Zincone (2006: 368–9) notes, these structural factors in favour of migration and amnesties clash with political and public rhetoric against migration, to produce significant continuities in policy, irrespective of the political hue of the governing coalition.

EUROPEAN UNION AND MIGRATION

Any account or analysis of migration in Europe which did not consider the role of the EU would be remiss. Geddes refers to European policy making in the migration area as involving both boundary-removing and boundary-building aspects. 'It seeks an area without internal frontiers within which people (meaning mainly EU citizens) can move freely coupled with restrictions on those forms of migration defined by state policies as unwanted' (Geddes 2003: 147; see also Koslowski 1998). In terms of the first aspect, boundary-removing, the founding treaty of the EU, the Treaty of Rome (1957), granted the right of free movement to EU citizens, something that was confirmed in the Single European Act and formally codified in the Treaty of Maastricht (for more details of intra-EU migration see Koslowski 1998: 160–7). Such moves on intra-EU movement did not produce similar activity in terms of extra-EU migration and asylum until the mid-1980s.

The EU migration policy is hybrid as it consists of intergovernmental and supranational elements. According to Geddes 'intra-EU migration (free movement for EU citizens) has been largely supranationalised while extra-EU migration (immigration and asylum) remains subject to inter-governmental co-operation in the main' (2000b: 636). Following the above differentiation, much recent work on EU migration policy focuses on the reasons for the move to EU cooperation and integration. Supra-nationalists believe that the EU is the most prominent feature of political globalisation in the region and has the potential for extending 'rights beyond borders' and thereby challenging and eroding the sovereignty of nation-states and migrant rights. In this vein, the EU member states are increasingly constrained by a transnationalisation of economic, political and social relations that demands new forms of organising and regulating immigration. Sassen insists that

> much as states have resisted and found it incompatible with their sovereign power, they have had to relinquish some forms of border control and have had to accept court rulings which support the human rights of immigrants and the civil rights of their citizens to sue their own government. (1999: xx)

The supranationalist and postnationalist position has undergone much criticism from scholars that stress the importance and resilience of the nation-state to control 'unwanted immigration' and those who are against the use of the EU as a device for attaining immigration policy objectives. Moreover, important counterarguments show that the supranational regu-lation in the migration field does not imply automatically a strengthening of migrants' rights, but like the Schengen and Dublin Accords, could be used to co-ordinate control and exchange information on illegal immigrants and asylum seekers.

The Schengen Agreement – which began in 1985, was implemented in 1990, and came into effect in 1996 – was the first step in this direction (although initially it was not formally a part of EU policy, being an agreement between France, Germany, Belgium, Luxembourg and the Netherlands). The agreement meant that internal borders between participating states were removed, so that journeys between Schengen countries were classed as internal. The agreement also provided for greater controls and security measures to deal with migration and asylum, including harmonised asylum application procedures and provisions that asylum seekers may only apply in one country (Koslowski 1998: 169). As Huysmans notes, the logic of the Schengen Agreement is that if internal borders are going to be removed, then external borders must be strengthened. 'The parties shall endeavour to approximate as soon as possible their visa policies in order to avoid any adverse consequences that may result from the easing of controls at the common frontiers in the field of immigration and security' (Schengen Agreement, quoted in Huysmans 2000: 759). The Schengen Agreement later became part of the *acquis* of the EU in the Amsterdam Treaty of 1999.

The Dublin Convention, agreed in 1990 (although not ratified until 1997), imposed tighter restrictions governing asylum applications. It provided rules for determining which member state had jurisdiction for particular asylum applications, and stated that if this application was rejected, the asylum seeker could not apply in any other member states. This was designed to eliminate asylum shopping, the submitting of multiple applications. In addition, member states were obliged to keep information on rejected applications in the European dactylographic comparison system (EURODAC) database, which established a system for the comparison of fingerprints of asylum applicants and illegal immigrants. This data-system of fingerprints equates migration policy with police work, prosecution and penalisation (EC no. 2725/2000 11/12/2000). As well as these provisions, there were particular responsibilities passed on to central and eastern European countries, such as Hungary, and the Czech and Slovak Republics. Whilst they were not members of the EU, they were required to adapt to the Dublin measures, effectively making these countries a migratory 'buffer zone'. This was reinforced by the 1992 Edinburgh Council agreement which encouraged asylum seekers to stay in the nearest safe country to their home (Koslowski 1998: 171). The convention also included provisions for rejecting 'manifestly unfounded' applications and established safe third countries. Central and eastern European countries were designated as safe, meaning that asylum seekers entering the EU from them could be returned to them (Geddes 2003: 133).

The above measures were agreed through informal intergovernmentalism, but the Amsterdam Treaty saw greater moves towards supranationalism, but not a wholesale embracing of it. '[T]he Amsterdam Treaty marked a historical shift towards a significantly augmented role for the EU and the supranational level' (Hansen 2005: 6). In addition to establishing a broad EU policy on free movement of persons, border controls and immigration and asylum measures, it allowed for EU policies concerning third country nationals and ethnic minorities (Hansen 2005; Geddes 2003). It should be noted that the UK, Denmark and Ireland negotiated complex opt-in, opt-outs of the relevant provisions. The Tampere summit in 1999, which followed Amsterdam, called for a common asylum policy. This was to be based on cooperation with countries of origin, determination of which state holds responsibility for an application and common standards of processing applications and treating applicants. It also proposed action on granting third country nationals rights equivalent to those of EU citizens and measures to combat xenophobia and racism (Geddes 2003: 137–9). Despite these rather grand ambitions, progress on the Tampere goals has been limited. Geddes argues that the process of decision-making hinders progress in this area. 'The requirement for unanimity acts as a break on common decision making' (Geddes 2003: 139).

The general tone and tenor of such policies, as they developed, was to restrict migration into the EU (Kostakopoulou 2000) to create 'Fortress Europe' (Geddes 2000a). Ugur argues that this aim manifested itself in EU policy as early as 1968 (Ugur 1995: 977). Other authors have argued that migration has come to be seen as a security issue, linked to terrorism and transnational crime (Huysmans 2000; Bigo 2001). Prior to the Amsterdam Treaty, Geddes notes that EU policies were 'unbalanced' in this area, paying much more attention to restricting immigration and rather less on dealing with legally resident third-country nationals and ethnic minorities. Language such as 'groundbreaking' and 'remarkable' (Hansen 2005: 18) has been used in referring to the swift development of anti-discrimination and anti-racism initiatives in the Treaty of Amsterdam. Hansen (2005: 58) has described the overall picture regarding EU migration policy as one marked by 'an awesome accumulation of contradictions'. He argues that the primacy of market considerations in the EU competes with, and largely dominates, a more pro-migrant agenda. In addition to this, the obligations of migrants and their adaptation to 'European' values are emphasised. The recent emphasis on anti-discrimination and anti-xenophobia initiatives seems to lie in stark contrast to the increasing use of detention for asylum seekers and illegal migrants. In many ways, it is argued that this reflects the balance of discourses in member states and that the move to greater supranationalism has not fundamentally altered the state-centric, exclusionary, security-based conception of migration policy (Hansen 2005: 58–62; Kostakopoulou 2000: 514).

The way in which the articulation of a European migration policy unfolds in relation to the wider politics of belonging, like the struggle over cultural, racial and socio-economic criteria for the distribution of rights and duties in a community, has implications for the understandings and conceptualisations of identity and citizenship in the European Union. The increasing liberalisation of free movement for nationals of the member states and the development of restrictive and control-oriented approaches to the free movement of third-country nationals creates discriminatory territorial admissions and reactivates exclusionary binary oppositions between 'us' and 'them', 'Europeans' and 'non-Europeans', 'citizens' and 'immigrants'.

However, by avoiding essentialist conceptualisations of immigration, and exploring the comparable construction of the immigrant as an 'Other' in direct, threatening opposition with the 'Self' as in nation or/and Europe, it becomes apparent that the discourses that constitute immigration on both levels share as a common denominator exclusionary practices (Buonfino 2004). Moreover, it seems that, progressively since the Amsterdam Treaty, the discourse on immigration has been characterised by a primacy of identity expressed through the repetitious reference to borders and control. The language that characterises immigration discourse objectifies it as a threat to the security of the EU and calls for efficient cooperation and 'collective restrictivism' (Ucarer 2001).

THE SECURITISATION OF MIGRATION

The cooperation between European countries aiming at the realisation of free movement within Europe for a large part took place on an informal intergovernmental level. Some depict this cooperation in terms of 'transnational relations between subnational actors' (Guiraudon 2003). Most of the time, officials of executive bodies of different states deliberated and formulated agreements that operated in the field of Justice and Home Affairs. The shared perceptions of these subnational actors on migration are characterised by elements of control and exclusion (Guiraudon 2003). A substantive part of research on migration policy and regulation which is often referred to as 'securitisation' indicates the increasing politicisation of the issue as a threat to internal cohesion and prosperity (Koslowski 1998). In the following section, we will elaborate the 'securitisation thesis' through the use of specific examples that illustrate the exclusionary role of security discourses in the area of migration.

We have already noted, above, the securitising elements of the Dublin Convention. In addition, in order to cut the numbers of illegal migrants arriving in Europe by sea, EU interior ministers have given the green light to set up a rapidly deployable force of border guards (Goldirova 2007). The rapid border intervention teams consist of some 450 national experts, made available at short notice of up to five working days to any member

CITIZENSHIP IN CONTEMPORARY EUROPE

state whose borders are under 'urgent and exceptional' strain by illegal migration. The deal obliges all 27 capitals to contribute to the EU teams as the prime goal is to combat illegal immigration in the Mediterranean and Atlantic coastal area. Additionally, Frontex, the EU's new border agency, is to set in motion a permanent coast patrols network for the EU's southern sea borders. Meanwhile, the number of migrants coming to the Spanish Canary Islands halved between 2006 and 2007 following tightened naval patrols (Mahony 2007). The percentage of boat migrants arriving on the Canary Islands dropped by 60 per cent in the first three months of 2007 to 1,525 from 3,914 during the same period last year. Frontex, is being credited with the drop in figures.

Moreover, there are debates that portray migration as a challenge to the welfare state and to the cultural composition of the nation, where the central argument is that migration is a danger to domestic society. An example that illustrates perfectly the above notion is Schengen, where there is a connection between immigration and asylum and terrorism, transnational crime and border control, and the regulation of migration in an institutional framework is portrayed as a provision for internal security (Bigo 2001).

The development of security discourse and policies in the area of migration is often advocated as the inevitable solution to the alarming instability that increasing numbers of illegal immigrants and asylum seekers are creating to the public order (Lodge 1993). This way, immigrants, asylum seekers, and refugees are conceptualised as a security problem where restrictive policies are thought to be necessary, and preventive institutions like the police take a prominent role in regulating the issue. As a result, the means to approach the status of refugees, immigrants and asylum seekers is not based on the human rights discourse but on the controlling and restricted agenda of security. Security policy generates modes of belongingness by influencing political integration and criteria of membership through the identification of existential threats. The community constructs its identity by developing concepts of what it considers to be 'good' and 'normal' life 'through the reification of figures of societal danger such as the criminal, the mentally abnormal and the invading enemy' (Huysmans 2000: 757). This means that discourses of danger and security practices derive their political significance from their capacity to stimulate people to contract into a political community and to justify or contest political authority on the basis of reifying dangers. For example, EU integration is perceived as the bulwark against a return to Europe's past of balance of powers and wars. Integration is thereby made an aim in itself because the alternative is a self-propelling process that by definition will destroy 'Europe' as a project and reopen the previous insecurity caused by balance of powers, nationalism and war (Waever 1996). Another example is the conservative discourse which presents multiculturalism as a cause of societal disintegration. It postulates the differentiation between 'them' and 'us' by identifying other cultures as threatening to the national cultural homogeneity. Migration has been characterised as one of the main factors for this 'cultural decadence' and the migrant is identified as the alien who is dangerous to the reproduction of the social life.

The securitisation of migration is reproduced in a variety of discourses that involve a plethora of agencies such as national governments, the media, extreme right parties, European transnational police networks, etc. But for the purpose of this analysis, we would like to focus on the way that migration is rendered problematic and has been securitised by the EU institutions.

EU and the securitisation of migration

The issue was no longer, on the one hand, terrorism, drugs, crime, and on the other, rights of asylum and clandestine immigration, but they come to be treated together in the attempt to gain an overall view of the interrelation between these problems and the free movement of persons within Europe. (Bigo 1994:164)

In this section we will discuss some of the exclusionary discourses that have been developed in relation to the stigmatisation of immigrants and their portrayal as a possible threat to internal security. The following analysis will examine the tendencies that create a defining line between external and internal borders, and accordingly a divisionary line between 'outsiders' and 'insiders'. It shows that the creation of internal and external borders could play a transformative role from the socio-economic project of the internal market to the internal security project (Huysmans 2000).

In order to present the issues of border control as a security question, a discourse which connects the internal market to internal security has been developed. Thus, the reinforcement of external borders is also about compensatory measures for the liberalisation of the EU's internal borders (Mitselegas 2002). The institutionalisation of police and customs co-operation and the discourses articulating this field produced a security continuum connecting border control, terrorism, international crime and migration.

Thus, it is not surprising that border policy, like visa policy, is also one of the most highly developed policy domains in the EU. Article 7 and Article 47 of the Schengen Convention implementing the Schengen

Agreement call for closer cooperation in the field of border controls (Shengen Information System at www.europa.eu.int). A May 2002 Commission Communication focused on integrated management of external borders, and the Seville European Council of June 2002 supported the findings of this Communication. Consequently, the Commission has funded a range of pilot projects and joint operations. The Communication identified five aspects of border management with the view to construct a European Corps of Border Guards. The five aspects included a common corps of legislation, a common co-ordination and operational cooperation mechanism, a common integrated risk analysis (especially through upstream liaison with third countries), staff trained in the European dimension and inter-operational equipment and burden sharing between the Member States (COM 2002).

Indeed, the last few European Council meetings have introduced and begun the implementation of a range of programmes under the general rubric of the EU's 'external policy'. In this respect, considerable financial assistance has been offered by the EU to third countries for 'reinforcing their external border and promoting institutional and administrative capacity for managing migration' (COM 2003a: 104). A special budget line (B7-667: 'Cooperation with Third Countries in the field of migration') within the general EU budget was established for the first time in 2001 in order to offer financial assistance outside the more generic development transfers (COM 2003a). In fact, in Thessaloniki it was agreed that €140 million would be spent on increased border checks and the creation of a database of EU visas and €250 million for assistance to countries that agree to accept the return of their nationals from EU countries (Migration News 2003). At present, migration is a nodal point in the internal security field, and more recently the security continuum has been extended from the development of the internal market to the enlargement of the EU to central and eastern European countries. On April 14, 2003, the Council announced that the accession countries would be given special attention (COM 2003b: 323). As noted above, these new members were in fact forced to accept the Shengen acquis and to satisfy the new EU visa directives in order to be accepted as EU-members, effectively functioning as the gatekeepers of Europe's eastern borders (Mitselegas 2002).

To sum up, people who want to go to Europe often experience that the effective border of the EU does not coincide with the geographical line around its territory. Getting a visa is subject to European guidelines that include a list of countries of origin. For citizens from some countries getting access is much easier than it is for others. The common denominator of favoured countries seems to be that they are not poor and not Islamic. European countries agreed on measures co-ordinating responsibilities in dealing with asylum applications. To effectuate these agreements, new instruments, such as data systems, were established. The migration policy developed in the EU is ambivalent, as it portrays immigrants and asylum seekers primarily in negative terms challenging societal and economical stability, but the politicisation of the issue generates multiple reactions and a plethora of debates.

THEORISING MIGRATION AND CITIZENSHIP

In contemporary political philosophy we can discern two lines of thinking that can be roughly distinguished between universalist (cosmopolitan, globalist) and particularist. Universalist approaches focus more on stressing different varieties of equal rights for all human beings or different varieties of egalitarian liberalism or basic rights (Rawls et al. 1986; Carens 1987; Shue 1980). Particularist approaches range from liberal nationalism (Tamir 1993; Kymlicka 2002), to advocates of social-democratic welfare-states (Føllesdal 1997; Walzer 1995), to more exclusive patriotism (McIntyre 1994).

Particularist responses to citizenship and migration

For Walzer, liberal tolerance requires not having open borders and refraining from interfering in the affairs of other states. Thus,

> the distinctiveness of cultures and groups depends upon closure [...] At some level of political organisation, something like the sovereign state must take shape and claim the authority to make its own admissions policy, to control and sometimes restrain the flow of immigrants. (1998: 39)

Citizenship here is understood as membership in a particular community and immigrants are seen as the ones who have to adjust to the norms and values of the state they enter. For communitarians, political membership and democracy beyond the state are seen as non-pragmatic and potentially erosive practices for national welfare systems. For example, Miller (1988a) thinks that redistributive principles will suffer beyond the boundaries of the state and will face problems of democratic legitimacy, whereas a common national identity is a prerequisite for such principles.

For cosmopolitans, the communitarian position is perpetuating an unjust world and therefore they can not provide a fair justification for closing the borders. The argument is that the establishment of fair conditions cannot include the endorsement of arbitrary borders. For Carens (1992), liberal democracies should in principle advance policies compatible with open borders, but he acknowledges that there are reasons – such as possible threat to public order or to national security – that could provide reasons for restricting immigration. Moreover, cosmopolitans criticise the view that borders create differences. As Bader says of Walzer,

> He wants states to be what they historically and actually have never been – linguistically and culturally homogenous worlds of common meaning, free associations based on democratic consent. Only in this way is he able to link state sovereignty to the democratic principle of sovereignty. (1995: 221)

This position by Walzer has been criticised by Lubans (1985) as a tendency for 'Romancing the Nation' and forgetting the heterogeneity that constitutes it. But Walzer argues that the importance of the state should not be dismissed as it is perceived to be the main distributor of welfare services.

Universalist responses to citizenship and migration

Goodin distinguishes between special duties which we have towards family members, friends, pupils, patients etc., and general duties which we have towards all human beings. He states that general duties are 'multiplied and magnified in special relationships and so become special duties' (Goodin 1988: 673). While he accepts that special duties towards our compatriots exist, Goodin also maintains that our general duties towards strangers go much further than Walzer allows for. General duties exist towards every human being. From this it follows that if there is an individual in need of protection then the responsibility to protect this individual is assigned to the set of states. In conclusion, Goodin states that

> boundaries matter [...] but it is the boundaries around people, not the boundaries around territories that really matter morally. Territorial boundaries are merely useful devices for 'matching' one person to one protector. Citizenship is merely a device for fixing special responsibility in some agent for discharging our general duties vis-à-vis each particular person. At root, however, it is the person and the general duty that we all have toward him that matters morally. (1988: 686)

Thus, while Walzer seems to reject the universal account of deontology, Goodin accepts it in a somewhat weaker form and recognizes the general duty to help (at least) those outsiders whose social bond with their own state has been severed.

The analysis of Veit Bader (1995) on the four paradoxes of state sovereignty shows how global liberalism is a more ethical proposition.

First, there is an intensified tension of globalisation on many levels that may lead even to the implosion of states. Second, different processes of decision-making take place on a regional, provisional and supra-state level. Third, because of this development, issues of taxation, currency, legislation and jurisdiction affect the concept of unitary sovereignty of a state. Fourth, the acceptance of humanitarian interventions has eroded dramatically the absolute sovereignty of a state. In this vein, Bader calls for a thorough rethinking of the concepts of statehood and citizenship which finds its completion in the global liberal approach.

> If communitarianism, for all its versions, pretends to be an identifiable position in practical philosophy, then it must mean that in all hard cases the particularist requirements of community must trump the universalist ones of justice. This priority rule clearly contradicts the strong moral intuitions that are elaborated in modern universalist moral theories and international and constitutional law: universalist principles and rights should not only trump prudentialist utility but also the ethics of particular communities. Otherwise, morality would be no more than a thin ideological mask of ethical or utilitarian welfare chauvinism. (Bader 1995: 216)

By accepting the naturalised notion of state-sovereignty, we are unable to understand its historicity and contingency associated with Westphalia. As Chris Brown pinpoints, 'it is precisely because certain kinds of theory draw distinctions between insiders and outsiders in the way that they do that the borders we find in the real world have the significance they have' (2000: 190). This practice of sovereignty impacts on our moral justifications as 'the social space of inside/outside is both made possible by and helps constitute a moral space of superior/inferior' (Campbell 1996: 199). In this vein, our perceptions about sovereignty construct a world that legitimises borders and positions justice within it. As Brown argues,

> There is nothing in the world of brute facts that requires us to draw a sharp distinction between our concern for the interests of our fellow-citizens and those of strangers – there are no 'natural' frontiers, moral or otherwise – although once we have drawn such a distinction, we have no difficulty in finding features of the world which legitimate our actions. (2000: 190)

The mainstream in theorising migration lies within the efforts of scholars who seek to find a middle way between the extremes of other traditions. We can distinguish the liberal communitarians who provide moral reasons for restrictive borders and liberal cosmopolitans who advocate the moral illegitimacy of such borders but in some cases they accept their necessity (Brown 1992). The tension within liberal approaches on migration seems to oscillate between an emphasis on the local and the universal. As we saw for communitarians, the problem lies in the overemphasis of the state as the provider of self determination. On the other hand, if we maintain the position for open borders, respect for universal human rights and undermine the state's capability for determining its own collective good then we may violate the rights of the people that would like to belong to a specific association and pursue a particular project of justice.

Both sets of theory are antiteleological in the sense that subjects are conceived to be apart from and prior to their ends, such that principles of justice are open to human construction (Sandel 1982: 175). Rather, for Rorty, solidarity might be required to extend our understanding to refugees and asylum seekers:

> It is to be achieved not by inquiry, but my imagination, the imaginative ability to see strange people as fellow sufferers. Solidarity is not discovered by reflection, but created [...] It is a matter of detailed description of what unfamiliar people are like and of rediscription of what we ourselves are like. (Rorty 1999: xvi).

Imaginative narratives can explore new ways of understanding and behaving towards migrants, in contrast to the closed, criminalised and securitised discourse on migration, borders and asylum promoted by the tabloid media and right-wing politicians. As Nyers argues, the language of emergency is restrictive to the

> practical ways in which order and normalcy can be re-instated. Critical questioning of both the unequal power relations and desirability of this order are de-emphasised, marginalised or ignored. Also de-emphasised is any attempt to question the purity and coherence of such key foundational concepts as citizenship and sovereignty. (Nyers 1999: 15)

What is really important for an ethical discussion of migration is to understand and deconstruct the ways that we perceive migrants in our daily practices. Accordingly, Nyers criticises the common humanitarian construction of refugees that characterises many liberal approaches to migration:

> One of the central difficulties of portraying refugees as 'mere humans' is that all notions of political agency are emptied from refugee subjectivity [...] refugees are silent – or rather, silenced because they do not possess the proper subjectivity (i.e. citizenship) through which they can be heard. (1999: 20)

Alternative forms of press like Indymedia, pro-migrants NGOs, and social movements can be used in order to give voice and present narratives from a migrant perspective. By giving the migrants the opportunity to make public their needs and demands, they can develop the political agency of the excluded. This also can advance our moral vocabularies where migrants are not simply 'helpless' or 'in the need of a home' as in the discourse of humanitarianism (Nyers 1999), but they can be 'active' 'political' and 'engaged'.

CONCLUSION

In the first section of this chapter we noted that for most of the countries we examined, migration did not appear to have increased over the last ten years. Indeed, asylum applications have all shown recent downturns and declines. It is somewhat curious, in this context, that migration should attract such controversy. Yet, the issue of migration throws into stark relief some central questions for citizenship. These include; who is to be considered a citizen; what responsibilities, if any, do we owe to non-citizens; can people who are not 'us' become citizens? These are difficult and controversial questions, which are given further twists by two processes: European integration and demographic changes. The market-building mechanisms of EU integration have given free movement to European citizens. Yet, such freedom is denied to non-Europeans. This raises a whole host of issues and problems for Europe in a context of enlargement, as seen in the debates and policies that surrounded the free movement rights of citizens of new accession states. Citizens of these states are not granted the same rights of free movement that, older, more established (richer? more western?) member states are, at least for a temporary period (Jileva 2002). In addition to these issues, is the fact that most European countries need migration. As we noted above, low birth rates and the shrinking of the working age population indicate that, even if European citizens and governments are less than comfortable with migration, it is something which almost demands a positive solution. We have suggested in this chapter that the contemporary debate is centred around a discourse of securitisation which does not offer a great deal of potential as a way forward. Whilst noting concerns of some communitarian, particularist authors about the threat from migration, we concluded the chapter by thinking about some alternative ways of thinking about this contentious issue which may offer a more productive and positive way of managing and dealing with these complex issues. We shall return to these themes of identity and citizenship in the next chapter.

CHAPTER 7

European citizenship and European identity

INTRODUCTION

The introduction of Union Citizenship by the Treaty on European Union stirred a heated debate on the political dimension of European integration, concerning issues such as legitimacy and democracy, European constitutionalism, European identity and the European public sphere (Weiler 1995; Meehan 1996; Kostakopoulou 1996; Closa 1998). Thus, European citizenship is considered to be a central theme in what has been called the 'normative turn' in European Studies (Weiler 1997).

The debate is characterised by two different sets of tensions inextricably linked with interpretations of citizenship: universalism and particularism. The critics of European citizenship see it as a symbolic and decorative institution (Everson 1995; d'Oliveira 1995). The reasons for this hostile reception are mostly related to the primacy of national citizenship and its derivative national order. In this vein, some scholars focused on the pre-Maastricht market citizenship which was designed to facilitate European integration at the expense of other, arguably, more important aspects of citizenship, like political participation and active engagement in the polity (Vink 2003). Also, European citizenship was perceived to have a weak affective dimension in contrast to its national identity counterpart which is firmly embedded within the nation-state environment and deploys 'pre-political elements' like the spiritual and cultural ties that bind the people together (Smith 1992). The lack of a European demos raised doubts about the appropriateness of such a venture and fears for forced processes of collective identity formation (Weiler 1995).

In the meantime, the absence of a primordial substratum and cultural commonalities is considered to be an advantage for pursuing a political community on a political base. Similarly, Kostakopoulou argues that a 'European citizenship constituted a unique experiment for stretching social and political bonds beyond national boundaries and for creating a political community in which diverse peoples become associates in a collective experience and institutional designers' (2007: 5). Further, for Closa (1998), the notion of a citizenship based on a form of commonality that was moulded under pre-democratic conditions is problematic because it adheres to exclusiveness and discrimination. In contrast, according to Closa (1998: 112), a site of democratic citizenship is one in which people live together under the asset of principled bonds, such as those identified by Robert Dahl including voting equality, effective participation, control of agendas and inclusiveness (1986: 221). From this perspective, European citizenship offers possibilities for greater political participation in different normative systems (human rights, EU) beyond the nation-state and multiple sites of identification and solidarity that could limit discrimination and marginalization.

In the next part of the chapter, we will present an overview of the evolution of European citizenship. We will note that debates about the European constitution have become central to debates around European integration and European citizenship. In order to better understand these debates, we will then examine different positions around European constitutionalism and its relation to the European demos and the European public sphere. Frequently, the lack of a definable European identity is held to be a terminal stumbling block both to further European integration and to a deeper, more meaningful European citizenship. In the third part, we will discuss the issues that render around European identity as well as the possibilities for advancing openness and accommodating differences within it. The chapter will conclude by considering the work of Jacques Derrida on European identity, examining the possibilities that it opens up for thinking differently about European identity.

EUROPEAN CITIZENSHIP: A HISTORICAL OVERVIEW

The general origin of European citizenship is considered to be the granting of free movement rights to workers in the original European Economic Community (EEC) Treaty. In this vein, European citizenship was understood as a 'market citizenship'; acting as a participant of the common market it was thus relevant to citizens in their capacity as workers, professionals and their families, moving across borders (Everson 1995: 73). Similarly,

> to the extent that citizenship could be regarded as being embedded within the context of the existing framework of the 'constitutionalised' European Community treaties, it was firmly linked to the common market concept,

and to the idea of the European Communities as a legal framework – at least in the first instance – for economic integration. (Bellamy et al. 2006: 10)

However, the political origins of the concept lie in the 1974 Paris summit, where a working group was established to examine the conditions under which citizens of the member states 'could be given social rights as members of the Community' (CEC 1974: item 11). For the next ten years the issue was

> punctuated by debates in the deadlocked Council over the question whether the Community was competent to legislate in this respect at all and the need to incorporate provisions requiring applicants to prove that they were in possession of sufficient resources and covered by a medical insurance scheme. (O'Leary 1999: 381)

In June 1984 the Fontainebleau European Council meeting resulted in the formation of the Adonnino Committee in order to reflect on a so-called 'People's Europe' to 'strengthen and promote its [the Community's] identity and its image both for its citizens and for the rest of the world' (CEC 1985: 5). The report dealt with aspects of political participation in the member states, the relationship between the citizen and the Community's legal instruments, the consultation of citizens on transfrontier issues and the right of consular assistance from other member states. Although the European Council approved the Committee's report, no further action was taken for the granting of European citizenship. After the fall of the Berlin Wall, a key question of the 1990 Dublin European Council was:

> how will the union include and extend the notion of Community citizenship carrying with it specific rights (human, political, social, the right of complete movement and residence, etc) for the citizens of Member States by virtue of these States belonging to the Union? (CEC 1990: 15–16)

The Spanish Prime Minister Felipe Gonzalez urged the inclusion of a conception of citizenship in the European Community/Convention (EC) Treaty, and by the time that the heads of government reconvened in Dublin, they agreed to an intergovernmental conference (IGC) on political union parallel with the one on the EMU. The discussions on European citizenship had as a focal point whether or not the rights inherent in the concept should have direct applicability. Denmark and the UK were against the idea that European citizenship would entitle individual citizens to force member states to respect their rights (Mazuccelli 1997: 145). After negotiations and modifications, the final text of the Maastricht Treaty heralds that: 'Every person holding the nationality of a Member State shall be a citizen of the Union' (CEC 1992). Union citizenship confers four main rights:

1. the 'right to move and reside freely within the territory of the Member States, subject to the limitations and conditions laid down in this Treaty and by the measures adopted to give it effect' (Article 8A);
2. the right to vote or stand in municipal elections for those citizens residing in Member States of which they are not nationals (Article 8B(1)); the right to vote or stand in European parliamentary elections for the same group of citizens (Article 8B(2));
3. EU citizens finding themselves in the territory of a third country where their own country is not represented have the right to diplomatic or consular protection by any Member State which is represented there (Article 8C);
4. the right to petition the European Parliament and to apply to the Ombudsman established under Article 138E.

In terms of citizenship issues, although many expected that citizenship would become a key element of the Amsterdam Treaty, it did not. The shadow of the Danish rejection of Maastricht had made states wary, lest strengthening Union citizenship be interpreted as weakening national citizenship (Halligan 1997). Thus, in October 1997 the Amsterdam Treaty introduced amendments to the principle of European citizenship in Articles 17 and 21 (formerly Articles 8 and 8[d]). The Amsterdam Treaty states unequivocally that 'citizenship of the Union shall complement and not replace national citizenship' which means that to be a national of a member state is a requirement to enjoy citizenship of the Union and European citizenship will complement the rights conferred by national citizenship. Furthermore, the Amsterdam Treaty has established a new right for European citizens. Every citizen of the Union can now write to the European Parliament, the Council, the Commission, the Court of Justice, the Court of Auditors, the Economic and Social Committee, the Committee of Regions and the Ombudsman in any of the twelve languages of the Treaties and receive an answer in the same language. Moreover, the Amsterdam Treaty has formally empowered the European Court of Justice (ECJ) to ensure the respect of fundamental rights and freedoms by the European Institutions (Shaw 2000). The treaty also introduces new legal and political protection that includes: the entitlement to take EU institutions to ECJ over any action they think breaches their rights and new Articles (F.1 in the Maastricht Treaty and 236 in the Rome Treaty) which gives the European Council the opportunity to deal with a member state in 'serious and persistent breach' of the general principles of rights, including suspending its voting rights (Duff 1997: 3–4). The Treaty also aims to enable people's elected representatives to act on their behalf through more efficient arrangements like scrutinising EU proposals by national parliaments and extending and simplifying the European's Parliament co-decision making powers vis-à-vis the Council of Ministers (Duff 1997: 174–8).

The next major negotiations, at Nice in December 2000, did not offer substantial changes to EU citizenship. The Nice summit 'was not the European Union's finest hour. Nor, however, was it an unmitigated disaster' (Ludlow 2004: 47). Most of the negotiations concerned the way in which decisions would be made after enlargement, and the resulting changes were 'technical' and 'limited' (European Commission 2001). In terms of citizenship rights, however, Nice extended qualified majority voting to free movement: henceforth, decisions about the right to move and reside freely within EU territory would no longer require the unanimous support of all member states. The member states did exempt passports, identity cards, residence permits, social security, and social protection from qualified majority voting. Provisions in those areas would continue to require unanimity, but decisions about free movement provisions could now be made more easily.

The Laeken summit of December 2001 took a special interest in increasing the EU's democratic legitimacy. In the Laeken Declaration the government leaders of the member states affirmed that, within 'the Union, the European institutions must be brought closer to its citizens. Citizens undoubtedly support the Union's broad aims, but they do not always see a connection between those goals and the Union's everyday action' (European Council 2001). Also, the Laeken summit established a constitutional Convention, whose work ultimately resulted in a draft constitutional treaty. For the Commission, a key task of the Constitution was 'to give European citizenship [...] its full meaning' (European Convention 2002). Representatives of the Committee of the Regions agreed that the Constitution should:

> flesh out European citizenship. The incorporation of the Charter of Fundamental Rights into the future constitutional text [...] will play a vital role in achieving this. The Charter will enable every national of an EU Member State to recognise European citizenship as a source of new rights and the expression of belonging to a new community. (European Convention 2002)

In order to do so the first comprehensive draft of the constitution specified that each EU citizen 'enjoys dual citizenship, national citizenship and

European citizenship; and is free to use either, as he or she chooses; with the rights and duties attaching to each' (European Convention 2002).

The Treaty establishing a Constitution for Europe was signed on 29 October 2004 by the heads of state or government of the twenty-five member states and the three candidate countries who had already unanimously adopted it on 18 June of the same year. In order for the Treaty to enter into force, it had to be adopted by each of the signatory countries, which according to their constitutional traditions could ratify the Treaty by either adopting the text by the state's parliamentary Chamber(s), or by holding a referendum (www.europa.eu.int). At the moment, Austria, Belgium, Cyprus, Germany, Greece, Hungary, Italy, Latvia, Lithuania, Malta, Slovakia, and Slovenia have ratified the Treaty by the 'parliamentary method', while in the case of Spain and Luxembourg the Treaty was adopted by using the 'referendum method' (www.europa.eu.int). However, the rejection of the Treaty in the French and Dutch referenda in 2005 froze the constitutional process and led to a 'period of reflection'. This period has come to an end and Angela Merkel has already made clear that the number one priority of the German Presidency of the EU (January–June 2007) will be re-launching the European Constitution. Angela Merkel told the Bundestag in December 2006 that she 'would consider it an historical failure if we do not succeed in working out the substance of the Constitutional Treaty by the time the next European elections take place' in 2009 (www.dw-world.de). At the European Council in June 2006 EU leaders agreed that Germany would present a report on the future of the Constitution in the first half of 2007, and that agreement on how to proceed with it would be reached before the end of 2008. Germany, along with the other seventeen countries which have ratified the Treaty, is adamant that the Constitution should eventually be implemented in the same form as originally agreed, or at least stay as close as possible to the current text. The constitution has thus become the key feature of contemporary discussions and debates about European integration and European citizenship. Questions about citizenship, diversity and integration are all captured and distilled into this debate. It is, therefore, important that we examine such debates in greater detail.

CONSTITUTION AND CONSTITUTIONALISM IN THE EU

As constitutions, constitutionalism and constitutional politics gained great momentum in the last decades in EU studies (Moravcsik and Nicolaidis 1998), it is pertinent to understand how these discourses form our understandings and conceptions of the European polity and the principles that it is based upon. It is possible, as Wilkinson states, that the

> constitutional discourse has been self consciously adopted not only amongst scholars, but by politicians, the judiciary and more recently the media on one level to give some overall coherence to the dis(array) of structures, norms and institutions: on another to infuse the project with a particular normative vision. (Wilkinson 2003: 452)

The starting point of this investigation is to situate the debate of the constitution within the context of the public debates that took place in the 1990s when one of the principle themes was the democratic legitimacy of the Union, which is often considered as its Achilles heel (Mayes and Palmowski 2004).

The Convention on the Future of Europe delivered its answers in an effort to contribute to the production of a document that would accommodate the diverse interests and positions within the polity. As Nicolaïdis argues,

> For the first time in the history of the EU, delegates from the whole continent but other than diplomats have engaged for more than a year in a public debate about the foundations of the European Union, its goals, its methods. The reach of the so-called dialogue with civil society may have been wanting, but they have conducted this debate in a highly open and transparent fashion, with the full paraphernalia of webcast and e-forum. Their mission fell somewhere between pragmatic simplification and radical refoundation: to give the Union a form of government adapted to its new size and ambitions and to do so whilst reinventing it as a democratic polity. (2004: 76)

However, if the constitutional debate is to be related to the underlying concern of democratisation and to the broader scope of integration then it is essential to take into account the theoretical and empirical assumptions which support these views.

Constitutionalism as a state-centred idea

For the proponents of constitutionalism as a state-centred construction, the components of a settled political community and the symbolic associations that evolve in a particular cultural setting in time cannot be transposed to non-state contexts such as the European Union. Such a belief has its origins in the modern Westphalian scheme which defines the role of the states as the major actors of the global political game. It has a resilient political and ideological currency and is 'also inscribed in and supported by the traditional division of labour within the study of law' (Walker 2002: 322). The scepticism or essentialism of political or methodological nationalists, or defensive internationalists, seeks to establish the proper legal character of the EU by explaining the transformation of structures and processes beyond the state within the traditional paradigm of international law as an external complement to internal state constitutionalism that doesn't undermine the continuous integrity of state sovereignty (Schilling 1996: 389). In other words, the member states are depicted as the 'master of the treaties' and are situated in a new legal order dressed in the clothes of a very old legal garment. Therefore constitutionalism at the EU level can only proceed with states as the key actors.

Accordingly, constitutionalism is envisaged as a set of mobile ideas that can be transferred and operate in similar ways in non-state settings as in state habitus. Shaw and Weiner (2000) criticise 'the often invisible touch of stateness'; the tendency to measure many of the supposed normative short-comings of post-state entities like deficits of democracy, legitimacy, accountability, equality and security in terms of a statist template and against the benchmark of a statist standard.

A similar view of constitutional scepticism argues that

> even a constitutional culture modestly weighted towards a homogenising ethic and a set of constitution-generating principles moderately disinclined to recognise group differences is enough to nurture a systemic bias against, or a deprioratisation of, social identity claims other than those which correspond with and reinforce the boundaries of the constitutional polity in question. (Walker 2002: 331)

This position is alternatively characterised as the deep diversity thesis (Fossum 2003: 3) and it is closely related to the tradition of communitarianism. Deep diversity describes a situation when many ways of belonging are acknowledged and accepted within the same state or polity. In this case acceptance is established through the political-legal and constitutional relations that are created for its promotion. In the case of the European Union,

> a political system whose hall-mark is deep diversity can be federal but cannot be based on one nation state [...] it doesn't presuppose a constitutional demos and the constitutional arrangement, therefore, doesn't need an explicit popular endorsement on a par with that of a full-fledged constitution. (Fossum 2003: 3)

The main principles that deep diversity assumes for the EU are: the non-European demos thesis, the principle of constitutional tolerance, and audit democracy. We will examine each in turn.

Firstly, regarding the non-European demos thesis, when the German

Constitutional Court assessed the question of whether the transfers of sovereignty to the EU pursuant to the Treaty of Maastricht were compatible with the basic laws of the Federal Republic which guarantee its democratic nature, it answered that there is not yet a sufficiently integrated European public sphere which could legitimise further transfers from the state to the supranational level. This meant that the member states should maintain

> sufficiently important spheres of activity of their own in which the people of each can develop and articulate itself in a process of political will-formation which it legitimates and controls, in order thus to give legal expression to what binds people together (to a greater or lesser degree of homogeneity) spiritually, socially and politically. (*Brunner* v *the European Treaty* 1994: 257)

In terms of constitutional tolerance, the supremacy of national identity and the locus for the consolidation of democracy within and among member states, Weiler argues that the EU provides a unique federal arrangement which lays its foundation on the principle of constitutional tolerance. As the 'Union is to remain a Union among distinct peoples, distinct political identities [...] the call to bond with those very others in an ever closer union demands an internalisation – individual and societal – of a very high degree of tolerance' (2001: 68). Based on the above two principles, the EU provides a 'a remarkable instance of civic tolerance to be bound by precepts articulated, not by "my people" but by a community composed of distinct political communities: a people, if you wish, of "others"' (Weiler 2002: 568).

The last criterion for the thesis of deep diversity is audit democracy, which is based upon the combination of accountability and representation, where the European institutions should respect and accommodate the interests of both states and citizens. As one author described it,

> audit democracy presupposes popularly elected bodies that are endowed with specific responsibilities for the monitoring and stock-taking of the Union's principles, institutional arrangements and activities and for the ensuring that these resonate with the popular needs. All higher-level institutions, courts, legislative, executive and administrative bodies would have to account for how they have expanded with their powers and prerogatives granted to them to the fulfilment of certain goals defined in the constitutional treaty. (Fossum 2003: 7)

To sum up our analysis to here, it seems that constitutionalism can be characterised as another contested concept, especially when it is analysed within the context of EU studies. But, by taking into account the theoretical framework that political and legal science offer, it seems that the communitarian, nationalist and intergovernmentalist discourses share overlapping articulations for the primacy of nation, demos and ethnos in their analysis of EU constitutionalism. Situating the debate at the opposite pole of the spectrum, in the following section we will critically engage with the discourse of supranationalism and liberal republicanism so as to explore their theoretical framework and its relevance to the European Constitution.

Constitutionalism as a supranationalist idea

The perspective comes from those who believe in the existence of a European demos. Supranationalists perceive the European Union as the instantiation of a progressive transfer of loyalties from the national level to the supranational. They emphasise the fact that member states have internally and externally been 'europeanised' through their participation and membership, and that this creates de facto solidarities between citizens of different states and encourages the mobility of students, professionals or firms. Such progressive 'europeanisation', in turn, is both the source and the consequence of development of a European public space where domestic politics converge to create a common European political culture and language and, in the end, a European 'civic nation' (Nicolaïdis 2004: 80).

Moreover, the belief that a European identity can co-exist harmoniously with the national and other local identities shows the degree of convergence with the intergovernmentalist position. In fact, supporting the construction of a collective identity through the use of common symbols like the European flag, passport, celebration day or Hymn for Europe, as well as histories in school curricula and the media to establish 'a common destiny', is a mere reproduction of 'the mystique and power of the nation state at the European level' (Nicolaïdis 2004: 80). It seems that the common denominator for both approaches, the emergence of a political community, is the glue that brings its members together flourishing in the grounds of a common identity. In the next section we situate the political positions of intergovernmentalists and supranationalists within the philosophical traditions that furnish their arguments, in order to analyse more effectively the limitations that these discourses set to the concept of the political.

Starting with a brief description of liberalism and then moving to its contextualisation within the discourse of constitutionalism, one could say that a constitution is the expression of individual freedom combined with the necessary order to achieve and protect that freedom. As discussed in Chapter One, for Rawl's liberal theory, the individual is an independent, autonomous and rational-bearing subject. Influenced by the Kantian tradition and with the fear that the desires of the powerful could limit freedom, Rawls privileges individual rights over all other principles, including that of the common good. The citizen pursues his own self-interest within a minimal set of limits where liberty, opportunity, income and wealth are to be distributed equally (Rawls 1971). Personal liberties are seen to be threatened by obligations, traditions and values that are advocated by communitarians, while the construction of universal maxims provides a moral environment for the subject to determine and pursue its own good. The problem with liberalism is that it is inadequately concerned with the idea of law authorship, as it is not uncomfortable with the presupposition that the idea of law is an external constraint on popular sovereignty. Republicanism, by contrast, in an effort to satisfy the authorship requirement, supports an ethical commonality where legal coercion is superfluous and it is replaced by custom and moral self-control (Honig 2001). In relation to law making, the liberal–legal tradition has been portrayed as 'an ideology in danger of becoming as tyrannical as the Leviathan it purported to restrain, and that way, paradoxically, bring about the precise end – despotism – it is designed to avoid' (Loughlin 2000: 5).

A liberal reading of identity formation within the legal framework of constitutional power would emphasise freedom, norm creation and innovation through the rationalisation of abstract principles of justice and the entrenchment of social rights as a product of a homogenous community. For the communitarian position, the emphasis would be the importance of belongingness and the demand of the law to secure and protect the values and the 'common good' of the community. But the problematic part of both discourses lies in the supposition of an already existing pre-political homogeneous community. In the former reading, the law-making is 'reproductive' of identity and in the earlier reading is 'purely productive' of identity (Lindahl 2003: 243). But, as Lindahl argues, the task should be 'conceptualising law-making as both reproductive and productive of identity' (2003: 244), that enables us to understand that within the context of legal theory of identity, neither a liberal nor a communitarian absolutism can inform us, but rather a combination of both will demonstrate its reflexive structure which must combine application and creation, responsiveness and innovation, identity and representation, belonging and freedom.

The role of law-making in the constitution of a non-fixed, open-ended identity, within the context of the EU, is an issue that will be discussed in detail in later sections of this chapter where we will present the debates that furnish more 'radical' and 'deliberate' forms of identity formation. For the time being this discussion will try to present notions of constitutionalism that take into account the *sui generis* nature of the Union in a postnational context.

CONSTITUTIONALISM AND POSTNATIONALISM

If the European polity suffers from a 'constitutional deficit', this needs to be addressed not simply by discussing the contents of a constitution for Europe, but also the political process through which such a constitution is put in place. The forms of such a process do not just depend on expediency and particular circumstances but can be the subject of principled discussion and of imaginative political psychology (Castiglione 1995: 74).

As EU constitutionalism has been substantively undertheorised by all standard accounts of constitutionalism, the attempts by writers such as Richard Bellamy and Dario Castiglione (1996), who try to combine theory and practice, are worthy of note. A basic premise of their work highlights the inadequacies of certain aspects of constitutional and democratic theory when they are uncritically transferred from the national level to the European context. More specifically, the changes in understandings and perceptions about the sovereignty of people, the homogeneity of the nation-state and the link between citizenship and rights cannot shift from one level to another without taking into consideration the discourses that affect and formulate theory.

In this vein, it is essential to engage with the constitutional discourse that places the EU in a postnational dimension of analysis. But before moving to the specifics of the theoretical framework of our investigation, we will discuss in laconic brevity some of the elements that constitute the notion of postnationalism. First, it should be noted that postnationalism is

neither a fixed or defined concept within academic writing and thinking, nor a certain and empirically observable phenomenon of law or politics [...] it can be defined dispositively as an open textured concept used to express many of the dynamic and *sui generis* elements of the EU as integration project involving the process of polity formation and in particular constitutional processes. (Shaw 1999: 589)

Secondly, the use of the term is not an effort to purport an idea that is the binary opposition of the state manifestations at a supra or sub level because of the transformations that occur at a state level; not merely an alternative articulation of identity formations or legal orders in another transnational, international or even subnational context. Third, in the context of the EU, the institutional dimension of the analysis departs from a narrow-minded portrayal of power management within the integration of states, to a study of an 'emerging non state polity'. Nevertheless, apart from the institutional dimension, the nature and the structure of the community are of equal importance. Under the auspices of postnationalism, issues of identity, affinity and attribution – the main characteristics of political communities – are investigated through the lenses of pluralism and com-plementarity rather than in monocultural, monolinguistic, and particular-istic terms.

In sum, a postnational apprehension of the legal power within the European context sustains ' a complex of overlapping interpenetrating or intersecting normative systems or regimes, amongst which relations of authority are unstable, unclear, contested or in the course of negotiation' (Cotterrell 1998: 381).

Constitutional patriotism

Habermas has written extensively on constitutional patriotism in an effort 'to rescue law and democracy from their supposedly permanent tension' (1996: 99). In this vein:

> constitutional patriotism elicits a post-national and rights-based type of allegiance, a sense of allegiance that is not derived from pre-political values and attachments stepped in a culture, tradition or way of life, but from a set of principles and values that are universal in their orientation, albeit contextualised, […] it elicits support and emotional attachment, because the universalistic principles are embedded in a particular context […] in which a set of universal principles are interpreted and entrenched within a particular institutional context. (Habermas 1996: 282)

In other words, the nature and the content of legal/constitutional norma-tive regulation should integrate the collective self-understanding of a particular, historical community with the universal criteria of rational legitimacy. Habermas suggests that

> discourses aimed at achieving self understanding are also an important component of politics. In such discourses, the participants want to get clear understanding of themselves as members of a specific nation, as members of a local community, as inhabitants of a region […] But […] the question that has priority in legislative politics is how a matter can be regulated in the equal interests of all […] Unlike ethical questions, questions of justice are not inherently related to a specific collectivity and its form of life. The law

of a concrete legal community must, if it is to be legitimate at least be compatible with moral standards that claim universal validity beyond the legal community (1996: 284).

For Habermas therefore, the structure of a political community is based on the possibility of intersubjective communication where people are able to recognise the contingency of particular norms and use their rationality to move beyond them. Relating constitutional patriotism to the EU polity, the proposal for a European consensus on principles of constitutional democracy, is the creation of an ethical discourse that is context-transcending and opens up the boundaries of a postnational polity.

For the dedicated advocates of the concept of constitutional patriotism, like Ferrajoli who combines the Habermasian concept with the particularities of the European Union,

> The sole democratic foundation of the unity and cohesion of a political system is its constitution, and the type of allegiance it alone can generate – the so called 'constitutional patriotism'. For this reason, it seems to me that the future of Europe as a political entity depends to a great extent on developing a constituent process open to public debate, aimed at framing a European constitution. (1996: 157)

Although it is a fascinating idea that constitutional politics could transform the understandings and the perceptions of citizens as they participate and communicate with each other for the construction of conditions of democracy, freedom and equality, it still is an ideal normative model of analysis. But, in order to be fair to the writings of Habermas, he recognises the fact that he works within a theoretical framework that is a 'regulative ideal'. He never said that we have already reached this ideal, nor that it is essential or even possible to obtain this goal (Mouffe 1996: 64). Rather, he argues that we should act and base our moral judgements as if this model of society is the representation of a perfect society. So, practically we are dealing with a dualism of a perfect society that lies on idealistic foundations and a real one that should identify its failures and pursue a more democratic way of living based on its ideal-type structure. The problematic task, though, appears to be that in an effort to secure an ideal model of society, Habermas has dismissed the power relations and antagonisms that constitute the political completely. In other words, as Mouffe has suggested, Habermas searches in vain for a view point 'above politics from which one could guarantee the superiority of democracy' (Mouffe 1994: 112).

However, if we want to be more pragmatic as well as more political, and overcome the obstacle of a supposedly rational consensus, then we should try to retrieve an alternative mode of understanding and doing constitutional politics in the EU.

Constitutionalism, postnationalism and radical forms of democracy

By departing from the Habermasian conceptualisation of a transcendental solution to the puzzle of constitutional democracy, one can integrate elements of radical democratic pluralism with the indeterminate transformations of a political community. We will begin our analysis with the work of James Tully, who has outlined the contours of an approach, which can be appropriated for the case of the European constitution. It shows how the premises of modern constitutionalism should be based on a discursive process and not on the essentialism of static constitutional arrangements.

For Tully,

> A constitution should be seen as a form of activity, an intercultural dialogue in which the culturally diverse sovereign citizens of contemporary societies negotiate agreements on their forms of association over time in accordance with three conventions of mutual recognition, consent and cultural community. (1995: 30)

Following his line of argumentation, it is understood that the plurality of political identities, values, traditions and ideas should be celebrated in an agonistic model of constitutional democracy. As he criticises the global juridification of economic freedom, the decline of democratic deliberation and decision-making within the representative institutions of the nation-state, as well as growing political apathy, he argues that 'these trends work together to insulate the global social and economic inequalities from public democratic discussion and reform' (Tully 2002: 217). Tully finds problematic both the neo-liberal Third Way advocated by thinkers like Giddens (1998), with the global fatalism that presents liberal democracy as the only way of political philosophy, and the Habermasian notion of transcendental rationalism. He claims that their mistake was to assume that the scope of political philosophy was to 'develop a comprehensive theory of justice or of procedures of public reasoning within which citizens themselves could reach agreement on definitive constitutional principles' (2002: 217). Tully argues that their positions have been criticised by a more agonistic and negotiated form of political dialogue which provides more space and recognition for the needs of our pluralistic global political communities. By deconstructing the constitutional essentials to any overall framework of fundamental principles of justice, and by supporting a negation of any transcendental solutions, the horizon of political possibilities is left contested and open for never-ending experimental practices. In this vein, he observes that:

> The orientation of practical philosophy should not be to reaching final agreements on universal principles or procedures, but to ensuring that constitutional democracies are always open to the democratic freedom of calling into question and presenting reasons for the renegotiation of the prevailing rules of law, principles of justice and practices of deliberation. Hence the first and perhaps the only universalizable principle of democratic deliberation is audi alteram partem 'always listen to the other side' for there is always something to be learned from the other side. (2002: 219)

Returning to the EU's constitutional and politico-legal evolution, we will turn to the framework developed by Kalypso Nicolaïdis who argues for the 'idea of a European demoi-cracy as a radical version of post-national thinking, which takes to their ultimate logic the implications of pluralism and the rejection of identity politics in the EU context'(2004: 81). Departing from the constraints of liberalism and cosmopolitical visions of a European utopia that neglects the presence and the demands of the others, she calls for a different vision for Europe that echoes the ideas of Balibar on the 'intermediary, transitory and dialogic' (2003: 313) role of Europe. By criticising the conventional modes of constitutional thinking, Nicolaïdis proposes 'three consecutive moves [...] First from common identity to the sharing of identities, secondly from a community of identity to a community of projects; and finally from multi level governance to multi-centred governance' (2004: 81).

Concerning identity, what is proposed is the transformation of Europe into a community where the respect and recognition of others will inform our political decisions and behaviours on the basis of an 'informed curiosity about the political lives of our neighbours and mechanisms for our voices to be heard in each other's forums [where] a multinational politics should emerge from the confrontation, mutual accommodation and mutual inclusion of our respective political cultures' (Nicolaïdis 2004: 81). Similarly, as Nicolaïdis pinpoints: 'the draft Constitution makes it amply clear that this political community does not rest on a shared identity, as is usually assumed with nation-states, but on shared projects and objectives' (2004: 82); then we should shift our focus to create a polity which stresses the importance of 'doing more than being' collectively. In other words, it is an EU that will advance the political in multifaceted, voluntary and differentiated ways rather than essentialist and holistic understandings of identity formations. Finally, a radical perception of constitutionalism:

> consists in translating an ethos of mutual recognition of identities and shared projects into legal and institutional terms. A demoi-cracy should not be based on a vertical understanding of governance, with supranational constitutional norms trumping national ones and supranational institutions standing above national ones. Instead, our demoi-cracy ought to be premised on the horizontal sharing and transfer of sovereignty. It involves a dialogue rather than a hierarchy between different legal or political authorities such as constitutional courts, national and European parliaments, national and European executives. (Nicolaïdis 2004: 83)

Combining these two insights, it is clear that constitutionalism is not about forging a teleological politico-legal evolution, but about proposing a different constitutionalism which advances an intercultural dialogue and a continuous process of negotiation and renegotiation based on social action. As was mentioned above, the values that should underpin common constitutionalism, informed by Tully's analysis, are those of mutual recognition, consent and cultural continuity. Thus, in the context of the EU Convention, as a gesture of mutual recognition, respect for difference and against assimilatory practices, the people of Europe should have been offered the opportunity to express their ideas, demands and even disagreements on the text as well as the procedures that furnish the production of the EU constitution. Moreover, following the intellectual framework of Nicolaïdis, the Convention should have abandoned the idea of singleness and unity, in favour of a search for mutual opening and mutual recognition of identities, identities that are not characterised by a restrictive monadic or exemplary trope of existing, but by a plural, diverse and conflictual trope of decision and action.

CONCEPTS OF EUROPEAN IDENTITY

As we have noted in previous chapters, the concept of identity is a vital one for citizenship. As we have seen above, questions and debates on the European constitution inherently involve issues concerning European identity. In the past ten years there has been a considerable body of literature devoted to the question of European identity. Is there a European identity? Does a European identity have to supplant the national ones? Can it transform them? Can a European identity be a postnational type of identity? All these issues have to be taken into consideration within their specific theoretical and empirical context in order to understand the complexity that characterises the quest for a European identity. In the following section we will explore what vision of Europe is being used and what European identity is being constituted in the construction of the European Union.

Europe of unity in diversity

The fundamental declaration 'Concerning European Identity', which was agreed at the 1973 Copenhagen summit by the, then, nine member states, stated that

> the Nine member countries of the European Communities have decided that the time has come to draw up a document on the European Identity. This will enable them to achieve a better definition of the relations with other countries and of their responsibilities and the place they occupy in world affairs. (CEC 1973)

The Copenhagen Declaration strongly emphasised the 'common European civilisation' based on a 'common heritage' and 'converging' approaches to life. This was the first institutional effort to create an official European identity with specific characteristics:

> The diversity of cultures within the framework of common European civilisation, the attachment to common values and principles, the increasing convergence of attitudes to life, the awareness of having specific interests in common and the determination to take part in the construction of a united Europe, all give the European identity its originality and its own dynamism. (CEC 1973)

They also decided to 'define the European Identity with the dynamic nature of the Community in mind' and they had

> the intention of carrying the work further in the future in the light of the progress made in the construction of a United Europe. Defining the European identity involves reviewing the common heritage, interests, and special obligations of the Nine, as well as the degree of the unity so far achieved within the Community. (CEC 1973)

Since Copenhagen, identity has appeared in a plethora of documents. The Tindermans Report on European Union in 1975 refers to a 'People's Europe' that is evident in the 'concrete manifestations of the European solidarity in everyday life' (CEC 1976). In 1983 in Stuttgart the heads of government signed the Solemn Declaration on European Union and invited the member states to advance 'European awareness and to undertake joint action in various cultural areas' (CEC 1983). Thus, the Commission began to promote cultural initiatives 'in order to affirm the awareness of a common cultural heritage as an element of European identity' (Shore 2000: 45). In this vein, the domain of culture becomes a central element that could raise consciousness and is used in many EU approaches. More specifically, there is a development of policy initiatives in education and training programmes that denote the importance of cultural cohesion. For example, the 1984 Television Without Frontiers Directive stressed the connection between integration and European cultural identity:

> Information is decisive, perhaps the most decisive, factor in European unification [...] European Unification will only be achieved only if Europeans want it. Europeans will only want it if there is such thing as European identity. A European identity will only develop if Europeans are adequately informed. At present, information via the mass media is controlled at national level. (cited in Shore 2000: 45)

At the European Council meeting in Fontainbleau, in 1984, the European Council considered it vital for the Commission to 'respond to the expectations of the people of Europe by adopting measures to strengthen and promote its identity and its image both for citizens and for the rest of the world' (CEC 1985). An *ad hoc* Committee was formed to prepare and put forward this idea. One of the main tasks of the Committee was to introduce symbols like a flag, an anthem, and European sport teams in order to enhance the European identity. Moreover, the Committee under the chairmanship of Pietro Adonnino, MEP, presented two reports in 1985 which included the strategies devoted to the promotion of the 'Idea of Europe'. Among these strategies, there were proposals for a European Academy of Science, school exchange programmes and a stronger European dimension in education.

The Commission, as the supranational institution of the EU, embraced these efforts and took a step further by stressing the importance of a new set of symbols that could be used for publicising the principles and the values upon which the Community is based. The Commission has argued that:

> Symbols play a key role in the consciousness-raising, but there is also a need to make the European Citizen aware of the different elements that go to make up his European identity, of our cultural unity with all its diversity of expression, and of the historic ties which links the nations of Europe. (CEC 1988)

One of the first strategies that had a symbolic character was the creation of a new emblem and flag that was hoisted outside the Commission headquarters at a formal ceremony in May 1986. The flag depicts a circle of twelve yellow stars set against a blue background, and the rationale is explained by the Council of Europe as the following:

> Twelve was a symbol of perfection and plenitude, associated with the apostles, the sons of Jacob, the tables of the Roman legislator, the labours of Hercules, the hours of the day, the months of the year, or the signs of the Zodiac. Lastly the circular layout denoted union. (Shore 2000: 47)

Moreover, the circle with the twelve gold stars is a Christian symbol representing the Virgin Mary's halo, and according to the Commission this is 'the symbol par excellence of European identity and European unification' (CEC 1988). Other symbols presented by the Committee for the make-up of European identity were the creation of a European passport, driving licence and car number plates as well as a European anthem and European stamps. Cultural symbolic references included the creation of the EC Youth Orchestra, the Opera centre, the European Literature Prize and over one thousand Jean Monnet Awards.

Furthermore, the Commission created days and months of commemoration like the European Weeks, the European Cultural Months and a series of European Years dedicated to EC-chosen themes. In this vein, 9 May, the anniversary of the Schuman Plan, was chosen as the official Europe Day that celebrates the significant historical moment of European integration.

This climate of unity has dramatically changed from 1990 and onwards. This cultural turn is clearly manifested in the Maastricht Treaty. The introduction of the 'Cultural article' (Article 128) states: 'The Community shall contribute to the flowering of the cultures of the Member States, while respecting their national and regional diversity and at the same time bringing the common cultural heritage to the fore' (CEC 1992). Related to this was the creation of a regional policy that was highly influential in shaping the EU's cultural policy and became an important basis of integration. Cultural programmes such as the Capital of Culture Award focused their attention from unity to diversity and regional policy tended to embrace these notions of diversity (Sassatelli 2002).

The adoption of a complex discourse of 'unity in diversity', recently chosen as the official motto of the EU, shows its adjustment to the wider discourses of globalisation, significant migration and national conflicts. This is expressed differently in the current framework of the EU which combines a liberal notion of universalistic values and a respect for diversity. For example, the Council of Europe, with a certain focus on human rights, stresses its commitment to unity in diversity with a touch of universalism. According to the official statement: 'diversity lies at the heart of Europe's cultural richness, which is our common heritage and the basis of our unity' (Sassatelli 2002: 29).

The choice of 'unity in diversity' is quite problematic as the EU has to present a common European identity that is distinctively European, which at the same time does not undermine national or regional identities. Romano Prodi, the former President of the European Commission, argues that

> Europe's destiny is not inherently Eurocentric, but one of universality and this universality should aspire a new cultural unity. This new unity must acknowledge 'otherness' and the ability of cultures to live together: This means the mutual acceptance among European of their cultural diversity. (2000: 46–7)

To draw onto the positions on European identity and of the relationship between unity and diversity, it is possible to discern four arguments. The first stresses the historical heritage of Greco-Roman and Christian culture. It is founded on the spirit of compromise and the love of freedom. Europe under this prism is conceptualised with a spirit or ethos of liberty and this is portrayed in the Euro-federalist literature that tries to combine notions of an underlying unity and a tolerance for diversity (Delanty and Rumford 2005). The second approach sees unity by overcoming differences. This is a project very popular with EU policy makers and it is manifested in cultural policies like the Cities of Culture programme and other cultural programmes supported by the Commission (Sassatelli 2002). The third position emphasises diversity where a plurality of national and regional cultures is recognised and its interaction is promoted. This view characterises the broad stance of the Council of Europe that perceives unity as the recognition of diversity (Van Ham 2001). The fourth position is inextricably linked with the work of Habermas who argues that a European identity should be related to values that can be internalised by all Europeans (1992). In this vein, the only common values are the constitutional ones because of the risks of nationalism and the divisionary practices of culture. Unity here is expressed in a limited universalism of values like critique and reflexivity where communicative structures balance out unity and diversity.

The much sited motto of the EU, 'unity in diversity', will be problematised in the following section, as it does not escape from the dilemma of universalism and particularism and re-invents exclusionary meanings and practices that marginalize the other. To the extent that this rhetoric promotes superfluous acceptance of the diversity in Europe and a xenophobic discourse where the unity of Europe consists in the separation of people in different cultures, it does not take into account discourses that are related to the political issues that constitute the identities of European people. This suggests that a European identity is articulated in discourses that are not referring to diversity or unity but to the political.

Community without community

The appeal to the 'common values and roots' of the European citizens 'as a key element of their identity and their membership of a society founded on freedom, democracy, tolerance and solidarity' (www.europa.eu.int 2000) certainly serves as an ideational support of the unification project. This effort to create a European identity aims to exclude the different. As Derrida reminds us, 'pure unity [...] is a synonym of death' (Caputo 1997: 13). In other words, an open identity cannot flourish without attending to the coming of difference.

The work of Jacques Derrida constitutes a challenging and alternative way of thinking about identity and European identity. Derrida asserts an aversion to the word community as well to the thing itself. His primary concern for the word relates to its connotations of fusion and identi-fication. Caputo analyses these meanings with reference to Derrida's etymological examination of community.

> Communio is a word for military formation and a kissing cousin of the word 'munitions': to have a communio is to be fortified on all sides, to build a 'common' (com) 'defence' (munis), as when a wall is put up around the city to keep the stranger or the foreigner out. The self-protective closure of 'community' then, would be just about the opposite of [...] preparation for the incoming of the other, 'open' and 'porous' to the other [...] A 'universal community' excluding no one is a contradiction in terms; communities always have an inside and an outside. (Caputo 1997: 108)

Thus, the word community is constructed on notions of 'us' versus 'them', and every use of the 'we' in this context should be problematised because it connotes the exclusion of the other.

Taking this discussion a bit further, we will argue that the homogeneous and self-identical notion of European identity is perilous as it closes all the passages for the coming of the other. This notion is developed by Jacques Derrida in his book entitled *The Other Heading* where he deconstructs the idea of an impermeable European identity by opening it up to difference. Accordingly, he argues that

> what is proper to a culture is not to be identical to itself. Not to not have an identity, but not to be able to identify itself, to be able to say 'me' or 'we'; to be able to take the form of the subject only in the non-identity to itself or, if you prefer, only in the difference *with itself*. (Derrida 1992: 9)

Thus, rigid and fixed notions of identity can't encapsulate the multiplicity of identifications and more importantly limit our understandings of identity formations.

For Derrida, the idea of Europe and European identity has to be internally differentiated in order to destabilise the 'we', because '"We" are those who cannot completely say "we", who cannot settle into being *chez soi*, at home with themselves. Whatever institutes community and identity, at the same time "forbids it from collecting itself" together' (Derrida 1995: 355). This is not a negation of identity but it is an invention of identity with a culture of self-differentiation, of differing with itself, where identity is an effect of difference. In other words,

> it is always in the figure of Western heading and of the final headland or point that Europe determines and cultivates itself; it is in this figure that Europe identifies itself, identifies with itself, and thus identifies its own cultural identity, in the being-for-itself of what is most proper to it, in its own difference as difference with itself, difference to itself that remains with itself, close to itself. Yes, difference *with itself, with the self*, that is maintained and gathered in its own difference, in its difference from-with [d'avec] the others, if one can say this, as difference to itself, different from itself for itself, in the temptation, risk, or chance of keeping at home (with itself) the turbulence of *with*, of calming it down in order to make it into a simple, interior border – well guarded by the vigilant sentinels of being. (Derrida 1992: 25–6)

The question of opening up to the other, of opening oneself to difference entails breaking with self-referential and essentialist notions of identity. The repetition and commemoration of values and principles of the EU as 'an area of freedom, security and justice' that valorises 'liberty, democracy and respect for human rights and fundamental freedom and of the rule of law' (EU 1997) is a discourse of exemplarity, a discourse of traditional modernity as well as a discourse of finality. But it is possible to conceptualise a European identity that integrates the heritage of the modern tradition with a sense of responsibility towards the other. As Derrida argues,

> It is necessary to make ourselves the guardians of an idea of Europe, of a difference of Europe, but of a Europe that consists precisely in not closing itself off in its own identity and in advancing itself in an exemplary way toward what is not. (1992: 29)

The articulation of difference within culture in *The Other Heading* for Derrida is the recognition of the other. He uses the navigational term as in the heading of a ship or a plane. Thus, it is an effort to acknowledge the heading of the other, to recognise and accept others that are heading elsewhere than we are. Moreover, the term is used as a 'delimitation of the idea of "planning ahead" in favour of an openness to the future that does without the guardrails of a plan, of a teleological orientation' (Caputo 1997: 116). By conceptualising a culture of identity that is characterised by a teleological development as well as by an inscribed arche, then this archeoteleological unity renders identity back to itself.

A European identity that is defined within the rationality of ancient Greek philosophy and the Western modern philosophy of Hegel establish notions of identity that are self-referential. For example, the Greek *logos* and its legacy for justice are inextricably linked with the clarity and beauty of presence and sameness, of order and totality where the rule of reason excludes any other and only ever finds itself. Derrida follows this fundamental accusation from its origins to its accomplishments in the philosophical positions of Hegel. Within Hegel's work, the dialectical notion of unity in difference is archeoteleological all the way. 'The self-presence of absolute knowledge and the consciousness of Being-near-to-itself in logos, in the absolute concept, will have been distracted from themselves only for the time of detour' (Derrida 1982: 71). The spirit loses itself only to better find itself again, it alters itself only to better identify itself: 'this way out of itself is the obligatory route of a return to itself' (Derrida 1982: 74). In this way, the self re-appropriates for itself any exterior strangeness thanks to an idealising and sublimating interiorisation which in the end leads everything back to peace, security and mastery of the 'at home-with-itself' that can never really lose itself. Thus, it never stops returning the other to the same, assimilating it, consuming it by taking it back to the self.

For Derrida, though, there is no essentialism or telos but only *différance*. Such a gesture takes into account all the unrecoverable resistances inscribed in itself, an outside always already within the inside, the other at the heart of the same, a stranger that never ceases to inhabit and work in the familiar order that excludes it, a stranger that comes to 'mine it like its proper stranger, to hollow it into an abyss from the vantage of an origin more original than it and independent of it, older than it within it' (Derrida 1987: 317–18). The movement of *différance* signals the index of an irreducible exterior, of a radical heterogeneity of the irreducibility of the other in its absoluteness, such that it can no longer integrate in a system. Here, we are dealing with something that can no longer be assimilated or integrated. It is an effort to produce in the discourse of sameness an 'otherwise', a modality without essence that never ceases to interrupt it in order to open it up for responsibility, in order to force it to accept the incommensurability of the Other. Thus, by deconstructing any logic of re-establishing mastery, we 'leave room for the incalculable, which attempts to calculate everything so that calculation should not get the better of everything' (Derrida 1991: 25). Because, in order to intervene in the logic of position is neither to substitute oneself for it nor to be opposed to it, but to open up 'another relation, a relation without relation, or without the basis of comparison' (Derrida 1987: 200). In affirming that 'différance is not a process of propriation in any sense whatever', it means as well that 'it is neither position (appropriation) nor negation (expropriation) but rather other' (Derrida 1982: 26). This logic is neither oppositional nor identifying, neither dualistic nor monistic or dialectic. It is a paradoxical logic of alterity, interruption or *différance*, which is neither contradiction nor separation. Thus, in out-playing a never-accomplished gesture, the mastery of the same that pretends to give reason with its other by positioning it within the interior of dialectic totality, tries to write itself another logic, a logic of the Other. It is the very thought of the Other that relativises the coherent discourse of the whole and any philosophical position of being.

To sum up, Derrida criticises the essentialist notions of identity because individuals constitute themselves by exposing themselves to the other in a relationship. Likewise

> these singular beings are themselves constituted by sharing, they are distributed and placed, or rather *spaced*, by the sharing that makes them *others*: other for one another, and other, infinitely other for the Subject of their fusion, which is engulfed in the sharing. (Nancy 1991: 25)

This dramatic breaking up with the teleological and autochthonous discourse of modernity is necessary for Europe so as not to close itself within its own identity and head towards the other.

ANOTHER EUROPEAN IDENTITY?

How is it possible to conceptualise a European identity that differs with itself? The first step is the recognition of the plurality of forms of being and the avoidance of teleological or eschatological conceptions of the political. If we base our decisions on a certain knowledge that is set on the advance or on the implementation of a programme then there is no room for experimentation and invention. Without the possibility of the invention we will end up in totalitarian notions of the political. In this vein, 'one must therefore try to invent gestures, discourses, politico-institutional practices that inscribe the alliance of these two imperatives'

(Derrida 1992: 44): the political decisions and the ethical responsibility to the other.

Today, for example, the projection of a unified concept of a cultural European identity is a simple particularity.

> The logical schema of this argument, the backbone of this national self-affirmation, the nuclear statement of the national 'ego' or 'subject' is to put it dryly: 'I am (we are) all the more national for being European, all the more European for being trans-European and international; no one is more cosmopolitan and authentically universal than the one, than this 'we', who is speaking to you. (Derrida 1992: 48)

Following this logic, Derrida argues that nationalism and internationalism are quite similar in their practices. This is manifested quite clearly in the examination of international organisations that are controlled by the largest and richest nations and advance notions on the universal notions of humanity that are quite particularistic. Europe, then, in these terms becomes responsible for the universe; for human rights and international law. This is manifested in the use of meta-narratives that ground Europe as the chosen and destined guardian of the Being, or Spirit or History. This dogmatism of identity should be avoided by experimenting with *différance* and *experience the impossible*. It is the 'impossible', as Europe should cultivate an identity that respects *différance* based on non-monologic accounts of it. This means that 'Europeans need to cultivate cooperation while avoiding "monopoly", a translation of their differences into a single over-arching standardisation' (Caputo 1997: 120). This apparent aporia calls for a genuine responsibility towards the other: a responsibility that constitutes moments of political decision where teleological solutions are not acceptable as they close the identity to itself. As Derrida argues:

> The value of universality here capitalises all the antinomies, for it must be linked to the value of *exemplarity* that inscribes the universal in the proper body of singularity, of an idiom or a culture, whether this singularity be individual, social, national, state, federal, confederal, or not. Whether it takes a national form or not, a refined, hospitable or aggressively xenophobic form or not, the self-affirmation of an identity always claims to be responding to the call of assignation of the universal. There are no exceptions to this law. No cultural identity presents itself as the opaque body of an untranslatable idiom, but always, on the contrary, as the irreplaceable *inscription* of the universal in the singular, the *unique testimony* to the human essence and to what is proper to man. (1992: 72–3)

But the acceptance of a genuine responsibility marks the acceptance of 'experience and experiment of the possibility of the impossible: the testing of the aporia from which one may invent the only possible invention, the impossible invention' (Derrida 1992: 41). Likewise, Europe has to open itself 'onto the *other shore of another heading*', in the very experience and experiment of the other,

> it has to begin to open itself, or rather to let itself open, or, better yet, to be affected with opening *itself* onto an other, onto an other that the heading can no longer even relate to itself as its other, *the other with itself*. (Derrida 1992: 76)

How is it possible to proceed towards an opening of itself to the other heading? First of all, it is an opening towards the one that 'never was and never will be Europe' (Derrida 1992: 77). It is an opening to the foreigners that are living in Europe. This opening is not a synonym for integration or assimilation but a recognition of their alterity and an invitation to cross our threshold. By avoiding teleological and self-enclosing notions of identity and community and by criticising efforts to do so, then the 'impossible' becomes possible. The impossibility to move beyond the uniqueness of our conceptualisations on democracy or justice or law, the impossibility to recognise and accept 'differences, idioms, minorities, singularities but also the universality of formal law, the desire for translation, agreement and univocity, the law of majority, opposition to racism nationalism and xenophobia' (Derrida, 1992: 78).

The above statement may seem paradoxical but it is exactly these antinomies that should be kept alive in any articulation of identity or community if we want to be genuine towards the Other. The difficulty here is to endure these antinomies and not try to resolve them by promoting assimilating policies or projects. It is a call for responsibility, 'for the responsibility to think, speak and act in compliance with this double contradictory imperative – a contradiction that must not be apparent or illusory antinomy but must be effective and, *with experience, through experiment*, interminable' (Derrida 1992: 79). The affirmation of 'responsibility', 'ethics', or 'decision' should never be based on pre-given or pre-planned programmes. It cannot be a matter of an already acquired knowledge, but of a genuine gesture towards the other. The Other than we, its shore, cannot be reached as it is the One that we do not know.

CONCLUSION

European citizenship represents a new legal reality that challenges the conventional link between stateness and citizenship and plausibly has radical implications for the future of democracy. However, the legal aspect of citizenship is not the only one that we should encounter as the concept includes a person's economic, social, cultural and political status within a polity. It seems, though, that European citizenship in most academic and political debates has been defined as a rights-based status rather than as a participatory political status. These debates do not take into account that the three elements of citizenship (set of rights and duties, participation and identity) are inexorably linked resulting in an impoverishment of the concept that leads to an analogous limited praxis. The Constitutional Treaty did not manage to bridge the gap between citizenship and political participation, as it didn't include citizenship in the drafting of the constitutional principles. A notion of active citizenship that brings forward broad debates on a variety of European issues is not considered in the EU. Constitutional practices that are not a product of a bottom-up process based on political dialogue with actors from the entire political spectrum cannot support a viable democratic system. If the traditional way to link identity to political participation is the creation of nationality, in the case of the EU we have the chance to experience and experiment with more flexible identities, such an identity dimension of citizenship that respects the Other and ensures equal recognition and participation for the less privileged.

Conclusion

In the Introduction we outlined two key themes of the book: (1) that any assessment of citizenship in contemporary Europe is heavily dependent upon which theoretical conception of citizenship is held, and (2) that citizenship should be seen in a connected way, such that the links between the different facets of citizenship can be seen. In this conclusion we will return to these two themes and attempt to provide some kind of overall assessment. However, we are not trying to provide a simple concise statement as to the status of citizenship in Europe. There are a number of reasons for this. Firstly, as we noted from the beginning, the European countries we have considered here have different histories and cultural, social, economic and political values. We could not possibly expect a single trajectory from such disparity. Yet, in addition, as we have seen in the above chapters, there are a range of cross-cutting, sometimes contradictory processes surrounding citizenship *within* European countries (migration policy in Italy, for example). If there is a simple conclusion, it is that the politics of citizenship in contemporary Europe are vital, diverse and complex. We will begin by reviewing the arguments and information in the main chapters, before going on to emphasise the interwoven nature of citizenship by probing the interrelationships of the empirical aspects of citizenship we have considered.

Trends and patterns?

One can usefully distinguish between empirical and theoretical trends (or material and ideational trends), in terms of citizenship. Practically, of course, both remain irrevocably interwoven, but for heuristic purposes we might here temporarily separate them. It is, of course, interesting to examine the extent to which the trends that we might identify in empirical issues, such as welfare state reform, or political participation, correspond or do not correspond with changes (or indeed, lack of changes) in terms of how citizenship in Europe is viewed theoretically

Empirical trends

In the first chapter of the empirical section, we examined political participation. What is perhaps most striking is that, despite all the caveats made above, there is something like a general pattern discernible. The pattern that we found was, in many respects, a curious one. In most European countries, participation in formal, or traditional, politics was in decline. This meant that fewer people were voting and joining political parties but increasing numbers of people were active in less formal repertoires of political activity and engagement. These patterns can be seen as either a rejection of a staid liberal politics of representation and a reinvigoration of the public sphere and political participation; or as a worrying decline in mass civic engagement and the onset of a divide between almost totally unengaged citizens and extremely active citizens.

When examining the politics of the welfare state and social citizenship provision, again, there was a rough pattern to be discerned. For most European countries, despite the widely held notion that the welfare state is in retreat, an unaffordable luxury in a competitive global economy, the evidence we presented showed only moderate declines in welfare state provision. We found declines in the levels of unemployment and sickness benefits, generally beginning in the 1980s. Yet, these declines in benefits vary, with Sweden and Germany experiencing small cuts, slightly larger cuts in the Netherlands and Denmark, and the only major cuts being seen in the UK. Pensions, however, had become more generous since the 1970s. Whether these small cuts observed suggest that the welfare state continues to provide social citizenship rights, despite pressures for retrenchment, or represents the beginning of a much more fundamental reorganisation of social policy remains to be seen.

Migratory patterns exhibited a larger degree of diversity. In Chapter Six we noted that overall migration over the last ten years appeared to be increasing for some countries (Italy, Spain and the UK), decreasing in Germany, and holding at roughly the same kinds of levels in the remaining countries (Belgium, Denmark, France, the Netherlands and Sweden). The sources of migration were also rather different. For most of the countries considered, the main source of migration is labour market migration, with up to three quarters of this being related to free movement of EU citizens. The exceptions to this are France, Italy and the Netherlands, where family reunification plays a larger role. Perhaps the only general trend we can identify in terms of migration flows is that, since the turn of the millennium, asylum seekers constitute an ever smaller source of migration. This is probably, in no small part due to the moves, from most European governments, to discourage asylum seekers, which in turn, relates to the Europeanisation, and securitisation of migration.

The development of a European Citizenship shows that there is evidence of a growing Europeanisation of citizenship, but its development suggests that if it is not supported from below, *by European citizens*, it will continue to be fragile and undemocratic. The historical overview of the concept shows that the institutional system includes provisions and aspirations that can create challenges and opportunities for new practices and paradigms. However, the democratic transformation of the concept requires an active European civil society that brings forward different cultural, social and political values for constructing a more inclusive and democratic Union.

Theoretical trends

In the past, citizenship represented the relationship between the individual and the territorial nation-state. The citizen is the bearer of rights and duties who has a say in the rules and practices of governance. Indeed, for communitarians any effort to open up the political imagery and propose forms of political membership beyond the state is perceived as naïve and futile. Accordingly, people's affinities and solidarities are constructed within a particular locus, the community in which they live. The problem with the glorification of the community is that most of the time it is constructed on the basis of exclusion and marginalisation of the elements that are perceived as threatening to its 'cohesion' and 'uniformity'. For the non-citizens the liberal nation-state symbolises the denial of political participation and self-rule. Thus, as the concept of modern citizenship was based on the cross-cutting of nomos and demos, non-nationals find themselves silenced and disempowered.

Yet, moving beyond these ethical and political concerns, the emergence of European citizenship and of the transnationalisation of political and social life manifest that citizenship increasingly cannot be confined to the community of the nation-state. In this respect, postnational citizenship denotes the commitment to institutional experimentation, attentiveness to the demands of heterogeneous groups and opening up to new forms of political community. The ongoing development of EU citizenship, for example, and points to the ongoing questioning of 'the national' within conceptions of citizenship

THE INTERRELATED NATURE OF CITIZENSHIP

A key theme of this book has been to emphasise the interrelated nature of citizenship; the ways in which different elements of citizenship interact with one another. These interactions shape the nature of citizenship in any given country at any given moment in time. There are numerous inter-relationships involved with citizenship. In this conclusion, for heuristic purposes, we will examine six.

Political participation and the welfare state

We noted in the introduction that a few authors have sought to point to the impact that political participation has upon the welfare state and vice versa. The power resource literature (Esping-Andersen 1990; Korpi 1989) emphasises the role that the political mobilisation of the working class had upon the development of the welfare state. Feminist authors have argued that the nature of welfare state institutions has an impact upon women's citizenship in a very general sense, influencing their political mobilisation and not just their social status (Orloff 1993; Hernes 1988).

In Chapter Four we noted that some countries had higher levels of political participation. It is interesting to see, as we did when considering how such patterns and trends might be explained, that those countries with the highest levels of political participation and interest are also those countries with the most generous social citizenship provisions and lower levels of poverty and inequality (such as Sweden and Denmark). Conversely, those countries with higher levels of poverty and inequality also have lower levels of political participation and interest (such as the UK). One potential explanation for such a relationship revolves around the social norms which institutions espouse; more generous welfare state institutions propagate solidaristic norms, which in turn encourage partici-pation (see Rothstein 1998; Lister 2007). Esping-Andersen (1990: 141) notes that the welfare state is normally seen as the thing which requires explanation, the dependent variable. However, it is important to recognise that the institutions of the welfare state are also factors in multiple social and political relationships. To emphasise, the nature of social citizenship, instantiated through the welfare state, is interrelated with citizenship in a political sense. How citizens express themselves as political subjects impacts upon the nature of the welfare state. In turn, the nature of social citizenship rights and the institutions of the welfare state seems to impact upon the ways in which citizens express themselves as political subjects.

Political participation and migration

The growing numbers of migrants in many European countries renders the whole concept of 'national citizenship' increasingly obsolete. The distinction, though, between citizens and migrants, or even worse 'insiders' and 'outsiders', creates an unjust and undemocratic polity that denies to certain groups the right to act politically within the state where they reside. Many social movements like SOS racismo, Associazione Ricreativa e Culturale Italiana (ARCI), Frassanito, No borders, No One is Illegal, have stressed the importance of political self-determination for the migrants as exclusionary policies advance practices of discrimination and precarisation of labour. In this way, the struggle for recognition as political subjects becomes a key element in the politics of migration.

Political participation and EU citizenship

The growing number of transnational networks, formal and informal, that express their demands at the European level points to the complexity as well as the innovative practices of European citizenship. Its evolution manifests the multiple interactions among national institutions, supranational institutions, NGOs, and social movements in an effort to redefine political structures and to negotiate new sites of identification through common political involvement. This practice could stimulate recognition for cultural diversity and acceptance of pluralism as the basis for the building of a political Europe. The future development of European citizenship is intertwined with the development of such networks of participation

Welfare state and migration

There are complex interactions between welfare policies and migration in Europe. Popular discourse suggests that generous European welfare states act as a pull effect for migration to Europe. This assertion does not hold up particularly strongly to empirical scrutiny, however, as the countries we identified in Chapter Six with the highest increases in migration flows (Spain, Italy and the UK) are, in comparative terms, amongst the least generous welfare states. This aside, migration and welfare policies may be connected in other ways. For example, as we discussed in Chapter Five, in southern European welfare states, like Italy and Spain, the family bears a high degree of responsibility for care provision. In a context of rising female labour force participation (in part, itself required by falling birth rates and a shrinking working-age population) in such countries, much domestic care and labour is performed by migrants. As we noted in Chapter Six, such imperatives, generated by the nature of social citizenship provision in such countries, clash with public and partisan political rhetoric which seeks to limit migration. Nowhere is this more clearly seen than in the Bossa-Fini law, where a range of measures designed to stem, regulate and control migration were introduced alongside the largest regularisation of illegal migrants, who performed domestic caring roles, ever seen in Europe. Despite this, as Ryner (2001) notes, the incorporation of such migrants, particularly temporary migrants, into social citizenship settlements is difficult – yet, restricting access is also problematic. More serious than any fiscal costs, may be the damage done to solidarity in terms of social citizenship provision. As Rothstein (1998) notes, if citizens perceive that there are some who are gaining from the welfare state and not contributing fully, then solidarity and the social consensus is weakened and this, at least in ideational terms, contributes to arguments for retrenchment of the welfare state.

Welfare state and EU citizenship

In Chapter Five we explicitly considered the argument that one of the reasons that the welfare state in Europe faces pressures for retrenchment is the process of Europeanisation itself. A number of authors discussed above (Hay 2004; Korpi 2003; Pierson 2001a) point to the ways in which EMU and the Growth and Stability Pact have brought pressures for fiscal retrenchment on European welfare states. The market-building function of the European project may be threatening social protection, and at the same time, the EU seems incapable, certainly hitherto, of fulfilling any social goals (Scharpf 2002) which might be seen as real benefits of citizenship of the EU. It may be the case that the disparity that exists between progress made on market integration and market-building and progress (or lack of) made on social protection may be one factor as to why citizens of the EU do not feel particularly engaged with or by the EU, as witnessed in the low levels of political participation at European Parliament elections.

Migration and EU citizenship

In Chapters Six and Seven we noted the central role that questions of identity play both in European citizenship and the politics of migration. The EU increasingly plays a large role in the politics of migration in Europe. The creation of European citizens seems to have also created 'non-Europeans', those to be excluded, or if not excluded (when migrant labour is required), then not welcomed. As the case of Turkey's potential accession to the EU shows, in the process of European integration the question as to who is European seems to play a prominent role. Yet, alongside such exclusionary discourses and practices, the EU's legal framework offers migrants options and openings for a more pro-migrant, or migrant-inclusive agenda (Geddes 2000b; Hansen 2005). Questions around European citizenship and migration are intimately linked.

In terms of a concrete conclusion, we cannot provide a single concise narrative about citizenship in contemporary Europe. As we have demonstrated in the chapters of this book, citizenship in contemporary Europe is marked by diverse, cross-cutting, complex, and frequently contradictory policies and trends. There are some indications that citizenship in Europe is becoming a narrower category, in that the rights which it confers are in some cases reduced and in others made more conditional. Who is to be thought of as a citizen comes under ever closer scrutiny and political participation is, in a number of key ways, in decline. Yet, those last two points capture perfectly the somewhat quixotic nature of contemporary citizenship; a decline in formal participation dovetails with increases in informal participation and the development of transnational, European, networks of activists and campaigners. Also, whilst the question as to who is a citizen comes under ever closer scrutiny in an age of mass migration, many countries are relaxing or have relaxed their qualifications for citizenship. European citizenship, too, offers potential to expand citizenship in new directions and questions the link to the nation that citizenship traditionally had. Theoretically, we do not see the dominance of a single perspective. Rather, contemporary European polities are marked by the overlapping of different, even contradictory, ideas about citizenship. Liberal, communitarian, republican, feminist, multicultural and post-national ideas all find expression in contemporary Europe.

References

Alcock, P. (2006), *Understanding Poverty*, 3rd edn, Basingstoke: Palgrave.

Aldrich, J. H. (1993), 'Rational Choice and Turnout', *American Journal of Political Science*, 37, pp. 246–78.

Anderson, Uwe (1990), 'Consultative institutions for migrant workers', in Z. Layton Henry (ed.), *Political Rights of Migrant Workers in Western Europe*, London: Sage, pp. 113–26.

Appadurai, A. (1991), 'Global ethnoscapes: notes and queries for a transnational anthropology', in R. G. Fox (ed.), *Recapturing Anthropology: Working in the Present*, Santa Fe, NM: School of American Research Press, pp. 191–210.

Appadurai, A. (1993), 'Patriotism and its Futures', *Public Culture*, 5 (3), pp. 411–23.

Arendt, H. (1958), *The Human Condition*, Chicago: University of Chicago Press.

Arendt, H. (1963), *On Revolution*, London: Faber.

Arendt, H. (1967), *The Origins Of Totalitarianism*, 3rd edn, London: Allen and Unwin.

Arendt, H. (1968), *Men In Dark Times*, New York: Harvest Books.

Aristotle (1981), *The Politics* (ed.) E. Baker, Oxford: Oxford University Press.

D'Art, D and T. Turner (2007), 'Trade Unions and Political Participation in the European Union: Still Providing a Democratic Dividend?', *British Journal of Industrial Relations*, 45 (1), pp. 103–26.

Atkinson, A. B. and J. Micklewright (1989), 'Turning the Screw: Benefits for the unemployed, 1979–1988', in A. Dilnot and I. Walker (eds), *The Economics of Social Security*, Oxford: Oxford University Press, pp. 17–51.

Aziz, R. (1992), 'Feminism and the challenge of racism: deviance or difference?', in H. Crowley and S. Himmelweit (eds), *Knowing Women: feminism and knowledge*, London: Polity, pp. 291–305.

Bader, V. (1995), 'Citizenship and Exclusion: Radical Democracy, Community, and Justice. Or, What is Wrong With Communitarianism?', *Political Theory*, 23 (2), pp. 211–46.

Balibar, E. (2003), 'Europe: Vanishing mediator', *Constellations*, 10 (3), pp. 312–38.

Bambra, C. (2006), 'Decommodification and the worlds of welfare revisited', *Journal of European Social Policy*, 16 (1), pp. 73–80.

Barber, B. (1984), *Strong democracy: participatory politics for a new age*, Berkeley, CA: University of California Press.

Bardi, L. (1992), 'Italy', *European Journal of Political Research*, 22 (4), pp. 449–60.

Barry, B. (2001), *Culture and Equality: An Egalitarian Critique of Multiculturalism*, Cambridge: Polity.

Bauböck, R. (1994), *Transnational citizenship: Membership and rights in international migration*, Aldershot: Edward Elgar.

Bauböck, R. (2003), 'Towards a political theory of migrant transnationalism', *International Migration Review*, 37 (3), pp. 700–23.

Baudrillard, J. (1983), *In the Shadow of Silent Majorities or, The End of the Social and Other Essays*, New York: Semiotext(e).

Beckett, A. (2005), 'Reconsidering Citizenship in the Light of the Concerns of the UK Disability Movement', *Citizenship Studies*, 9 (4), pp. 405–21.

Bellamy, R. and D. Castiglione (1996), *Constitutionalism in transformation: European and theoretical perspectives*, Oxford: Blackwell.

Bellamy, R. and A. Warleigh (eds) (2001), *Citizenship and Governance in the European Union*, London: Continuum.

Bellamy, R., D. Castiglione and J. Shaw (2006), 'Introduction: From National to Transnational Citizenship', in R. Bellamy, D. Castiglione and J. Shaw (eds), *Making European Citizens. Civic Inclusion in a Transnational Context*, Basingstoke: Palgrave, pp. 1–30.

Belsey, C. (2002), *Poststructuralism: A Very Brief Introduction*, Oxford: Oxford University Press.

Berlin, I. (1969), *Four Essays on Liberty*, Oxford: Oxford University Press.

Beuchler, S. M. (1995), 'New Social Movement Theories', *The Sociological Quarterly*, 36 (3), pp. 441–64.

Bigo, D. (1994), 'The European International Security Field: Stakes and Rivalries in a Newly Developing Area of Police Intervention', in M. Anderson and M. den Boer (eds), *Policing across National Boundaries*, London: Pinter, pp. 161–73.

Bigo, D. (2001), 'Migration and Security', in V. Guiraudon and C. Joppke (eds), *Controlling a New Migration World*, London: Routledge, pp. 121–49.

Blair, T. and G. Schröder (1999), *Europe: The Third Way/Die Neue Mitte*, accessed at http://www.conscience-politique.org/international/thirdway.htm on 24/05/07.

Boli, J. and J. Thomas (eds) (1999), *Constructing World Culture: International Nongovernmental Organizations Since 1875*, Stanford, CA: Stanford University Press.

Bolten, J. (1991), 'From Schengen to Dublin: The New Frontiers of Refugee Law', in H. Meijer, J. J. Bolten and A. Cruz (eds), *Schengen. Internationalisation of Central Chapters of the Law of Aliens, Refugees, Privacy, Security, and the Police*, Antwerp: Kluwer, pp. 95–121.

Boyer, R. and D. Drache (eds) (1996), *States against markets: The limits of globalisation*, London: Routledge.

Brewer, M., A. Goodman, J. Shaw and A. Shephard (2005), *Poverty and Inequality in Britain: 2005*, London: The Institute for Fiscal Studies. Available at http://www.ifs.org.uk/comms/comm99.pdf

Brown, C. (1992), *International Relations Theory, New Normative Approaches*, New York: Columbia University Press.

Brown, C. (2000), 'On the Borders of (International) Political Theory', in N. O' Sullivan (ed.), *Political Theory in Transition*, London: Routledge, pp. 190–208.

Brubaker, R. (1992), *Citizenship and Nationhood in France and Germany*, Cambridge, MA: Harvard University Press.

Brunner v the European Treaty (1994) 31 Common Market Law Report, pp. 251–62.

Buonfino, A. (2004), 'Politics, Discourse and Immigration as a Security Concern in the EU: a tale of two Nations, Italy and Britain', Paper presented at the PSA Annual Conference in Lincoln, 5–8 April 2004.

Burk, J. (2000), 'The Citizen Soldier and Democratic Societies: A Comparative Analysis of America's Revolutionary and Civil Wars', *Citizenship Studies*, 4 (2), pp. 149–65.

Calabrese, A. (2005), 'Communication, global justice and the moral economy', *Global Media and Communication*, 1 (3), pp. 301–15.

Calhoun, C. (1991), 'Indirect Relationships and Imagined Communities: Large Scale Social Integration and the Transformation of Everyday Life', in P. Bourdieu and J. Coleman (eds), *Social Theory for a Changing Society*, Boulder, CO: Westview, pp. 95–121.

Campani, G. and A. De Bonis (2003), *Migration Policies in Italy*, available at http://www.emz-berlin.de/projekte_e/pj32_1pdf/MigPol/MigPol_Italy.pdf (accessed 04/06/07).

Caputo, J. D. (1997), *Deconstruction in a Nutshell: A Conversation with Jacques Derrida*, New York: Fordham University Press.

Carens, J. H. (1987), 'Aliens and Citizens: The Case for Open Borders', *Review of Politics*, 49 (2), pp. 251–73.

Carens, J. H. (1997), 'Liberalism and Culture', *Constellations*, 4 (1), pp. 35–47.

Castiglione, D. (1995), 'Contracts and Constitutions', in R. Bellamy, V. Bufacchi and D Castiglione (eds), *Democracy and Constitutional Culture*, London: Lothian Foundation Press, pp. 75–102.

Castles, F. G. (2004), *The Future of the Welfare State: Crisis Myths and Crisis Realities*, Oxford: Oxford University Press.

Castles, S. (2006), 'Guestworkers in Europe: A Resurrection?', *International Migration Review*, 40 (4), pp. 741–66.

Checchi, D. and J. Visser (2005), 'Pattern Persistence in Trade Union Density: A Longitudinal Analysis 1950–1996', *European Sociological Review*, 21 (1), pp. 1–21.

Childs, S. and M. L. Krook (2006), 'Should Feminists Give Up on Critical Mass? A Contingent Yes', *Politics and Gender*, 2 (4), pp. 522–30.

Clasen, J. and N. Siegel (eds) (2007), *Investigating Welfare State Change: The 'Dependent Variable Problem'*, in *Comparative Analysis*, Cheltenham: Edward Elgar.

Closa, C. (1998), 'Some Foundations for the Normative Discussion on Supranational Citizenship and Democracy', in U. K. Preuss and F. Requejo (eds), *European Citizenship, Multiculturalism, and the State*, Baden-Baden: Nomos Verlagsgessellschaft.

Closa, C. (1998), 'Supranational Citizenship and Democracy: Normative and Empirical Dimensions', in M. LaTorre (ed.), *European Citizenship: An Institutionalist Challenge*, The Hague: Kluwer, pp. 415–33.

Cohen, J. L. (1985), 'Strategy or Identity: New Theoretical Paradigms and Contemporary Social Movements', *Social Research*, 52 (4), pp. 663–716.

Cohen, J. L. (1999), 'Changing Paradigms of Citizenship and the Exclusiveness of the Demos', *International Sociology*, 14 (3), pp. 245–68.

Cohen, R. and S. Vertovec (1999), 'Introduction', in R. Cohen and S. Vertovec (eds), *Migration, Diasporas, and Transnationalism*, Cheltenham: Edward Elgar, pp. xiii–xxviii.

Colombo, A. and G. Sciortino (2004), 'Italian immigration: the origins, nature and evolution of Italy's migratory systems', *Journal of Modern Italian Studies*, 9 (1), pp. 49–70.

Commission of the European Communities [CEC] (1973), Bulletin of the European Community, no. 12-1973.

CEC (1974), Bulletin of the EC, 12-1974/7.

CEC (1976), Bulletin of the EC, Supplement 1/76.

CEC (1983), Bulletin of the EC, 6, 24.

CEC (1985), Bulletin of the EC, Supplement 7/85.

CEC (1988), Bulletin EC, Supplement 2/88.

CEC (1990), Bulletin of the EC, 6-1990.

CEC (1992), Treaty on the European Union, Luxemburg: Office for Official Publications of the European Communities.

CEC (2002), *Communication from the Commission to the Council and the European Parliament, Towards integrated management of the external borders of the member states of the European Union*, May 7, no. 233.

CEC (2003), *Communication from the Commission to the Council and the European Parliament, Wider Europe – Neighbourhood: A New Framework for relations with our Eastern and Southern Neighbours*, no. 104.

CEC (2003a), *Call for proposals 2003,Budget line: Co-operation with the Third Countries in the Area of Migration*.

CEC (2003b), *Communication from the Commission to the Council and the European Parliament in view of the European Council in Thessaloniki, On the development of a common policy on illegal immigration, smuggling and trafficking of human beings, external borders and the return of illegal residents*, June 3, no. 323.

CEC (2005), 'Report From The Commission To The Council, The European Parliament, The European Economic And Social Committee And The Committee Of The Regions on equality between women and men', Brussels: Commission of the European Communities.

Constant, B. ([1816] 1988), *Political Writings* (ed.) B. Fontana, Cambridge: Cambridge University Press.

Cotterrell, R. (1998), 'Why Must Legal Ideas Be Interpreted Sociologically', *Journal of Law and Society*, 25 (2), pp. 179–92.

Council Regulation (EC) no. 2725/2000 11/12/2000

Crick, B. (1999), 'The Presuppositions of Citizenship Education', *Journal of Philosophy of Education*, 33 (3), pp. 337–52.

d'Oliveira, J. (1995), 'Union Citizenship: Pie in the Sky?', in A. Rosas and E. Antola (eds), *A Citizens' Europe: In Search of a New Order*, London: Sage, pp. 58–84.

Dagger, R. (2002), 'Republican Citizenship', in E. F. Isin and B. S. Turner (eds), *Handbook of Citizenship Studies*, London: Sage, pp. 145–58.

Dahl, R. (1986), *Democracy, Liberty and Equality*, Oslo: Norwegian University Press.

De Tocqueville, A. ([1835-40] 2000), *Democracy in America*, Indianapolis, IN: Hackett Publishing Company.

Delanty, G. (2002), 'Communitarianism and Citizenship', in E. F. Isin and B. S. Turner (eds), *Handbook of Citizenship Studies*, London: Sage, pp. 159–74.

Delanty, G. and C. Rumford (2005), *Re-Thinking Europe: Social Theory and the Implications of Europeanisation*, London: Routledge.

Delanty, G. (2000), *Citizenship in a Global Age: Society, Culture, Politics*, Buckingham: Open University Press.

Della Porta, D. and M. Diani (1999), *Social Movements: An Introduction*, Oxford: Blackwell.

Derrida, J. (1982), *Margins of Philosophy*, Chicago: Chicago University Press.

Derrida, J. (1987), *The Post-Card: From Socrates to Freud and Beyond*, Chicago: Chicago University Press.

Derrida, J. (1992), *The Other Heading: Reflections on Today's Europe*, Bloomington, IN: Indiana University Press.

Derrida, J. (1995), *Points … Interviews 1974–1994*, Stanford, CA: Stanford University Press.

Di Pascale, A. (2002), 'The New Regulations on Immigration and the Status of Foreigners in Italy', *European Journal of Migration and Law*, 4 (1), pp. 71–7.

Dietz, M. (1998), 'Context Is All: Feminism and Theories of Citizenship', in A. Phillips (ed.), *Feminism and Politics*, Oxford: Oxford University Press, pp. 378–400.

Dilnot, A. W. and C. N. Morris (1983), 'Private Costs and Benefits of Unemployment: Measuring Replacement Rates', *Oxford Economic Papers*, 35 Supplement: The Causes of Unemployment, pp. 321–40.

Dolan, F. E. (2003), 'Battered Women, Petty Traitors, and the Legacy of Coverture', *Feminist Studies*, 29 (2), pp. 249–77.

Downs, A. (1957), *An Economic Theory of Democracy*, New York: Harper and Row.

Dryzek, J. (1996), 'Political Inclusion and the Dynamics of Democratization', *American Political Science Review*, 90 (3), pp. 475–87.

Dryzek, J. (2000), *Deliberative Democracy and Beyond: Liberals, Critiques, Contestations*, Oxford: Oxford University Press.

Duff, A. (1997), *The Treaty of Amsterdam: Text and Commentary*, London: Sweet and Maxwell/Federal Trust.

Elshtain, J. B. (1987), *Women and War*, Brighton: Harvester Press.

Elshtain, M. B. (1998), 'Antigone's Daughters', in A. Phillips (ed.), *Feminism and Politics*, Oxford: Oxford University Press, pp. 363–77.

Entzinger, H. (2003), 'The Rise and Fall of Multiculturalism: The Case of the Netherlands', in C. Joppke and E. Morawska (eds), *Toward Assimilation and Citizenship*, Basingstoke: Palgrave, pp. 59–86.

Esping-Andersen, G. (1990), *The Three Worlds of Welfare Capitalism*, Cambridge: Polity.

Etzioni, A. and J. H. Marsh (eds) (2003), *Rights vs. Public Safety after 9/11*, Oxford: Rowman and Littlefield.

Etzioni, A. (1995), *The Spirit of Community: rights, responsibilities and the communitarian agenda*, London: Fontana.

Etzioni, A. (2004), *The Common Good*, Cambridge: Polity.

EurActive (2004), 'European Parliament Elections 2004: Results', available at http://www.euractiv.com/en/elections/european-parliament-elections-2004-results/article-117482

European Commission (2000), Culture, accessed at http://europa.eu.int/comm/culture/culture

European Commission (2001), The Treaty of Nice: A Comprehensive Guide. Brussels.

European Convention (2002), Preliminary Draft Constitutional Treaty, CONV 369/02.

European Council (2001), The Future of the European Union: Laeken Declaration.

European Social Forum, presentation at www.indymedia.org (17.11.02).

European Social Forum, thematic organisation of the ESF at www.attac.org. (25.11.02).

European Union (1997), *Treaty of Amsterdam*, Preamble.

Everson, M. (1995), 'The Legacy of the Market Citizen', in J. Shaw and C. More (eds), *New Legal Dynamics of European Union*, Oxford: Clarendon Press, pp. 73–90.

Falk, R. (1994), 'The making of global citizenship', in B. Steenbergen (ed.), *The Condition of Citizenship*, London: Sage, pp. 127–40.

Faulks, K. (2000), *Citizenship*, London: Routledge.

Feder Kittay, E. (2000), 'A Feminist Public Ethic of Care Meets the New Communitarian Family Policy', *Ethics*, 111 (3), pp. 523–47.

Ferrajoli, L. (1996), 'Beyond Sovereignty and Citizenship: A Global Constitutionalism', in R. Bellamy (ed.), *Constitutionalism, Democracy and Sovereignty: American and European Perspectives*, Aldershot: Avebury, pp. 151–60.

Ferrera, M. (1996), 'The "Southern Model" of Welfare in Social Europe', *Journal of European Social Policy*, 6 (1), pp. 17–37.

Føllesdal, A. (1997), 'Do welfare obligations end at the boundaries of the Nation State?', in R. Koslowski and A. Føllesdal (eds), *Restructuring the Welfare State*, Berlin: Springer, pp. 145–63.

Fossum, E. (2003), 'Still a Union of Deep Diversity? The Convention and the Constitution for Europe', *ARENA Working Papers* at www.arena.uio.no.

Fox, J. (2005), 'Unpacking Transnational Citizenship', *Annual Review of Political*

Science, 8, pp. 171–201.

Franklin, J. (2000), 'What's wrong with New Labour politics?', *Feminist Review*, 66, pp. 138–42.

Franklin, M. (1996), 'Electoral Participation', in L. LeDuc, R. Niemi and P. Norris (eds), *Comparing Democracies: Elections and Voting in Global Perspective*, Thousand Oaks: Sage, pp. 148–68.

Franklin, M. (2001), 'How Structural Factors Cause Turnout Variations at European Parliament Elections', *European Union Politics*, 2001, 2 (3), pp. 309–28.

Fraser, E. and N. Lacey (1993), *The Politics of Community: A Feminist Critique of the Liberal-Communitarian debate*, Toronto: University of Toronto Press.

Galston, W. (1991), *Liberal Purposes: Goods Virtues and Duties in the Liberal State*, Cambridge: Cambridge University Press.

Garrett, G. (1998), *Partisan Politics in the Global Economy*, Cambridge: Cambridge University Press.

Geddes, A. (2000a), *Immigration and European Integration: Towards Fortress Europe*, Manchester: Manchester University Press.

Geddes, A. (2000b), 'Lobbying for migrant inclusion in the European Union: New Opportunities for Transnational Advocacy', *Journal of European Public Policy*, 7 (4), pp. 632–44.

Geddes, A. (2003), *The Politics of Migration and Immigration in Europe*, London: Sage.

Giddens, A. (1982), *Profiles and Critiques in Social Theory*, London: Macmillan.

Giddens, A. (1998), *The Third Way: Renewal of Social Democracy*, Cambridge: Polity.

Gilbert, N. (2004), *Transformation of the Welfare State: The Silent Surrender of Public Responsibility*, Oxford: Oxford University Press.

Goldirova, R. (2007), 'EU agrees rapid reaction anti-immigration units,' *EU Observer*, Brussels, 23 April 2007.

Goodin, R.E. (1988), 'What is So Special about Our Fellow Countrymen?', *Ethics*, 98 (4), pp. 663–86.

Goodin, R. E., B. Headey, R. Muffels and H. J. Dirven (1999), *The Real Worlds of Welfare Capitalism*, Cambridge: Cambridge University Press.

Green-Pedersen, C. (2004), 'The Dependent Variable Problem within the Study of Welfare State Retrenchment: Defining the Problem and Looking for Solutions', *Journal of Comparative Policy Analysis*, 6 (1), pp. 3–14.

Green, D. P. and I. Shapiro (1994), *Pathologies of Rational Choice Theory*, New Haven: Yale University Press.

Guiraudon, V. (2003), 'The Constitution of a European Immigration Policy Domain: A Political Sociology Approach', *Journal of European Public Policy*, 10 (2), pp. 263–82.

Gutmann, A. and D. Thompson (1996), *Democracy and Disagreement*, London: Belknap Press.

Haas, E. (1958), *The Uniting of Europe: Political, Social and Economic Forces, 1950–1957*, Stanford, CA: Stanford University Press.

Habermas, J. (1987), *Theory of Communicative Action*, Boston, MA: Beacon Press.

Habermas, J. (1992), 'Citizenship and National Identity: Some Reflections on the Future of Europe', *Praxis International*, 12 (1), pp. 1–19.

Habermas, J. (1996), *Between Facts and Norms: Contributions to a Discourse Theory of Law and Democracy*, Cambridge, MA: MIT Press.

Hagemann-White, C. (2007), 'Statement for the Panel "Elimination of all forms of violence against women: follow-up to the Secretary-General's in-depth study at national and international levels"', Presented to the *Commission on the Status of Women, United Nations*, accessed at http://www.un.org/womenwatch/daw/csw/csw51/panelvaw/Hagemann-VAW%20Panel.pdf

Hall, S. (1995), *Nationality, Migration Rights and Citizenship of the Union*, Dordrecht: Martinus Nijhoff.

Halligan, B. (1997), 'Issues for Ireland', in B. Tonra (ed.), *Amsterdam: What the Treaty Means*, Dublin: Institute of European Affairs.

Hamilton, A., J. Madison and J. Jay ([1788] 2003), *The Federalist Papers*, New York: Signet Classic.

Hansen, P. (2005), 'A Superabundance of Contradictions: The European Union's Post-Amsterdam Politics on Migrant "Integration", Labour Immigration, Asylum and Illegal Immigration', *ThemES - Occasional Papers and Reprints on Ethnic Studies*, no. 28.

Hansen, R. and J. Koehler (2005), 'Issue definition, political discourse and the politics of nationality reform in France and Germany', *European Journal of Political Research*, 44 (5), pp. 623–44.

Hay, C. and D. Marsh (eds) (2000), *Demystifying Globalization*, Basingstoke: Palgrave.

Hay, C. (1997), 'Divided by a Common Language: Political Theory and the Concept of Power', *Politics*, 17 (1), pp. 45–52.

Hay, C. (2002), *Political Analysis*, Basingstoke: Palgrave.

Hay, C. (2004), 'Common trajectories, variable paces, divergent outcomes? Models of European capitalism under conditions of complex economic inter-dependence', *Review of International Political Economy*, 11 (2), pp. 231–62.

Hay, C. (2006a), 'What's Globalization Got to Do with It? Economic Inter-dependence and the Future of European Welfare States', *Government and Opposition*, 41 (1), pp. 1–22.

Hay, C. (2006b), 'Globalization, Economic Change and the Welfare State: The "Vexatious Inquisition of Taxation"?', in C. Pierson and F. Castles (eds), *The Welfare State Reader*, 2nd edn, Cambridge: Polity, pp. 200–25.

Held, D. and A. Leftwich (1984), 'A Disciple of Politics', in A. Leftwich (ed.), *What is Politics?*, Oxford: Blackwell, pp. 139–59.

Held, D. (1995), *Democracy and the Global Order: From the Modern State to Cosmopolitan Governance*, Oxford: Polity.

Held, D. (2006), *Models of Democracy*, Cambridge: Polity.

Hernes, H. M. (1988), 'Welfare State Citizenship of Scandinavian Women', in K. Jones and A. Jonasdottir (eds), *The Political Interests of Gender*, London: Sage, pp. 187–213.

Heron, E. and P. Dwyer (1999), 'Doing The Right Thing: Labour's Attempt to Forge a New Welfare Deal Between the Individual and the State', *Social Policy and Administration*, 33 (1), pp. 91–104.

Herreros, F. (2004), *The Problem of Forming Social Capital: Why Trust?*, Basingstoke: Palgrave.

Hicks, A. (1999), *Social Democracy and Welfare Capitalism*, Ithaca, NY: Cornell University Press.

Hill, G. (1993), 'Citizenship and Ontology in the Liberal State', *The Review of Politics*, 55 (1), pp. 67–84.

Hills, J. (2004), *Inequality and the State*, Oxford: Oxford University Press.

Himmelfarb, G. (1974), *The Idea of Poverty: England and the Early Industrial Age*, New York: Alfred A. Knopf.

Hobhouse, L. T. ([1911] 1999), *Liberalism*, Kitchener, ON: Batoche.

Honig, B. (2001), 'Dead Rights, Live Futures', *Political Theory*, 29 (6), pp. 792–805.

hooks, b. (1981), *Aint I a woman? Black women and feminism*, Boston, MA: South End Press.

hooks, b. (1984), *Feminist Theory: From margin to center*, Boston, MA: South End Press.

Huysmans, J. (2000), 'The European Union and the Securitisation of Migration', *Journal of Common Market Studies*, 38 (5), pp. 751–77.

IDEA (2006), 'Voter Turnout by Gender', accessed at http://www.idea.int/gender/vt.cfm (accessed 28/06/06).

Inglehart, R. (1990), *Culture Shift in Advanced Industrial Society*, Princeton, NJ: Princeton University Press.

Inter-Parliamentary Union (2006), *Women in National Parliaments*, available at http://www.ipu.org/wmn-e/classif.htm.

Itzigsohn, J. (2000), 'Immigration and the boundaries of citizenship: the institutions of immigrants' political transnationalism', *International Migration Review*, 34 (4), pp. 1126–54.

Jackman, R. W. (1987), 'Political Institutions and Voter Turnout in the Industrial Democracies', *American Political Science Review*, 81 (2), pp. 405–24.

Jacobs, L., B. Barber, L. Bartels, M. Dawson, M. Fiorina, J. Hacker, R. Hero, H. Heclo, C. J. Kim, S. Mettler, B. Page, D. Pinderhughes, K. L. Schlozman, T. Skocpol, and S. Verba (2004), 'American Democracy in an Age of Rising Inequality', *Task Force in Inequality and American Democracy*, American Political Science Association. Available at http://www.apsanet.org/imgtest/taskforcereport.pdf.

Jefferson, T. (1999), *Thomas Jefferson: Political Writings* (eds) J. Appleby and T. Ball, Cambridge: Cambridge University Press.

Jileva, E. (2002), 'Visa and free movement of labour: the uneven imposition of the EU acquis on the accession states', *Journal of Ethnic and Migration Studies*, 28 (4), pp. 683–700.

Joppke, C. (2001), 'The Legal-Domestic Sources of Immigrant Rights: the United States, Germany, and the European Union', *Comparative Political Studies*, 34 (4), pp. 339–66.

Joppke, C. (2004), 'The retreat of multiculturalism in the liberal state', *The British Journal of Sociology*, 55 (2), pp. 237–57.

Joppke, C. (2007), 'Beyond National Models: Civic Integration Policies for

Immigrants in Western Europe', *West European Politics*, 30 (1), pp. 1–21.

Katz, R. S. and P. Mair (eds) (1994), *How parties organize. Change and adaptation in party organizations in western democracies*, London: Sage.

Katz, R. S. and P. Mair (1995), 'Changing Models of Party Organization and Party Democracy: The Emergence of the Cartel Party', *Party Politics*, 1 (1), pp. 5–29.

King, D. and J. Waldron (1988), 'Citizenship, Social Citizenship and the Defence of Welfare Provision', *British Journal of Political Science*, 18 (4), pp. 415–43.

Korpi, W. and J. Palme (2003), 'New Politics and Class Politics in the Context of Austerity and Globalization: Welfare State Regress in 18 Countries 1975–95', *American Political Science Review*, 97 (3), pp. 425–46.

Korpi, W. (1989), 'Power Politics and State Autonomy in the Development of Social Citizenship', *American Sociological Review*, 54 (3), pp. 309–28.

Korpi, W. (2003), 'Welfare State Regress in Western Europe: Politics, Institutions, Globalization and Europeanization', *Annual Review of Sociology*, 29, pp. 589–609.

Koslowski, R. (1998), 'European Union Migration Regimes, Established and Emergent', in C. Joppke (ed.), *Challenge to the Nation-State – Immigration in Western Europe and the United States*, Oxford: Oxford University Press, pp. 153–88.

Kostakopoulou, D. (2007), 'European Union Citizenship: Writing the Future', *European Law Journal*, 13 (5), pp. 623–46.

Kostakopoulou, T. (1996), 'Towards a Theory of Constructive Citizenship in Europe', *Journal of Political Philosophy*, 4 (4), pp. 337–58.

Kostakopoulou, T. (2000), 'The "Protective Union": Change and Continuity in Migration Law and Policy in Post-Amsterdam Europe', *Journal of Common Market Studies*, 38 (3), pp. 497–518.

Kratochwil, F. (1994), 'Citizenship: On the Border of Order', *Alternatives*, 19 (4), pp. 485–506.

Kukathas, C. and P. Pettit (1990), *Rawls: A Theory of Justice and its Critics*, Cambridge: Polity.

Kumlin, S. (2002), 'Institutions-experiences-preferences: How welfare state design affects political trust and ideology', in B. Rothstein and S. Steinmo (eds), *Restructuring the Welfare State: Political Institutions and Policy Change*, Basingstoke: Palgrave, pp. 20–50.

Kumlin, S. (2004), *The Personal and the Political. How Personal Welfare State Experiences Affect Political Trust and Ideology*, Basingstoke: Palgrave.

Kurthen, H. (1995), 'Germany at the Crossroads: National Identity and the Challenges of Immigration', *International Migration Review*, 29 (4), pp. 914–38.

Kymlicka, W. and W. Norman (1994), 'Return of the Citizen: A Survey of Recent Work on Citizenship Theory', *Ethics*, 104 (2), pp. 352–81.

Kymlicka, W. (1995), *Multicultural Citizenship: A Liberal Theory of Minority Rights*, Oxford: Oxford University Press.

Kymlicka, W. (1997), 'Do We Need A Liberal Theory of Minority Rights? Reply to Carens, Young, Parekh and Forst', *Constellations*, 4 (1), pp. 72–87.

Kymlicka, W. (2002), *Contemporary Political Philosophy*, 2nd edn, Oxford: Oxford University Press.

Laclau, E. and C. Mouffe (1985), *Hegemony and Socialist Strategy: Towards a Radical*

Democratic Politics, London: Verso.

Lefort, C. (1988), *Democracy and Political Theory*, Cambridge: Polity.

Levi, M. (1996), 'Social and Unsocial Capital: A Review Essay of Robert Putnam's Making Democracy Work', *Politics and Society*, 24 (1), pp. 45–55.

Lewis, J. (2002), 'Gender and Welfare State Change', *European Societies*, 4 (4), pp. 331–57.

Lijphart, A. (1997), 'Unequal Participation: Democracies Unresolved Dilemma', *American Political Science Review*, 91 (1), pp. 1–14.

Lindahl, H. (2003), 'Aquiring a Community: The Acquis and the Institution of European Legal Order', *European Law Journal*, 9 (4), pp. 433–50.

Lindberg, L. N. and S. A. Scheingold (1970), *Europe's Would be Polity*, Englewood Cliffs, NJ: Prentice-Hall.

Lister, M. (2005), 'Marshalling social and political citizenship: Towards a unified conception of citizenship', *Government and Opposition*, 40 (4), pp. 471–91.

Lister, M. (2007), 'Institutions, Inequality and Social Norms: Explaining Variations in Participation', *British Journal of Politics and International Relations*, 9 (1), pp. 20–35.

Lister, R. (2001), 'Citizenship and Gender', in K. Nash and A. Scott (eds), *Blackwell Companion to Political Sociology*, Oxford: Blackwell, pp. 323–32.

Lister, R. (2003), *Citizenship: Feminist Perspectives*, 2nd edn, Basingstoke: Palgrave.

Locke, J. ([1683] 1993), *Two Treatises of Government*, London: Everyman.

Lodge, J. (1993), 'Internal Security and Judicial Cooperation', in J. Lodge (ed.), *The European Community and the Challenge of the Future*, London: Pinter, pp. 315–39.

Loughlin, M. (2000), *Sword and Scales: An Examination of the Relationship Between Law and Politics*, Oxford: Hart Publishing.

Lubans, D. (1985), 'Romance of the Nation State', in C. Beitz, M. Cohen, T. Scanlon and A. J. Simmons (eds), *International Ethics*, Princeton, NJ: Princeton University Press, pp. 238–46.

Ludlow, P. (2004), *The Making of the New Europe: The European Councils in Brussels and Copenhagen 2002*, Brussels: EuroComment.

Luxembourg Income Study (LIS) Key Figures (2007), accessed at http://www.lisproject.org/keyfigures.htm on 22/05/07.

Macedo, S. (1990), *Liberal Virtues: Citizenship, Virtue, and Community in Liberal Constitutionalism*, Oxford: Oxford University Press.

MacIntyre, A. D. (1984), *After Virtue: A Study in Moral Theory*, Notre Dame, IN: University of Notre Dame Press.

MacIntyre, A. D. (1994), 'Is Patriotism a Virtue', in M. Daly (ed.), *Communitarianism: Belonging and Commitment in a Pluralistic Democracy*, Belmont, CA: Wadsworth.

Magnusson, W. (1994), *The Search for Political Space: Globalisation, Social Movements, and the Urban Political Experience*, Toronto: University of Toronto Press.

Mahony, H. (2007), 'Border agency cuts African migrant numbers', *EU Observer*, Brussels, 13 April 2007.

Mair, P. and I. van Biezen (2001), 'Party Membership in Twenty European Democracies, 1980–2000', *Party Politics*, 7 (1), pp. 5–21.

Mandaville, P. (1999), 'Territory and translocality: discrepant idioms of political identity', *Millennium: Journal of International Studies*, 28 (3), pp. 653–73.

Mann, A. (1987), 'Ruling Class Strategies and Citizenship', *Sociology*, 21 (3), pp. 339–54.

Mansbridge, J. (1990), 'The Rise and Fall of Self-Interest in the Explanation of Political Life', in J. J. Mansbridge (ed.), *Beyond Self Interest*, Chicago: University of Chicago Press, pp. 3–22 .

Mansbridge, J. (1999), 'Should Women Represent Women and Blacks Represent Blacks: A Contingent Yes', *The Journal of Politics*, 61 (3), pp. 628–57.

Marshall, T. H. (1963), 'Citizenship and Social Class', in *Sociology at the Crossroads and other essays*, London: Heinemann, pp. 67–127.

Martin, J. (1996), 'Measures Of Replacement Rates For The Purpose Of International Comparisons: A Note', *OECD Economic Studies*, 26, pp. 91–125.

Martin, J. (2000), 'What Works Among Active Labour Market Policies: Evidence From OECD Countries' Experiences', *OECD Economic Studies*, 30, pp. 79–113.

Mayes, F. and J. Palmowski (2004), 'European Identities and the EU – The ties that bind the people of Europe', *Journal of Common Market Studies*, 42 (3), pp. 573–98.

Mazzucelli, C. (1997), *France and Germany at Maastricht: Politics and Negotiations to Create the European Union*, New York: Garland.

Mead, L. (1986), *Beyond Entitlement: The Social Obligations of Citizenship*, New York: Free Press.

Meehan, E. (1993), *Citizenship and the European Community*, London: Sage.

Meehan, E. (1997), 'Political Pluralism and European Citizenship', in P. Lehning and A. Weale (eds), *Citizenship, Democracy and the New Europe*, London: Routledge, pp. 69–85.

Melluci, A. (1985), 'The Symbolic Challenge of Contemporary Movements', *Social Research*, 52 (4), pp. 789–816.

Melluci, A. (1996), *Challenging Codes*, Cambridge: Cambridge University Press.

Migration News, September 2003.

Milbrath, L. W. (1965), *Political Participation: How and Why Do People Get Involved in Politics?*, Chicago: Rand McNally and Company.

Mill, J. S. ([1869] 1989), *On Liberty*, Cambridge: Cambridge University Press.

Miller, D. (1988a), 'Socialism and Toleration', in S. Mendus (ed.), *Justifying Toleration: Conceptual and Historical Perspectives*, Cambridge: Cambridge University Press.

Miller, D. (1988b), 'The Ethical Significance of Nationality', *Ethics*, 9 (4), pp. 647–62.

Miller, D. (1992), 'Community and Citizenship', in S. Avineri and A. de Shalit (eds), *Communitarianism and Individualism*, Oxford: Oxford University Press, pp. 85–100.

Miller, M. J. (1986), 'Policy Ad-Hocracy: The paucity of coordinated perspectives and policies', *Annals of the American Academy of Political and Social Science*, 485 (1), pp. 64–75.

Miller, M. J. (1989), 'Political participation and representation of non citizens', in R. W. Brubaker (ed.), *Immigration and the Politics of Citizenship in Europe and North*

America, New York: University Press of America, pp. 129–43.

Mitselegas, V. (2002), 'The Implementation of the EU Acquis on Illegal Immigration by the Candidate Countries of Central and Eastern Europe: Challenges and Contradictions', *Journal of Ethics and Migration Studies*, 28 (4), pp. 665–82.

Moravcsik, A. and K. Nicolaïdis (1998), 'Federal Ideas and Constitutional Realities in the Treaty of Amsterdam', *Journal of Common Market Studies*, 36, Annual Review, pp. 13–38.

Morris-Jones, W. H. (1954), 'In Defence of Apathy: Some Doubts on the Duty to Vote', *Political Studies*, 2 (1), pp. 25–37.

Mouffe, C. (1992a), 'Feminism, Citizenship, and Radical Democratic Politics', in J. Butler and J. Scott (eds), *Feminists Theorizing the Political*, London: Routledge, pp. 369–84.

Mouffe, C. (1992b), 'Citizenship and Political Identity', *October*, 61, pp. 28–32.

Mouffe, C. (1993), *The Return of the Political*, London: Verso.

Mouffe, C. (1994), 'For a Politics of Nomadic Identity', in G. Robertson, M. Mash, L. Tickner, J. Bird, B. Curtis and T. Putnam (eds), *Travellers' Tales: Narratives of Home and Displacement*, London: Routledge, pp. 105–13.

Mouffe, C. (1996), 'Deconstruction, Pragmatism and the Politics of Democracy', in C. Mouffe (ed.), *Deconstruction and Pragmatism*, London: Routledge, pp. 1–12.

Mulhall, S. and A. Swift (1992), *Liberals and Communitarians*, Oxford: Blackwell.

Murphy, J. B. (2007), 'Against Civic Education in Public Schools', *International Journal of Public Administration*, 30 (6&7), pp. 651–70.

Murray, C. (1984), *Losing Ground: American Social Policy 1950–1980*, New York: Basic Books.

Murray, C. (2006), 'The Two Wars Against Poverty', in C. Pierson and F. Castles (eds), *The Welfare State Reader*, 2nd edn, Cambridge: Polity, pp. 96–106.

Nancy, J. L. (1991), *The Inoperative Community* (ed. and trans.) P. Connor, Minneapolis, MN: University of Minnesota Press.

Needham, C. (2005), 'Introduction: Do Parties Have A Future?', *Parliamentary Affairs*, 58 (3), pp. 499–502.

Ney, S. (2000), 'Are You Sitting Comfortably … Then We'll Begin: Three Gripping Policy Stories About Pension Reform', *Innovation: The European Journal of Social Science Research*, 13 (4), pp. 341–71.

Nicolaïdis, K. (2004), 'The New Constitution as European Demoi-cracy?', *Critical Review of International Social and Political Philosophy*, 7 (1), pp. 76–93.

Norris, P. (1999), 'Gender: A Gender-Generation Gap?', in G. Evans and P. Norri (eds), *Critical Elections: British Parties and Voters in Long-term Perspective*, London: Sage, pp. 148–63.

Norris, P. (2002), *Democratic Phoenix: Reinventing Political Activism*, Cambridge: Cambridge University Press.

Nozick, R. (1974), *Anarchy, State and Utopia*, Oxford: Blackwell.

Nyers, P. (1999), 'Emergency or Emerging Identities? Refugees and Transformations in World Order', *Millennium: Journal of International Studies*, 28 (1), pp. 1–26.

O'Brien R., A. M. Goetz, J. Aart, and M. Williams (eds) (2000), *Contesting Global*

Governance: Multilateral Economic Institutions and Global Social Movements
Cambridge: Cambridge University Press.

O'Leary, S. (1999), 'The Free Movement of Persons and Services', in P. Craig and
G. De Búrca (eds), *The Evolution of EU Law*, Oxford: Oxford University Press.

O'Neill, J. (1997), 'The civic recovery of citizenship', *Citizenship Studies*, 1 (1), pp.
9–32.

Organisation for Economic Co-operation and Development [OECD] (1995),
Employment Outlook 1995, Paris: OECD.

OECD (2007), *International Migration Outlook*, Paris: OECD.

Ohmae, K. (1990), *Borderless World*, London: Collins.

Oldfield, M. (1990), *Citizenship and Community: Civic Republicanism and the Modern
World*, London: Routledge.

Oldfield, M. (1994), 'Citizenship: An unnatural practice?', *Political Quarterly*,
61 (2), pp. 177–87.

Olson, M. (1971), *The Logic of Collective Action: Public Goods and the Theory of
Groups*, Cambridge, MA: Harvard University Press.

Orloff, A. S. (1993), 'Gender and the Social Rights of Citizenship: The Comparative Analysis of Gender Relations and Welfare States', *American Sociological
Review*, 58 (3), pp. 303–28.

Orloff, A. S., J. O'Connor and S. Shaver (1999), *States, Markets, Families: Gender,
Liberalism and Social Policy in Australia, Canada, Great Britain, and the United
States*, Cambridge: Cambridge University Press.

Orton, M. and K. Rowlingson (2007) ,'A Problem of Riches: Towards a new Social
Policy Research Agenda on the Distribution of Economic Resources', *Journal of
Social Policy*, 36 (1), pp. 59–77.

Parekh, B. (2000), *Rethinking Multiculturalism: Cultural Diversity and Politica Theory*,
London: Macmillan.

Parry, G., G. Moyser and N. Day (1992), *Political Participation and Democracy in
Britain*, Cambridge: Cambridge University Press.

Pateman, C. (1988), 'The Patriarchal Welfare State', in A. Gutmann (ed.), *Democracy and the Welfare State*, Princeton, NJ: Princeton University Press, pp. 231–60.

Pateman, C. (1989), *The Disorder of Women*, Cambridge: Polity.

Pattie, C., P. Seyd and P. Whiteley (2004), *Citizenship in Britain: Values, Participation
and Democracy*, Cambridge: Cambridge University Press.

Pettit, P. (1997), *Republicanism: a theory of freedom and government*, Oxford: Clarendon Press.

Pfau-Effinger, B. (2005), 'Culture and Welfare State Policies: Reflections on a
Complex Interrelation', *Journal of Social Policy*, 34 (1), pp. 3–20.

Phillips, A. (1993), *Democracy and Difference*, Cambridge: Polity.

Pichardo, N. A. (1997), 'New Social Movements: A Critical Review', *Annual
Review of Sociology*, 23, pp. 411–30.

Pierson, C. (2006), *Beyond the Welfare State: The New Political Economy of Welfare*,
Cambridge: Polity.

Pierson, P. (1994), *Dismantling the Welfare State. Reagan, Thatcher and the Politics of
Retrenchment*, Cambridge: Cambridge University Press.

Pierson, P. (1996), 'The New Politics of the Welfare State', *World Politics*, 48 (2), pp. 143–79.

Pierson, P. (ed) (2001a), *The New Politics of the Welfare State*, Oxford: Oxford University Press.

Pierson, P. (2001b), 'Coping with Permanent Austerity: Welfare State Restructuring in Affluent Democracies', in P. Pierson (ed.), *The New Politics of the Welfare State*, Oxford: Oxford University Press, pp. 410–56.

Pierson, P. (2001c), 'Post-industrial pressures on the mature welfare states', in P. Pierson (ed.), *The New Politics of the Welfare State*, Oxford: Oxford University Press, pp. 80–104.

Piper, N. and A. Uhlin (2004), 'New perspectives on transnational activism', in N. Piper and A. Uhlin (eds), *Transnational activism in Asia: Problems of power and democracy*, London: Routledge, pp. 1–25.

Piven, F. F. and R. A. Cloward (1989), *Why Americans Don't Vote*, New York: Pantheon Books.

Plamenatz, J. (1963), *Man and society : a critical examination of some important social and political theories from Machiavelli to Marx*, Vol 2, London: Longman.

Pocock, J. G. A. (1975), *The Machiavellian moment: Florentine political thought and the Atlantic republican tradition*, Princeton, NJ: Princeton University Press.

Prodi, R. (2000), *Europe as I See it*, Cambridge: Polity.

Prokhovnik, R. (1998), 'Public and Private Citizenship: From Gender Invisibility to Feminist Inclusiveness', *Feminist Review*, 60, pp. 84–104.

Putnam, R. (1993), *Making democracy work: civic traditions in modern Italy*, Princeton, NJ: Princeton University Press.

Putnam, R. (2000), *Bowling Alone: The Collapse and Revival of American Community*, New York: Simon and Schuster.

Rawls, J. (1972), *A Theory of Justice*, Oxford: Clarendon Press.

Rawls, J. (1988), 'The Priority of Right and Ideas of the Good', *Philosophy and Public Affairs*, 17 (4), pp. 251–76.

Rawls, J., C. Beitz, T. Pogge, B. Barry and R. Dworkin (1986) *Law's Empire*, London: Fontana.

Reich, R. (1992), *The Work of Nations*, New York: Vintage Books.

Richardson, D. (1998), 'Sexuality and Citizenship', *Sociology*, 32 (1), pp. 83–100.

Riker, W. and P. C. Ordeshook (1968), 'A Theory of the Calculus of Voting', *American Political Science Review*, 62 (1), pp. 25–42.

Risse-Kappen, T. (ed.) (1995), *Bringing transnational relations back in: Non-state actors, domestic structures and international institutions*, Cambridge: Cambridge University Press.

Rorty, R. (1999), *Contingency, Irony and Solidarity*, Cambridge: Cambridge University Press.

Rothstein, B. (1998), *Just Institutions Matter*, Cambridge: Cambridge University Press.

Rothstein, B. (2001), 'Social Capital in the Social Democratic Welfare State', *Politics and Society*, 29 (2), pp. 206–40.

Rousseau, J.-J. ([1762] 1987), *The Basic Political Writings*, Indianapolis, IN: Hackett

Publishing Company.

Rubery, J., D. Grimshaw and H. Figueiredo (2005), 'How to close the gender pay gap in Europe: towards the gender mainstreaming of pay policy', *Industrial Relations Journal*, 36 (3), pp. 184–213.

Ryner, M. (2001), 'European welfare state transformation and migration', in M. Bommes and A. Geddes (eds), *Immigration and Welfare: Challenging the Borders of the Welfare State*, London: Routledge, pp. 51–71.

Ryner, M. (2002), *Capitalist Restructuring, Globalisation and the Third Way: Lessons from the Swedish Model*, London: Routledge.

Sandel, M. J. (1984), 'The Procedural Republic and the Unencumbered Self', *Political Theory*, 12 (1), pp. 81–96.

Saskia, S. (1999), *Guests and Aliens*, New York: The New Press.

Sassatelli, M. (2002), 'Imagined Europe: The Shaping of a European Cultural Identity through EU Cultural Policy', *European Journal of Social Theory*, 6 (1), pp. 25–45.

Sassen, S. (1996), *Losing Control?: Sovereignty in an Age of Globalisation*, New York: Columbia University Press.

Sassen, S. (2003), 'The Repositioning of Citizenship: Emergent Subjects and Spaces for Politics', *The New Centennial Review*, 3 (2), pp. 41–66.

Scharpf, F. W. (1996), 'Negative Integration: States and the Loss of Boundary Control', in G. Marks, F. W. Scharpf, P. C. Schmitter and W. Streeck (eds), *Governance in the European Union*, London: Sage, pp. 15–39.

Scharpf, F. W. (2002), 'The European Social Model: Coping with the Challenges of Diversity', *Journal of Common Market Studies*, 40 (4), pp. 645–70.

Schilling, T. (1996), 'The Autonomy of the Community Legal Order: An Analysis of Possible Foundations', *Harvard International Law Journal*, 37 (2), pp. 389–410.

Schmitter, P. C. (1996), 'Examining the Future of Euro-polity with the Help of New Concepts', in G. Marks, F. W. Scharpf, P. C. Schmitter and W. Streek (eds), *Governance in the European Union*, London: Sage, pp. 121–50.

Schuck, P. H. (2002), 'Liberal Citizenship', in E. F. Isin and B. S. Turner (eds), *Handbook of Citizenship Studies*, London: Sage, pp. 131–44.

Sciortino, G. (2004), 'Immigration in a Mediterranean Welfare State: The Italian Experience in Comparative Perspective', *Journal of Comparative Policy Analysis*, 6 (2), pp. 111–29.

Scruggs, L. and J. Allan (2004), 'Political Partisanship and Welfare State Reform in Advanced Industrial Societies', *American Journal of Political Science*, 48 (3), pp. 496–512.

Scruggs, L. and J. Allan (2006), 'Welfare-state decommodification in 18 OECD countries: a replication and revision', *Journal of European Social Policy*, 16 (1), pp. 55–72.

Scruggs, L. (2004), Welfare State Entitlements Data Set: A Comparative Institutional Analysis of Eighteen Welfare States, accessed at http://sp.uconn.edu/~scruggs/wp.htm.

Scruggs, L. (2006), 'The Generosity of Social Insurance, 1971-2002', *Oxford Review of Economic Policy*, 22 (3), pp. 349–64.

Shaw, C. K. Y. (2003), 'Quentin Skinner on the Proper Meaning of Republican Liberty', *Politics*, 23 (1), pp. 46–56.

Shaw, J. and A. Wiener (2000), 'The Paradox of European Polity', in M. Green Cowles and M. Smith (eds), *The State of the European Union: Risks, Resistance and Revival*, Oxford: Oxford University Press, pp. 64–89.

Shaw, J. (1999), 'Postnational Constitutionalism in the European Union', *Journal of European Public Policy*, 6 (4), pp. 579–97.

Shaw, J. (2000), 'Constitutional Settlements and the Citizen After the Treaty of Amsterdam', in K. Neunreither and A. Wiener (eds), *European Integration After Amsterdam: Institutional Dynamics and Prospects for Democracy*, Oxford: Oxford University Press, pp. 290–317.

Shearer, I. A. (1994), *Starke's International Law*, 11th edn, London: Butterworths.

Shore, C. (2000), *Building Europe: The Cultural Politics of European Integration*, London: Routledge.

Shue, H. (1980), *Basic Rights*, Princeton, NJ: Princeton University Press.

Skinner, Q. (1983), 'Machiavelli on the Maintenance of Liberty', *Politics*, 18 (2), pp. 3–15.

Skinner, Q. (1984), 'The Idea of Negative Liberty: Philosophical and Historical Perspectives', in R. Rorty, J. B. Schneewind and Q. Skinner (eds), *Philosophy in History: Essay on the Historiography of Philosophy*, Cambridge: Cambridge University Press, pp. 193–211.

Skinner, Q. (1986), 'The Paradoxes of Political Liberty', in S. M. McMurrin (ed.), *The Tanner Lectures on Human Values*, Salt Lake City, UT: University of Utah Press.

Skinner, Q. (1992), 'On Justice, the Common Good and the Priority of Liberty', in C. Mouffe (ed.), *Dimension of Radical Democracy: Pluralism, Citizenship, Community*, London: Verso, pp. 211–24.

Skocpol, T. (2003), *Diminished Democracy: From Membership to Management in American Civic Life*, Norman, OK: University of Oklahoma Press.

Smith, A. D. (1992), 'National Identity and the idea of European Unity', *International Affairs*, 68 (1), pp. 55–76.

Smith, M. P. (2001), *Transnational Urbanism: Locating Globalization*, Oxford: Blackwell.

Smith, S. B. (1986), 'Hegel's Critique of Liberalism', *American Political Science Review*, 80 (1), pp. 121–39.

Solé, C. (2004), 'Immigration policies in Southern Europe', *Journal of Ethnic and Migration Studies*, 30 (6), pp. 1209–21.

Soss, J. (1999), 'Lessons of welfare: Policy design, political learning and political action', *American Political Science Review*, 93 (2), pp. 363–80.

Soysal, Y. N. (1994), *Limits of Citizenship: Migrants and Postnational Membership in Europe*, Chicago: University of Chicago Press.

Soysal, Y. N. (1997), 'Changing Parameters of Citizenship and Claims-Making: Organised Islam in European Public Spheres', *Theory and Society*, 26 (4), pp. 509–27.

Spiro, P. J. (1997), 'Dual Nationality and the Meaning of Citizenship', *Emory Law*

Journal, 46 (4), pp. 1412–85.

Stryker, S. (1980), *Symbolic Interactionism*, Menlo Park, CA: Benjamin-Cummings.

Tamir, Y. (1993), *Liberal Nationalism*, Princeton, NJ: Princeton University Press.

Tarrow, S. and D. della Porta (2005), 'Conclusion: Globalization, complex internationalism, and transnational contention', in S. Tarrow and D. della Porta (eds), *Transnational protest and global activism*, Lanham: Rowman and Littlefield, pp. 227–46.

Tarrow, S. (2001), 'Transnational Politics: Contention and Institutions in International Politics', *Annual Review of Political Science*, 4, pp. 1–20.

Tarrow, S. (2005), *The New Transnational Activism*, Cambridge: Cambridge University Press.

Taylor, C. (1994), 'The Politics of Recognition', in A. Gutmann (ed.), *Multi-culturalism, Examining the Politics of Recognition*, Princeton, NJ: Princeton University Press, pp. 25–74.

Taylor, P. (1996), *The European Union in the 1990s*, Oxford: Oxford University Press.

Taylor-Gooby, P. (1991) 'Welfare State Regimes and Welfare Citizenship', *Journal of European Social Policy*, 1 (2), pp. 93–105.

Taylor-Gooby, P. (1999), 'Policy Change at a Time of Retrenchment: Recent Pension Reform in France, Germany, Italy and the UK', *Social Policy and Administration*, 33 (1), pp. 1–19.

Torfing, J. (1999), *New Theories of Discourse*, Oxford: Blackwell.

Torres, M. (1998), 'Transnational Political and Cultural Identities: Crossing Theoretical Borders', in F. Bonilla, E. Melendez, R. Morales and M. de los Angeles Torres (eds), *Borderless Borders: U.S. Latinos, Latin Americans, and the Paradox of Interdependence*, Philadelphia, PA: Temple University Press, pp. 169–82.

Trifiletti, R. (1999), 'Southern European welfare regimes and the worsening position of women', *Journal of European Social Policy*, 9 (1), pp. 49–64.

Tully, J. (1995), *Constitutionalism in an Age of Diversity*, Cambridge: Cambridge University Press.

Tully, J. (2002), 'The Unfreedom of the Moderns in Comparison to their Ideals of Constitutional Democracy', *Modern Law Review*, 65 (2), pp. 204–28.

Tully, J. (2005), 'Two Meanings of Global Citizenship: Modern and Diverse', The Meanings of Global Citizenship Conference, Liu Centre and Trudeau Foundation, UBC, paper accessed at http://web.uvic.ca/polisci/tully/publications/index.htm.

Turner, B. (1994), 'Postmodern Culture / Modern Citizens', in B. van Steenbergen (ed.), *The Condition of Citizenship*, London: Sage, pp. 153–68.

Ucarer, E. (2001), 'Managing Asylum and European Integration: Expanding Spheres of Exclusion?', *International Studies Perspectives*, 2 (3), pp. 288–304.

Ugur, M. (1995), 'Freedom of Movement vs. Exclusion: A Reinterpretation of the "Insider"-"Outsider" Divide in the European Union', *International Migration Review*, 29 (4), pp. 964–99.

Van Ham. P. (2001), 'Europe's postmodern identity: a critical appraisal', *International Politics*, 38 (2), pp. 229–52.

Vandenberg, A. (2000), 'Cybercitizenship and digital democracy', in A. Vandenberg (ed.), *Citizenship and Democracy in a Global Era*, New York: St. Martin's Press, pp. 289–306.

Veikou, M. and A. Triandafyllidou (2001), 'Immigration policy and its implementation in Italy: the state of the art', in A. Triandafyllidou (ed.), *Migration Pathways. A Historic, Demographic and Policy Review of Four Countries of the European Union*, Brussels: European Commission Research Directorate, pp. 63–84.

Verba, S. and N. Nie (1972), *Participation in America: Political Democracy and Social Equality*, New York: Harper and Row.

Verba, S., K. L. Schlozman and H. E. Brady (1995), *Voice and Equality: Civic Voluntarism in American Politics*, London: Harvard University Press.

Vincent, R. J. (1992), 'The Idea of Rights in International Ethics in Traditions of International Ethics', in T. Nardin and D. R. Mapel (eds), Cambridge: Cambridge University Press, pp. 250–69.

Vink, M. P. (2005), *Limits of European Citizenship*, Basingstoke: Palgrave.

Vink, M. P. (2007), 'Dutch "Multiculturalism" Beyond the Pillarisation Myth', *Political Studies Review*, 5 (3), pp. 337–50.

Visser, J. (2006), 'Union Membership Statistics in 24 countries', *Monthly Labour Review*, 129 (1), pp. 38–49.

Voet, R. (1998), *Feminism and Citizenship*, London: Sage.

Waever, O. (1996), 'European Security Identities', *Journal of Common Market Studies*, 34 (1), pp. 103–32.

Waldron, J. (2003), 'Security and Liberty: The Image of Balance', *Journal of Political Philosophy*, 11 (2), pp. 191–210.

Walker, N. (2002), 'The Idea of Constitutional Pluralism', *Modern Law Review*, 65 (3), pp. 317–59.

Wallace, H. (1993), 'Deepening and Widening: Problems of Legitimacy for the EC', in S. Garcia (ed.), *European Identity and the Search for Legitimacy*, London: Pinter, pp. 95–105.

Walzer, M. (1983), *Spheres of Justice*, New York: Basic Books.

Walzer, M. (1995), 'Response to Veit Bader', *Political Theory*, 23 (2), pp. 247–49.

Wapner P. (1996), *Environmental Activism and World Civic Politics*, Albany, NY: State University of New York Press.

Ward, D. (1995), *Rewriting Democracy: The Role of Public Information in Europe's Information Society*, London: Maclennan Ward Research.

Warkentin C. and K. Mingst (2000), 'International Institutions, the state and global civil society in the age of the world wide web' *Global Governance*, 6 (2), pp. 237–57.

Weiler, J. H. H. (1995), 'Does Europe Need a Constitution? Reflections on Demos, Telos and the German Maastricht Decision', *European Law Journal*, 1(3), pp. 219–58.

Weiler, J. H. H. (2001), 'Federalism without Constitution: Europe's Sonderweg', in K. Nicolaïdis and R. Howse (eds), *The Federal Vision: Legitimacy and Levels of Governance in the US and the EU*, Oxford: Oxford University Press, pp. 54–71.

Weiler, J. H. H. (2002), 'A Constitution for Europe: Some Hard Choices', *Journal of Common Market Studies*, 40 (4), pp. 563–80.

White, S. (2004), 'Welfare Philosophy and the Third Way', in J. Lewis and R. Surender (eds), *Welfare State Change: Towards a Third Way*, Oxford: Oxford University Press, pp. 25–46.

Whiteford, P. (1995), 'The use of replacement rates in international comparisons of benefit systems', *International Social Security Review*, 48 (2), pp. 3–30.

Wilkinson, M. (2003), 'Civil Society and the Re-imagination of European Constitutionalism', *European Law Journal*, 9(4), pp. 451–72.

Wilkinson, R. G. (1996), *Unhealthy Societies: The Afflictions of Inequality*, London: Routledge.

Williams, J. (2000), *Lyotard and the Political*, London: Routledge.

Williams, S. (1991), 'Sovereignty and Accountability in the European Community', in S. Hoffman and R. A. Keohane (eds), *The New European Community: Decision Making and Institutional Change*, Boulder, CO: Westview Press, pp. 155–76.

Wincott, D. (2001), 'Reassessing the Social Foundations of Welfare (State) Regimes', *New Political Economy*, 6 (3), pp. 409–25.

Wincott, D. (2006), 'Paradoxes of New Labour Social Policy: Toward Universal Child Care in Europe's "Most Liberal" Welfare Regime?', *Social Politics*, 13 (2), pp. 286–312.

Women and Work Commission (2006), *Shaping a Fairer Future: Executive Summary*, Department of Trade and Industry. Available at http://www.womenandequalityunit.gov.uk/women_work_commission/index.htm.

World Bank (1994), *Averting the Old Age Crisis*, Oxford: Oxford University Press.

Young, I. M. (1988), 'Five Faces of Oppression', *Philosophical Forum* 19 (4), pp. 270–90.

Young, I. M. (1989), 'Polity and Group Difference: A Critique of the Ideal of Universal Citizenship', *Ethics*, 99 (2), pp. 250–74.

Young, I. M. (1995), 'Polity and Group Difference', in R. Beiner (ed.), *Theorising Citizenship*, Albany, NY: State University of New York Press, pp. 175–208.

Yuval Davis, N. (1997), 'Women, Citizenship and Difference', *Feminist Review*, 57, pp. 4–27.

Zincone, G. (2006), 'The Making of Policies: Immigration and Immigrants in Italy', *Journal of Ethnic and Migration Studies*, 32 (3), pp. 347–75.

Index